MEN'S TRANSITIONS TO PARENTHOOD

Longitudinal Studies
of Early Family Experience

Edited by

Phyllis W. Berman
Frank A. Pedersen

National Institute of Child Health
and Human Development

33542

LEA LAWRENCE ERLBAUM ASSOCIATES, PUBLISHERS
1987 Hillsdale, New Jersey   Hove and London

Lawrence Erlbaum Associates, Inc., Publishers
365 Broadway
Hillsdale, New Jersey 07642

Library of Congress Cataloging-in-Publication Data

Men's transitions to parenthood.

Papers from a conference organized by the National
Institute of Child Health and Human Development,
spring 1984.
Bibliography: p.
Includes indexes.
1. Fathers—United States—Longitudinal studies—
Congresses.   2. Father and child—United States—
Longitudinal studies—Congresses.   3. Infants—United
States—Longitudinal studies—Congresses.
4. Parenthood—United States—Longitudinal studies—
Congresses.   I. Berman, Phyllis W.   II. Pedersen,
Frank A.   III. National Institute of Child Health and
Human Development (U.S.)

HQ756.M46   1987   306.8'742   86—29165
ISBN 0-89859-814-1

Printed in the United States of America
10 9 8 7 6 5 4 3 2 1

Contents

List of Contributors   vii

Preface   ix

1 **Introduction: A Perspective on Research
   Concerning Fatherhood**   1
   Frank A. Pedersen

The Father as Marker of Socioeconomic Status **2**
Father-Absence Studies **3**
Correlational Studies
    of Father and Child Characteristics **4**
Other Trends Affecting Research on Fatherhood **5**
Descriptive Studies of Father–Infant Interaction **7**
The Leading Edge in Research on Fatherhood **8**
References **10**

2 **Predicting Strain in Mothers and Fathers
   of 6-Month-Old Infants:
   A Short-Term Longitudinal Study**   13
   S. Shirley Feldman

Method **16**
Results **24**
Discussion **28**
Acknowledgments **33**
References **33**

3   **Mothering, Fathering, and Marital Interaction in the Family Triad During Infancy: Exploring Family System's Processes**   **37**
Jay Belsky and Brenda L. Volling

Methods *43*
Results and Discussion *45*
Conclusions *59*
Acknowledgments *61*
References *61*

4   **Father–Infant Interaction Among Men Who Had Contrasting Affective Responses During Early Infancy: Follow-Up Observations at 1 Year**   **65**
Frank A. Pedersen, Martha J. Zaslow, Richard L. Cain, Joan T. D. Suwalsky, Beth Rabinovich

Methods *70*
Results *72*
Discussion *80*
Summary *85*
References *86*

5   **Separate and Together: Men's Autonomy and Affiliation in the Transition to Parenthood**   **89**
Frances Kaplan Grossman

Method *95*
Conclusions *110*
Acknowledgments *110*
References *110*

6   **Interrelationships Within the Mother–Father–Infant Triad**   **113**
Jane R. Dickie

An Empirical Study of the Context for Parenting *123*
Methods *123*
Results *124*
Implications of Findings for Potential Intervention *138*
References *141*

7   Men's Involvement in Parenthood:
Identifying the Antecedents
and Understanding the Barriers   145
   Carolyn Pape Cowan and Philip A. Cowan

A Five-Domain Model of Family Structure   146
Becoming a Family Project   150
Father Involvement, Satisfaction, and Stress   154
A Family System View of Supports
   and Barriers to Father Involvement   165
Conclusions   170
Acknowledgments   171
References   171

8   Father–Infant Caregiving and Play
with Preterm and Full-Term Infants   175
   Michael W. Yogman

Method   179
Results   183
Discussion   188
Acknowledgments   193
References   193

9   Fathers and Their At-Risk Infants:
Conceptual and Empirical Analyses   197
   Ross D. Parke and Edward R. Anderson

Theoretical Assumptions   197
Fathers and Triads: Expanding
   the Context of Development   200
Beyond the Triad: Extra-Familial
   Support Systems and the At-Risk Infant   206
The Role of Historical Time   210
Conclusions   211
Acknowledgments   211
References   212

10   Research on Men's Transitions to Parenthood:
An Integrative Discussion   217
   Phyllis W. Berman and Frank A. Pedersen

Methodological Issues   218
Substantive Issues   223
Conclusions   238

Acknowledgment *241*
References *241*

Author Index   **243**

Subject Index   **251**

List of Contributors

Edward R. Anderson—*University of Illinois*

Jay Belsky—*Pennsylvania State University*

Phyllis W. Berman—*National Institute of Child Health and Human Development*

Richard L. Cain—*National Institute of Child Health and Human Development*

Carolyn Pape Cowan—*University of California*

Philip A. Cowan—*University of California*

Jane R. Dickie—*Hope College*

S. Shirley Feldman—*Stanford University*

Frances Kaplan Grossman—*Boston University*

Ross D. Parke—*University of Illinois*

Frank A. Pedersen—*National Institute of Child Health and Human Development*

Beth Rabinovich—*National Institute of Child Health and Human Development*

Joan T. D. Suwalsky—*National Institute of Child Health and Human Development*

Brenda L. Volling—*Pennsylvania State University*

Michael W. Yogman—*Children's Hospital*

Martha J. Zaslow—*National Institute of Child Health and Human Development*

Preface

After many years of neglect, research on fathers is proliferating. Rapid changes are now taking place; new aspects of fathers' behavior are being examined; new issues are being raised; and new methods are being devised. In the spring of 1984 a 2-day conference was organized by the National Institute of Child Health and Human Development to explore theoretical and methodological questions concerning men's development of parental attitudes, behaviors, and roles from their children's prenatal period through early infancy. Most of the researchers who participated in the conference are still working with longitudinal projects that continue to trace the development of fathers throughout their children's early years. This book presents the work of eight of these investigators. The volume is dedicated to the memory of Dr. Mortimer B. Lipsitt, the past director of the National Institute of Child Health and Human Development, who died November 10, 1985. We are grateful for his leadership and continued support for this research.

Phyllis W. Berman
Frank A. Pedersen

Introduction: A Perspective on Research Concerning Fatherhood

Frank A. Pedersen
National Institute of Child Health and Human Development

It is customary to introduce a scholarly tome by reciting a litany of reasons why scientists have ignored a particular topic, creating the raison d'être for the pages that follow. The area of fatherhood, however, no longer qualifies as a neglected phenomena. Scholarly studies of fathers by behavioral scientists are now in their third decade. A more visible index of the timeliness of the topic is that lay publications, such as manuals of the genre "how to be an effective parent," include suggestions and advice for fathers. Even Benjamin Spock's revision of *Baby and Child Care* now recognizes that relevant nurturing contributions can be made by fathers. Fatherhood is indeed "in" among both behavioral scientists and the objects of their scientific interest, fathers themselves.

Our point of departure from literature for the layman is that the goal of this volume is to establish statistically reliable generalizations about men's transitions to parenthood using methods with scientific respectability. This goal also is a progression from past research on fathers, but it is one that follows naturally from appreciation of the results obtained from previous strategies for understanding fatherhood. Broadly speaking, three distinct phases in past research can be discerned that implicate fathers as potentially significant influences upon family experience and a child's development: (a) The father as marker of socioeconomic status (SES); (b) father-absence studies; and (c) correlational studies of father and child characteristics.[1]

---

[1]Lamb (1986) has presented an overlapping perspective on these historical trends in research on fathers.

THE FATHER AS MARKER OF
SOCIOECONOMIC STATUS

One of the most important ways in which fathers were first addressed in human development research and psychological phenomena generally was that they established the family's SES. Classical indexes of SES, such as the Hollingshead scale (Hollingshead & Redlich, 1958), involve evaluation of paternal attainments alone, educational level, and occupational prestige. Although this practice recognizes the significance of the father's provider role (and nothing else), more often than not the causal import on any outcome is attributed to the abstract concept of SES. Nonetheless, socioeconomic status is surely one of the most potent variables in the social sciences, and virtually every research problem must include attention to the possible mediating influence of SES upon outcome measures. Socioeconomic status has been documented to have a decisive impact on a range of critical events, including children's intellectual development, emotional and behavioral problems, friendship patterns, sex-role development, the prevalence of medical risk factors such as prematurity or other perinatal complications, attitudes and behaviors that parents regard as appropriate for rearing children, and the educational opportunities that are available to children (see Hess, 1970, for a comprehensive review of this area). Indeed, social class is so powerful an influence that Sameroff and Chandler (1975) contended that it can mask or modify virtually any variable of putative psychological significance. In an important early statement of the influence of social class (Hollingshead & Redlich, 1958), not only was the prevalence of mental disease linked to social class, but also the course of treatment for individuals with the same disease was different depending on the patient's social class.

Despite the fact that SES has been shown to have a profound influence on psychological variables, fathers were shadowy figures for understanding the more proximal factors affecting development and outcomes. Yet, something must have been critically linked to the father because it was he that defined the family's SES. In research that implicated SES with the child's development, the father was a kind of latent variable obscured by an abstract number that defined a family's level in the social order. In more recent research addressing the family's socioeconomic level and children's experiences, a great deal of progress has been made in defining what it is about the father that affects family life in different social strata. A father's job conditions, for example, and his personality are posited to be reciprically affected, and this is thought to influence the kind of care a child receives (Kohn & Schooler, 1983).

FATHER–ABSENCE STUDIES

A research strategy that promised more direct inference regarding the influence of fathers on children's development was based on the father-absence paradigm. That is, comparisons were made of children reared in single-parent families headed by the mother with those reared in conventional two-parent families. A pioneering study was done by Sears (1951), comparing doll play fantasises of 3- to 5-year-old children whose fathers either were at home or were absent from the home because of military service during World War II. Following that pattern, a plethora of research reported different developmental outcomes for children growing up either with or without fathers. Generally, adverse outcomes among children who were without fathers were usually interpreted as due to diminished availability of the father as a socialization influence or as an identification figure. Over the years, negative effects of the father's absence, especially for male children, were reported in such areas as intellectual level, academic attainment, cognitive style, sex-role identification, conscience and moral development, delay of gratification, delinquent behavior, and heterosexual interaction patterns in adolescent girls. The most extensive review and integration of this research literature was written by Biller (1974). Subsequently, an incisive review was published by Shinn (1978), focusing on the effects of father absence on cognitive development alone.

Herzog and Sudia (1973) reviewed and criticized the conclusions drawn from father-absence research conducted prior to 1969. They contended that relatively few studies were available meeting criteria for rigor and appropriate controls, and that among the more carefully executed studies the results were far from consistent. Moreover, many of the effects attributed to the presence or absence of the father were as likely due to circumstances that only indirectly involved the father–child relationship. For example, deleterious effects of father absence associated with divorce might more readily be attributed to marital discord and instability that preceded the father's separation from the mother and child rather than the direct loss to the child of the father as a socialization influence and role model. The latter conclusion was recently documented in longitudinal research by Block, Block, and Gjerde (1986) that included pre-separation assessments; children reared in homes that eventually experienced divorce were distinguishable from control children reared in stable families even before the divorce occurred. Perhaps the strongest criticism posed by Herzog and Sudia was that comparison groups must be matched for SES, and that few studies met this condition. More recent research with very large samples, e.g., 26,000 four-year-olds (Broman, Nichols, & Kennedy, 1975) have found no decrement in IQ for father-absent children after controlling for SES (see also Svanum, Bringle, & McLaughlin, 1982).

What constitutes appropriate controls for SES when evaluating the effects of father absence is not a simple matter. If a major role of fathers in many families is to provide economic resources, it is dubious to apply statistical controls to adjust for that effect. Statistical controls for SES, however, do help determine whether fathers have effects on children's development above and beyond that explained by SES.

Because of such quandries and, more critically, because whatever effects can be reliably identified as due to father absence are still "explained" only by speculation and inference, the argument has been presented that a deficit-based research paradigm provides limited information about the actual behavior of fathers in families (Pedersen, 1976; Svanum et al., 1982). A more productive research strategy is to examine the behavior of fathers detailed in ways other than merely by their absence. A similar point was made earlier by Yarrow (1964) with regard to the research area called *maternal deprivation,* the rearing of children in institutional environments.

CORRELATIONAL STUDIES OF
FATHER AND CHILD CHARACTERISTICS

A third research strategy involves explicit recognition of individual differences in components of the father–child relationship. It also seeks to establish statistical connections between such variability and different developmental outcomes for the child. To illustrate, harsh disciplinary techniques, especially physical punishment, administered by the father has been found to be associated with heightened rates of aggressive behavior for middle-class children (Eron, Walder, & Lefkowitz, 1971). In studies of this nature, disciplinary practices are frequently appraised with parental interviews, whereas child-aggression rates typically are measured through an independent source of information, such as peer nominations. A variant on this procedure is to elicit the child's report of parental behavior through questionnaires, projective tests, and so on, and to establish correlations with characteristics of the child.

Conceptually, the correlational strategy represents several major improvements over attempts to find group differences between children reared in globally different environments. First, it involves a model based on individual differences in socialization practices as well as on child outcomes. Second, there is an attempt to specify proximal influences on development, features of the immediate parent–child relationship, rather than merely to infer possible causal influences from group outcomes. Finally, a correlational model allows for other potentially modifying circumstances. For example, a father's punitive disciplinary techniques might have a particularly potent effect in combination with certain patterns of maternal behavior. On the whole, a vastly more differentiated model of psychological influences can be entertained.

Correlational studies have uncovered a variety of significant associations between paternal and child characteristics. It should be noted, of course, that much more effort has gone into seeking associations between maternal behaviors and child development, and, in some research, maternal and "parental" sources of influence are considered synonymous (see Maccoby & Martin, 1983, for a review of this area). Illustrative studies addressing father and child attributes include research by Hoffman (1975), who found that the extent to which fathers expressed prosocial moral values correlated significantly with their son's and daughter's prosocial behavior, measured by peer nomination. For mothers, similar correlations were significant only for daughters. Radin (1973) found that observed paternal nurturance in the home setting was significantly related to cognitive competence in preschool white boys, particularly middle-class youngsters. Cognitive competence was measured on a standard test, the Stanford–Binet.

By far the strongest challenge to correlation-based studies of parent and child attributes was posed by Bell (1968). Bell called attention to the indeterminate directionality of influence in studies of this nature, pointing out that it was merely an assumption that parental behavior "socializes" the child. Correlational relationships between harsh disciplinary techniques and child aggressiveness, Bell asserted, were as likely a "child effect" upon the parent. For example, a child might be prone to highly active, rambunctious behavior on a congenital or genetic basis; if the parent experienced difficulty in asserting control over such a child, the parent might more frequently escalate controlling behaviors and resort to more extreme forms of control including physical punishment. An interactional pattern yielding a positive correlation between parental punishment and child aggressiveness might as likely be due to parental reactivity to the child as it might be a parental cause of child aggressiveness. Bell's theoretical challenge had a wide impact upon the field of developmental psychology, leading eventually to *transactional* or mutual regulatory models of interaction (Sameroff & Chandler, 1975) in which it was recognized that both parent and child reciprocally influence one another in the course of the child's development.

OTHER TRENDS AFFECTING
RESEARCH ON FATHERHOOD

In the late 1960s and 1970s two new trends emerged in the methodology and substance of developmental research, both of which encompassed budding interest in fatherhood. The first was a disaffection with measurement of either parental or child characteristics based upon self-report procedures, such as interviews and questionnaires, along with a consequent increase in emphasis upon observational procedures. The second trend was a burgeoning of interest in infancy. Both trends converged in the first observational studies of father–infant interaction.

The disaffection with self-report procedures, the interview in particular, can be traced to research findings that challenged their accuracy and validity on matters subject to independent verification. Perhaps the ultimate study of children's socialization based almost entirely upon interview data was by Sears, Maccoby, and Levin (1957). An effort at replication and extension of these findings, conceptualized in terms of social learning principles, proved disappointing, and an incisive critique of its methodological techniques was forthcoming (Yarrow, Campbell, & Burton, 1968). Direct observation had always been a central part of the scientific method as applied to developmental studies, and is evident in Darwin's 2-year record of observations of his son published in 1877 (cited by Cairns, 1983). From the behaviorism of John B. Watson through the important discriptive studies of children during the 1930s, observational methods were primary. The redirection of this effort, however, was toward observation of parental behavior as it became clear that parents' reports of their own practices were of uncertain validity.

The second trend was an expanded interest in infancy. What apparently spurred this greater interest was a heightened appreciation of the adaptive capacities of the young infant, the social, sensory, motor, and cognitive capacities that had been underestimated in past studies of infants. Vigorous research was conducted on the compentencies of the infant and how they emerged. Indeed, a full handbook of infancy research was compiled by Osofsky (1979).

A prime example of the convergence of observational methods applied to the study of parental (maternal) behavior and the new found appreciation of the adaptive capacities of the young infant is found in the important research of Mary Ainsworth (1963, 1964). Ainsworth and John Bowlby, following a long tradition that derives from psychoanalytic theory, conceptualized the quality of the mother–infant attachment relationship as critical for the infant's future development. They directed attention to both the signaling capacities of the infant and attributes of the mother, such as her sensitivity to the infant's needs, that promoted a secure attachment relationship. One of the earliest studies of infant attachment (Schaffer & Emerson, 1964) as well as Ainsworth's own reports of infant attachments in a Third World setting (Ainsworth, 1963) showed that, given the opportunity, infants readily formed multiple attachment relationships. From an evolutionary perspective, which is part of the conceptual roots of attachment theory, creatures with such prolonged periods of helplessness as humans probably require the capacity for multiple attachments for sheer survival.

Thus, attachment theory, although obviously directed primarily to the mother–infant relationship, still provided a stronger theoretical basis for examining the father–infant relationship than did any conceptual alternative.

DESCRIPTIVE STUDIES OF FATHER–INFANT INTERACTION

A number of observational studies of father–infant interaction were conducted in the late 1970s. On the whole, these took the form of comparisons between mothers and fathers in amount, style, and content of interactive behavior, often with subcomparisons for male and female infants studied from the newborn period through toddlerhood. Observational settings in which studies were conducted included natural home environments, the hospital setting a few days after delivery, and laboratory situations that, to varying degrees, either attempted to simulate the natural environment or manipulate circumstances to maximize the occurrence of events being studied. Laboratory settings also permitted video recording of the participants under optimal conditions, which, in turn, permitted more fine-grained analyses of behavioral events and their sequences.

A sampling of observational studies of paternal interactions includes work by Lamb (1976, 1977), who called attention to the high rates of affiliative behaviors that were more characteristic of infants at home with their fathers than with their mothers, that paternal physical contact was most often associated with play, and that the father and male child had a special affinity for one another evident in the second year of life. Clarke-Stewart (1978) compared fathers and mothers when interacting with their toddler in the home setting. She pointed out that mothers generally interacted at higher rates than fathers did, especially in providing greater amounts of verbal stimulation and caregiving. Fathers' play behavior was more often physical and arousing, whereas mothers' play behavior was more often didactic and utilized toys. Yogman et al. (1977) described detailed analyses of short periods of face-to-face play in a laboratory setting during infants' first half year of life; mothers were found to be more verbal in their interaction, whereas fathers more frequently interacted tactually. Parke and Sawin (1980) observed mothers and fathers feeding and playing with their infants in the hospital setting and again at home at ages 6 weeks and 3 months. Mothers engaged more often in caregiving, whereas fathers engaged in more social stimulation which, they noted, might be a precursor of the father's emerging role as playmate. Parke and Sawin also were among the first to study the sequential character of father–infant interaction and to compare it with similar measures of mother and infant.

Pedersen (1980), reviewing several observational studies in the infancy and toddler period, noted that although researchers often highlight the areas of difference between mothers and fathers, studies show many more variables on which mother and father do not differ significantly from one another. Moreover, although research of this nature focuses upon interesting central tendencies of behavior, the results tend to draw attention away from the variability that different fathers show, the range of adaptations that exist within contemporary families.

THE LEADING EDGE IN RESEARCH ON FATHERHOOD

Most recent developments in research on fatherhood suggest three final developments: (a) individual differences in paternal adaptations appear to be receiving more attention, (b) longitudinal studies are more prevalent, and (c) paternal adaptations are being viewed within the context of other family members and other relationship parameters. The research studies presented in this volume follow this pattern.

In the context of earlier studies featuring a correlational strategy, individual differences in paternal behavioral patterns were noted, and child developmental outcomes were viewed as dependent variables. More recent work appears to try to establish a psychological basis for variation in paternal adaptations. In the language of experimental studies, the father's behavior with the child has become the dependent variable. To illustrate, Russell (1978) investigated the possibility that a father's sex-role identification (measured on the Bem scale) is related to the amount of time he spent in either caregiving or social play with young children. Measures of parental behavior based on interviews were used with a sample of Australian families. Psychologically androgynous fathers were found to be significantly more involved in both caregiving and play than masculine fathers; androgynous and feminine fathers combined were more involved in caregiving and play than masculine and undifferentiated fathers combined. Mother's scores on the sex role identification scale were not significantly related to their time spent in caregiving and play, a finding that Russell interpreted as due to more rigid cultural definitions of the maternal role.

In a conceptually related study, Palkovitz (1984) examined paternal sex role identification (also with the Bem scale) in relation to the observed interactions of fathers with their 5-month-old infants. Consistent with Russell's findings, psychologically androgynous fathers showed the highest rates of involvement with their infants. Contrary to generalizations suggested from gender-comparison studies, androgynous fathers engaged in high rates of both playful behavior and caregiving activities. Palkovitz also found that fathers tended to conform to patterns and expectations that their spouses maintained were appropriate for men, but only when spouses were present in the situation.

As with all cross-sectional correlational studies, the two just mentioned suffer from not knowing whether the father's androgynous sex-role identification may be understood as a true predictor variable. If causal inferences are entertained, it is important to evaluate the father's sex-role identification prior to potential influence by the child's unique characteristics, the birth events, and the current relationship with the child. Whether A (the father's sex-role identification) affects B (his amount of caregiving and play) cannot be determined when the question is examined cross-sectionally. Except with longitudinal assessments one cannot rule out that it is equally possible for fathers to become highly involved with caregiving and play for reasons other than sex-role identification, and then subsequently score high on measures of psychological adrogeny. Thus, B may cause A, or both may co-vary because of another variable, C. Longitudinal designs allow a slightly stronger causal inference because of the temporal precedence of A, one of the key criteria for inferring cause (Cook & Campbell, 1979).

In several of the chapters that follow, researchers were guided by a focus upon individual differences and an attempt to identify predictor variables that temporally preceded the father's relationship with his own child. Longitudinal designs can greatly increase interpretive credibility as long as outcomes, the dependent variables, do not contaminate the predictor variables.

The final element in research at the leading edge is that paternal adaptations are being viewed within the context of other family members and other relationship parameters. Whereas much of past research on mother–infant adaptations was viewed in isolation from the father—except for appropriate controls for socioeconomic level—current research efforts are more sensitive to the interplay of family relationships that may influence parental adaptations. To illustrate, it is possible that aspects of the marital relationship, the sense of support and confirmation that is received from one's spouse, may impinge upon the mother's or father's parental effectiveness. The traditional view, apparent in Bowlby's (1951) early writings, was that the father's primary contribution to the family was to provide economic resources and emotional support to the mother:

> Fathers have their uses even in infancy. Not only do they provide for their wives to enable them to devote themselves unrestrictedly to the care of the infant and toddler, but, by providing love and companionship, they support her emotionally and help her maintain that harmonious contented mood in the aura of which the infant thrives. (p. 13)

Two questions that are related to Bowlby's view of the father as a source of emotional support to the mother are whether there are consequences of variation in the father's capacity or willingness to be supportive and whether the father, too, can derive benefit from emotional support for his nurturing role from the wife/mother. These questions prompt attention to a range of new issues regarding the nature of emotional support and its delineation from the broader concept of marital satisfaction.

Both Aldous (1977) and Furstenberg (1985) noted that research that contemplates influences between marital and parental functioning crosses conventional disciplinary boundaries. Traditionally, the study of marital relationships has been the province of family sociology, a discipline that has had little interest in the parenting of young children; developmental psychology, on the other hand, has not considered the marital relationship as a meaningful influence upon parent–child interaction. The expansion of our understanding of parental functioning to include influences upon it by other family members, as well as relationships between family members other than the parent, requires new conceptual models. Examples of efforts in that direction are represented by Belsky (1981) and Minuchin (1985) and are apparent in several of the chapters that follow.

In this chapter, an overview of past approaches to research on fatherhood has been presented, and a sampling of research findings was included in relation to particular research strategies. The economic provider role of the father does not appear so central as in earlier periods, whereas the father's direct interactive experience, even with very young children, is now central. Longitudinal approaches to understanding the father's contribution to family experience are favored, and the conceptualization of early experience in the family has been elaborated to recognize the interplay of different family members and their relationships upon the emergent role of the father. The chapters that follow are prime examples of these new research approaches.

REFERENCES

Ainsworth, M. D. S. (1963). The development of infant–mother interaction among the Ganda. In B. M. Foss (Ed.), *Determinants of infant behavior* (Vol. 2 pp. 67–112). New York: Wiley.

Ainsworth, M. D. S. (1964). Patterns of attachment behavior shown by the infant in interaction with his mother. *Merrill-Palmer Quarterly, 10,* 51–58

Aldous, J. (1977). Family interaction patterns. *Annual Review of Sociology, 3,* 105–135.

Bell, R. Q. (1968). A reinterpretation of the direction of effects in studies of socialization. *Psychological Review, 75,* 81–95.

Belsky, J. (1981). Early human experience: A family perspective. *Developmental Psychology, 17,* (1), 3–23.

Biller, H. B. (1974). *Paternal deprivation.* Lexington, MA: Heath.

Block, J. H., Block, J., & Gjerde, P. F. (1986). The personality of children prior to divorce: A prospective study. *Child Development, 57,* 827–840.

Bowlby, J. (1951). *Maternal care and mental health.* Geneva: WHO.

Broman, S. H., Nichols, P. L., & Kennedy, W. A. (1975). *Preschool IQ: Parental and early developmental correlates.* Hillsdale, NJ: Lawrence Erlbaum Associates.

Cairns, R. B. (1983). The emergence of developmental psychology. In P. H. Mussen (Ed.), *Handbook of child psychology* (Vol. 1, pp. 41–102). New York: Wiley.

Clarke-Stewart, K. (1978). And daddy makes three: The father's impact on mother and young child. *Child Development, 49,* 466–478.

Cook, T., & Campbell, D. (1979). *Quasi-experimentation: Design and analysis issues for field settings.* Chicago: Rand McNally.

Eron, L. D., Walder, L. O., & Lefkowitz, M. M. (1971). *Learning of aggression in children.* Boston: Little, Brown.

Furstenberg, F. F. (1985). Sociological ventures in child development. *Child Development, 56,* 281–288.

Herzog, E., & Sudia, C. E. (1973). Children in fatherless families. In B. M. Campbell & H. N. Ricciuti (Eds.), *Review of child development research* (Vol.3, pp. 141–232). Chicago: University of Chicago Press.

Hess, R. D. (1970). Social class and ethnic influences on socialization. In P. H. Mussen (Ed.), *Carmichael's manual of child psychology* (3rd ed., pp. 457–557). New York: Wiley.

Hoffman, M. L. (1975). Altruistic behavior and the parent–child relationship. *Journal of Personality and Social Psychology, 31,* 937–943.

Hollingshead, A. B., & Redlich, F. C. (1958). *Social class and mental illness: A community study.* New York: Wiley.

Kohn, M. L., & Schooler, C. (1983). *Work and personality: An inquiry into the impact of social stratification.* Norwood, NJ: Ablex.

Lamb, M. E. (1976). Interactions between eight-month-old children and their fathers and mothers. In M. E. Lamb (Ed.), *The role of the father in child development* (pp. 307–327). New York: Wiley.

Lamb, M. E. (1977). The development of mother–infant and father–infant attachments in the second year of life. *Developmental Psychology, 13,* 637–648.

Lamb, M. E. (1986). The changing roles of fathers. In M. E. Lamb (Ed.), *The father's role: Applied perspectives* (pp. 3–27). New York: Wiley.

Maccoby, E. E., & Martin, J. A. (1983). Socialization in the context of the family: Parent-child interaction. In P. H. Mussen (Ed.), *Handbook of child psychology* (Vol. 4, 4th ed., pp. 1–101). New York: Wiley.

Minuchin, P. (1985). Families and individual development: Provocations from the field of family therapy. *Child Development, 56,* 289–302.

Osofsky, J. D. (Ed.). (1979). *Handbook of infant development.* New York: Wiley.

Palkovitz, R. (1984). Parental attitudes and fathers' interactions with their 5-month-old infants. *Developmental Psychology, 20* (6), 1054–1060.

Parke, R. D., & Sawin, D. B. (1980). The family in early infancy: Social interactional and attitudinal analyses. In F. A. Pedersen (Ed.), *The father–infant relationship: Observational studies in the family setting* (pp. 44–70). New York: Praeger.

Pedersen, F. A. (1976). Does research on children reared in father-absent families yield information on father influences? *Family Coordinator, 25,* 457–464.

Pedersen, F. A. (1980). Overview: Answers and reformlated questions. In F. A. Pedersen (Ed.), *The father-infant relationship: Observational studies in the family setting* (pp. 147–163). New York: Praeger.

Radin, N. (1973). Observed paternal behaviors as antecedents of intellectual functioning in young boys. *Developmental Psychology, 8,* 369–376.

Russell, G. (1978). The father role and its relation to masculinity, femininity, and androgyny. *Child Development, 49,* 1174–1181.

Sameroff, A. J., & Chandler, M. J. (1975). Reproductive risk and the continuum of caretaking casualty. In F. D. Horowitz (Ed.), *Review of child development research* (Vol. 4, pp. 187–244). Chicago: University of Chicago Press.

Schaffer, H. R., & Emerson, P. E. (1964). The development of social attachments in infancy. *Monographs of the Society for Research in Child Development, 29* (Serial No. 94).

Sears, P. S. (1951). Doll play aggression in normal young children: Influence of sex, age, sibling status, father's absence. *Psychological Monographs, 65* (No. 6).

Sears, R. R., Maccoby, E. E., & Levin, H. (1957). *Patterns of child rearing.* Evanston, IL: Row Peterson.

Shinn, M. (1978). Father absence and children's cognitive development. *Psychological Bulletin, 85,* 295–324.

Svanum, S., Bringle, R. G., & McLaughlin, J. E. (1982). Father absence and cognitive performance in a large sample of six- to eleven-year-old children. *Child Development, 53,* 136–143.

Yarrow, L. J. (1964). Separation from parents during early childhood. In M. L. Hoffman & L. W. Hoffman (Eds.), *Review of child development research* (Vol. 1, pp. 89–136). New York: Russell Sage Foundation.

Yarrow, M. R., Campbell, J. D., & Burton, R. (1968). *Child rearing, an inquiry into research and methods.* San Francisco: Jossey-Bass.

Yogman, M. W., Dixon, S., Tronick, E., Als, H., Adamson, L., Lester, B., & Brazelton, T. B. (1977, April). *The goals and structure of face-to-face interaction between infants and fathers.* Paper presented at the meeting of the Society for Research in Child Development, New Orleans.

Predicting Strain in Mothers and Fathers of 6-Month-Old Infants
A Short-Term Longitudinal Study

S. Shirley Feldman
Stanford University

Role transitions and life-event changes have long been recognized as stressful (George, 1980; Holmes & Rahe, 1967), for they may require the performance of new and distinctive tasks (Duvall, 1971), the redefinition of behaviors and beliefs (Abrahams, Feldman, & Nash, 1978; Parsons & Bales, 1955), and even the reorientation and reorganization of personality (Feldman, Biringen, & Nash, 1981; Lidz, 1976). Consequently, the behavioral, attitudinal, and relational patterns that are developed for one stage of life may no longer be functional at a later stage.

One of the most dramatic transitions in the family life cycle, experienced by more than 80% of all adults, occurs between the stages of expectancy and parenthood. Adults themselves list the bearing of children and the establishment of a family as important turning points in their lives (Lowenthal & Chiriboga, 1972). For many, becoming a parent affects the development of self-concept and self-esteem (Neugarten, 1968), contributes to life satisfaction and dissatisfaction (Campbell, 1975), and gives a sense of worth and meaning to life (Erikson, 1950).

The advent of parenthood necessitates the adoption of demanding and often unfamiliar roles that differ in kind and extent for fathers and mothers. The man usually assumes the major responsibility for providing financial and physical security for his now-expanded family—a role he may have previously shared with his wife. In addition, the role of husband requires considerable redefinition in accord with his wife's exacting new roles and the increased demands on her time and energy. The woman, on the other hand, is typically primary caregiver to the child and remains responsible for that care, regardless of whether she administers it or delegates it to others. Profound changes occur in virtually every aspect of a woman's life. Paid work is usually terminated toward the end of the pregnancy and shared responsibility at work is replaced with sole responsibility at home. The direct goal-oriented problem solving of the workforce is disfunctional for the mother who must give priority to her baby's needs before achieving closure on her home-making or her work-related tasks. The former balance between work and leisure is now upset by the full-time "on-call" role of mother. Social (and work) contacts with other adults are outnumbered by interactions with a dependent, non-verbal child. Even familiar roles such as wife or daughter require extensive redefinition. Clearly, the role changes explicit and implicit during the transition to parenthood are of considerable magnitude and breadth.

In light of extensive psychological disruption, behavioral change and role redefinitions demanded by the transition to parenthood, a sense of strain might seem to be a highly likely outcome, at least during the first months. However, the individual's perception of the meaning and response to parenthood as a life-event change is as important for adaptation as the actual role transition itself (Lowenthal, Thurnher, & Chiriboga, 1975). Accordingly, the range of reactions to first-time parenthood is diverse, ranging from severe depression through various degrees of stress and strain, to a total sense of well-being (Magnus, 1980).

The focus of this chapter is on individual differences in subjectively experienced strain by mothers and fathers of young infants. This topic is of considerable importance for not only is strain a highly unpleasant state for those experiencing it, but it also has effects on parental competence. Stress and strain diminish psychological energy available for interaction with others and render the person less sensitive and less attuned to the needs of others (Belsky, Robins, & Gamble, 1984). Serious consequences may result for the young infant whose well-being depends on responsive, nurturant interactions by his parents (Belsky, 1984).

To date, there have been three approaches to studying adjustment to the transition to parenthood. Clinicians have focused on the intrapsychic needs and conflicts of expectant men and women and of couples who have recently become parents (Benedek, 1970; Bibring, Dwyer, Huntington, & Valentine, 1961; Colman, 1969; Curtis, 1955; Deutscher, 1970; Gordon & Gordon, 1957; Hartman & Nicolay, 1966; Loesch & Greenberg, 1962; Retterstol, 1968; Robin, 1962; Senn & Hartford, 1968; Wainwright, 1966). Although rich in clinical insights, the subjectivity of the data and the small and frequently atypical subject populations (e.g., men in therapy, or unmarried women) limits generalizing from these results.

A second body of evidence has been provided by family sociologists studying the hypothesis of "parenthood as crisis" (LeMasters, 1957). The best of these studies are large-scale longitudinal investigations of shifts in attitudes between pregnancy and parenthood (Feldman, 1971; Myerowitz & Feldman, 1966; Ryder, 1973). This evidence is largely restricted to marital satisfaction.

Recently, more broad-based longitudinal studies have been carried out on the transition to parenthood from a psychological perspective (Cowan & Cowan, 1983; Grimm & Venet, 1966; Grossman, Eichler, & Winickoff, 1980; Leifer, 1977; Nilsson & Almgren, 1970; Shereshefsky & Yarrow, 1974). In many of these studies, individual differences in personal and marital adjustment (as well as in parenting behavior) are predicted from diverse antecedents assessed during pregnancy. With one notable exception (Grossman et al., 1980), however, this literature neglects the fathers' adjustment at parenthood and focuses exclusively on the reaction of women. The inattention to fathers is lamentable: Not only is fatherhood important to men (Fein, 1978; Tasch, 1952) but fathers are becoming more actively involved in interacting with and caring for their children (Parke & O'Leary; 1976, Russell & Radin, 1983). Thus, adjustment to such a major new role as fatherhood is worthy of study in its own right.

Perhaps an even more compelling reason to study men as well as women as they become parents is the recognition that for most people the transition to parenthood is a family event, not just an individual event. The family (the husband and wife) is a social system marked by interdependent roles and reciprocal relations. Any perturbation of the social system, such as the birth of an infant, impacts on each member individually and on the system qua system. To understand the behavior of one family member, the reactions and behaviors of the other members must be recognized and assessed. Thus, to understand how parents adjust to the transition to parenthood it is necessary to supplement the data on individuals by studying how the reactions of husbands influence wives, and wives influence husbands.

The study to be reported in this chapter attempts to predict strain in adjustment at parenthood from measures assessed during expectancy. It differs from other psychological research in this area in two ways: First, both men and women are studied; second, the characteristics and reactions of the spouse during pregnancy are considered as potentially prognostic of strain at parenthood.

METHOD

Subjects

The subjects of the study were 30 highly educated American-born Caucasian primigravidae and their husbands, first seen during the last trimester of pregnancy. Initially, 34 couples were seen, but 3 couples moved from the area, and a fourth couple declined to return. Couples were recruited from prenatal exercise classes. About 70% of the couples volunteered after hearing the description of the studies.

The age of the women when first seen ranged from 21 to 35 years, with a mean age of 27.9 years (SD = 3.8). Seventy-four percent were between 24-32 years of age. Men's ages ranged from 23 to 40, with a mean of 31.0 years (SD = 4.3). Seventy-eight percent of the men were between 25-35 years old.

More than half the women were working at the time of the first session, 29% had given up work during the third trimester, and the remainder had stopped work earlier. The women were (or had been) employed as teachers and nurses (30%), office workers (21%), programmers and accountants (12%), managers (9%), advanced degree students (19%), and technicians (9%). Ten women (32%) had returned to work (half-time or more) by the time they were seen for the second session, when their infants were 6 months old. Among the men, 35% were professionals, 32% held managerial positions, 26% had technical jobs, and 6% were in sales.

The pregnancy was planned by 65% of the sample, and by the time of the first session, was wanted by 95% of the sample. Both the women and men were immersed in the pregnancy experience; they attended prenatal classes and read books on pregnancy, childbirth, and parenting, and the men attended the birth of their child. As fathers, despite assumption of the traditional breadwinner role, these men were psychologically invested in their offspring. They played with them nightly (100%), and looked after the infant on a regular or "as needed" basis.

Procedure

Subjects were seen twice, first during the third trimester of their wives' pregnancies and again 7-9 months later, when their babies were 6-8 months old. Information obtained during expectancy concerned six general areas: sex typing, the marital relationship, adjustment to expectancy, financial and job-related concerns, relations with parents and in-laws, and background information. Expectant fathers and their wives participated separately in lengthy interviews (2-2½ hrs.), and completed three rating scales, the Bem Sex Role Inventory (BSRI) the Bem Satisfaction Scale, (Bem, 1976), and the Household Tasks Checklist.

During the second visit, five scales were administered: the Mood Scale; the BSRI; the Bem Satisfaction Scale; Personal Change Ratings of health, energy, and appearance; and the Social Change Scale. Each subject was also observed interacting with his or her child, separately in a play situation, and jointly with spouse while being interviewed concerning reactions to parenthood. After the interview, subjects were given a form on which they were requested to list what they liked most and least about parenthood.

Measures Assessed During Expectancy

The Bem Sex Role Inventory (BSRI; Bem, 1974) is a Likert-type scale consisting of 20 feminine, 20 masculine, and 20 neutral personality traits. Scores for each adjective range from 1 = not at all like me to 7 = almost always like me.

An expressive personality trait score based on 12 feminine items (alpha = .87) included the following: sympathetic, sensitive, compassionate, understanding, tender, affectionate, gentle, tender, warm, cheerful, eager to soothe hurt feelings, and loves children. An instrumental personality trait score based on 17 masculine items (alpha = .90) included the following: acts as leader, assertive, dominant, strong personality, forceful, aggressive, willing to take a stand, independent, defends beliefs, willing to take risks, individualistic, has leadership abilities, self-sufficient, decisive, ambitious, self-reliant, and competitive.

Expectancy Interview.   An extensive, open-ended interview tapped the following content areas: motivation for parenthood, attitudes and reactions to expectancy (including health, appearance, behavior, moods, dreams), the marital relationship, relationship with parents (past and present) and parents-in-law, the development of maternal/paternal feelings, anticipation of changes, and the kind of parents subjects thought they would become.

Each interview was read in its entirety at least six times by two or more independent coders. After each reading, coders rated three to five scales in a given area (e.g., marriage, pregnancy adjustment) using 4- or 5-point rating scales. The resulting scales, listed here, are described in Table 2.1. Further details appear elsewhere (Feldman, Nash, & Aschenbrenner, 1983). Inter-rater agreement was 86%, with any discrepancies resolved by discussion.

Reaction to pregnancy was assessed in nine scales including overall reaction to expectancy, reaction to pregnant body, detachment or turning away from involvement with people and activities, anxiety, mood changes, emotional rehearsal (including daydreams, fantasies of being parent) changes in self-concept, stress (excluding marital problems), and weight of responsibility.

TABLE 2.1
Summary of Interview Scales and the Major Questions on Which They Were Based

Marriage

1. *Quality of marital relationship* (1 = poor to 5 = excellent)
   Direct questions included how satisfying is the marriage, number and intensity of disagreements, ease or difficulty of communication, and satisfaction from sexuality. Less direct questions included what's important to you, most and least satisfying, most on mind, dreams and nightmares, sources of anxiety.

2. *Problems in marital relationship* (1 = few, if any, 4 = many)
   Areas included poor quality of marriage, increased stress in the relationship during expectancy, feelings of estrangement from spouse, sexual difficulties, increase in number of arguments, and mood changes.

3. *Empathy with Spouse* (1 = hardly at all, 4 = great deal)
   empathy, ease of communication

Reaction to Expectancy

1. *Overall adjustment* (1 = negative, 5 = very positive)
   Direct questions included nature of expectancy, differences from expectations of it. Less direct questions included what's important to you, what's most and least satisfying, reactions to prenatal classes and quickening, changes in mood and self-concept, fears, anxiety, etc.

2. *Reaction to wife's body changes* (1 = very negative, 5 = very positive)
   (NB this scale was independent from 1.)
   Questions tapped feelings about wife's pregnant appearance, her body changes, feelings of self-consciousness, thought when touching wife's abdomen, concern about wife's future figure, sexuality.

3. *Detachment* (1 = no change, 3 = a lot of change)
   Feelings of detachment, turning focus inward on self, less focus on relationships with spouse, parents, friends.

4. *Anxiety* (1 = not anxious, 4 = very anxious)
   Fears, anxieties, arguments with spouse, description of the expectancy experience; prenatal class experience; health, anxiety about sex; reaction to quickening; superstitions, unpleasant thoughts, nightmares; and worry about baby, relationship, spouse's labor and delivery; and readiness for parenthood (NB financial anxiety excluded from this scale).

5. *Stress* (1 = not stressed, 4 = very stressed)
   Financial difficulties, fears, anxieties, arguments with spouse, description of the expectancy experience; prenatal class experience; health; anxiety about sex; reaction to quickening; superstitions, unpleasant thoughts, nightmares; worry about baby, relationship, labor and delivery; and readiness for parenthood (marital problems excluded from this scale).

6. *Weight of responsibility* (1 = minimal, not a worry, 4 = major pressure)
   Based on thoughts most on mind, sources of dissatisfaction, things least enjoyed, unpleasant thoughts, source of couple conflicts, change in self-concept, least satisfying aspect of marriage, anticipated problems, three wishes.

TABLE 2.1
(Continued)

Reaction to Expectancy

---

7. *Mood changes* (1 = more moody, 3 = no change, 5 = more positive or even)
   Based on mood change, frequency and basis of arguments, recent changes in self.
8. *Change in self-concept* (1 = minimal, 3 = a lot of change)
   Scored from two direct questions: Do you think you've changed and do you think differently of yourself. Change in self-concept was always in a positive direction (e.g., more responsible, more motherly).
9. *Emotional rehearsal for parenthood* (1 = not at all, 4 = a lot)
   Included daydreaming, fantasies, maternal/paternal feelings, reactions to quickening, feelings of protectiveness, what the subject enjoyed thinking about, anticipation of first two weeks after birth, and anticipation of type of parent will be. Open-ended questions were also included.

Relationship with Significant Others

---

1. *Relation with mother* and *Relation with father* (1 = poor to 5 = very good)
   These separate scales include past and current relations, parents enjoyment of parenthood while subject was growing up, change in relationship since expectancy, and anticipation of parents as grandparents.
2. *Relation with parents-in-law* (1 = poor to 5 = very good)
   Includes current relations with in-laws and anticipation of in-laws as grandparents. As scores regarding mother- and father-in-law were very highly correlated (r = 70) these scores were combined.

Other

---

1. *Salience of job* (1 = low, 3 = high)
   Included description of job and attitude to job, and open-ended questions such as sources of satisfaction and dissatisfaction, interests not shared with spouse, who and what are most on mind, pleasant and unpleasant thoughts, and self-description.

Background/Demographics

---

1. *Plannedness of pregnancy* (1 = unplanned, 3 = planned)
   Both members of the marital dyad received identical scores for this measure.
2. *Age of subject*

Relationships with significant others were assessed by three scales about the marriage, and five about other family members. These included quality of marital relations, problems in the marriage, empathy with spouse, relationship with mother and father (separate scales) and present relations with in-laws, and frequency of contact with parents and in-laws.

Other measures derived from the interview included job salience, plannedness of pregnancy, and background information on the respondents.

The Bem Satisfaction Scale (Bem, 1976) consisted of 39 statements, on which the subject rated his/her self-satisfaction. Scores ranged from 1 = very dissatisfied to 5 = very satisfied with that part of myself. In addition to a general self-satisfaction score (the average of 39 items) three subscores were examined. Satisfaction with open emotional qualities (9 items $K\text{-}R20$ = .79) included such items as my ability to express affection, my self-understanding, the tolerance I show for others' shortcomings. Satisfaction with autonomy/competence (9 items, $K\text{-}R20$ = .74) included such items as my ability to make decisions, the sense of accomplishment I feel, the amount of independence I show. Satisfaction with tending marital relation (5 items $K\text{-}R20$ = .71) included such items as the amount of effort I put into having a good relationship with my spouse, and the effort I put into helping my spouse realize his/her goals.

The Household Responsibilities Checklist consisted of eight items, which subjects rated on the extent to which they took responsibility relative to their spouse. Scores ranged from 1 = spouse does most to 4 = subject does most. The Masculine Household Task score was the mean of the four items (bringing in income, budgeting, carpentry, car repair; $K\text{-}R20$ = .64). The Feminine Household Task score was the mean of three items (housework, shopping, cooking; $K\text{-}R20$ = .90). The fourth feminine item, furniture arrangement, did not correlate with the other three items and was not included.

Responsiveness to an unfamiliar baby was observed from behind a one-way mirror while the subject was in a waiting room. Six-second timed observations were made of proximal and distal bids, with high inter-observer reliability r = .93 (see Feldman & Nash, 1978 for more information).

Predictors from Expectancy

To reduce the number of predictors we created a priori conceptual clusters of variables and then subjected them to factor analysis, separately for men and women. The results are shown in Table 2.2. Five of the factors were similar for men and women including the sex-typed factors (instrumentality, expressiveness), relationship with parents and in-laws, and positive expectancy experience. The marriage and stress factors differed for men and women. In each case, a single factor emerged for one sex and two factors emerged for the other sex.

In addition to the eight factor scores, the following six items were maintained as predictors: emotional rehearsal for parenthood (interview), change in self-concept to feeling more parent-like, scores on both masculine and feminine household tasks, mother's age and plannedness of pregnancy. Thus there were a total of 14 potential predictors.

TABLE 2.2
Description of the Factor Scores Used as Predictors of Parent's Stress

Items Entered into Factor Analysis	Source of Data	Factor Label and Loadings	
		Women	Men
Marriage		Good Marriage	Empathic Marriage
Quality of relationship	Interview	.69	.43
Empathy with spouse	Interview	.34	.98
Satisfaction with relation to spouse	Satisfaction Scale	.66	.27
			Marital Tension
Problems in marriage	Interview	-.37	0.53
Detachment from spouse	Interview	-.62	1.0
Expressiveness		Expressiveness	Expressiveness
Expressive personality traits	BSRI	.80	.77
Satisfaction with emotional response	Satisfaction Scale	.76	.59
Responsiveness to unfamiliar baby	Observation	.40	.38
Instrumentality		Instrumentality	Instrumentality
Instrumental personality traits	BSRI	.95	.58
Satisfaction with autonomy/competence	Satisfaction Scale	.42	.95
Salience of job	Interview	.41	.44
Relation with Parents		Parental Relations	Parental Relations
Relationship with mother	Interview	.97	.78
Relationship with father	Interview	.54	.79
Frequency of contact	Interview	.22	.76

TABLE 2.2
(Continued)

Items Entered into Factor Analysis	Source of Data	Factor Label and Loadings	
		Women	*Men*
Marriage		Good Marriage	Empathic Marriage
Relation with In-laws		In-law Relations	In-law Relations
Relations with in-laws	Interview	.60	.55
Frequency of contact	Interview	.20	.23
Experience of Expectancy		Positive Expectancy	Positive Expectancy
Overall adjustment to pregnancy	Interview	.93	.63
Reaction to (wife's) body	Interview	.35	.69
Mood changes	Interview	.37	.41
Stress		Financial Stress	General Stress
Stress (excluding stress in marriage)	Interview	.65	.81
Weight of responsibility	Interview	.67	.65
		Nonfinancial stress	
Anxiety	Interview	.62	.64

Measures Assessed During Parenthood

The Mood Scale, a Likert-type scale, consisted of 21 items describing mood states with scale points range from 1 = hardly ever to 5 = very often. The outcome variable, strain at parenthood, was the mean score of five items: overwhelmed, tense or keyed up, inadequate, sad for no reason, and discouraged.

These five items were selected on an a priori basis, and then factor analyzed (using principal components analysis with iteration) three times: for men, for women, and for the combined sample. The factor analysis confirmed that the items comprised a single cluster with factor loadings ranging from .50 to .89. Inter-item correlations yielded an alpha of .73 for women, .76 for men, and .70 for the total sample.

Many other measures were collected at parenthood. Because they were used only to check the validity of the outcome measure, strain at parenthood, they are listed briefly. More information about these measures can be found elsewhere (Feldman & Nash, 1984; Feldman et al., 1983).

Rating Scales.   The BSRI and Satisfaction Scales (described previously) were readministered with the addition of three items to the satisfaction scale concerning self as parent. In addition, subjects described personal changes in health, energy, and appearance, amount and type of social changes and the extent to which they were bothered or pleased by them. Subjects rated their parenting style, listed the things they liked most and least about being a parent, and described division of parenting responsibilities at home.

Observational Measures.   Parents' behavior with their infants was observed in three situations. While each subject and his or her infant was in a playroom furnished with a one-way observation mirror, observers using 6-second time-sampling noted each instance of parental caretaking during a free-play situation and a structured-play situation. Interobserver reliability was 97%. The total number of instances of caretaking in these two situations formed Caretaking during play.

In the same playroom, parents were then interviewed together concerning reactions to parenthood. Using event-sampling, observers noted each parent's affect while interacting with the infant, distance from the baby, playing, caretaking, and responses to fussing. Caretaking during the interview was the number of instances of caretaking observed. Affective interaction was a rating ranging from 3 = low to 10 = high based on affect and distance from baby. Interobserver agreement was 87%, with discrepancies between raters resolved by discussion.

Validity of the Measure "Strain at Parenthood"

For women, strain at parenthood correlated with low self-satisfaction ($r = -.46$, $p < .01$), low instrumentality ($r = -.54$, $p < .001$), many adverse social changes ($r = -.37$, $p < .05$), particularly in relationship to husband ($r = -.54$, $p < .001$), recent declines in energy ($r = -.36$, $p < .05$), and appearance ($r = -.39$, p $< .05$). In terms of parenting measures, strain correlated with low affective interaction ($r = -.37$, $p < .05$) but high caretaking ($r = .40$, $p < .05$) during an interview, a self-reported parenting style that was patient ($r = .46$, $p < .01$), low in playfulness ($r = -.41$, $p < .001$), high in feeling worried/puzzled ($r = .44$, $p < .01$), and a relatively short list of things liked most about the baby ($r = -.29$, $p < .10$).

For men, concurrent correlates of strain at parenthood were less extensive. Strain was associated with greater involvement in childcare as observed during a play session ($r = .31$, $p < .05$), during an interview when the wife was also present ($r = .42$, $p < .05$), and in a self-report measure of behavior at home ($r = .44$, $p < .01$). Strained men reported that as parents they were puzzled/worried by the baby ($r = .35$, $p < .05$), arranged their lives around the infant ($r = .43$, $p < .01$), but were low in satisfaction with parenthood ($r = -.35$, $p < .05$). Further, in men as in women, strain was associated with adverse social changes in their lives ($r = -.41$, $p < .05$), particularly in the relationship with their wives ($r = -.37$, $p < .05$).

RESULTS

The mean strain score for the sample was 2.02 with similar scores for men and women ($X = 1.92$ and $X = 2.12$ respectively, $t = 1.30$, $p > .20$). Thus the sample as a whole experienced only a low level of strain.

To obtain predictors of strain on parents, the outcome measure was correlated with all 14 expectancy variables, separately for men and women. Because of the relatively small sample size, only the strongest five correlates were entered as predictors in stepwise multiple linear regression analyses. Only those items for which the F of the equation at entry was greater than 2.8 ($p < .05$) are reported. This procedure for identifying predictors of strain may capitalize on chance findings. To minimize interpreting chance findings a series of backward or stepdown regression analyses were carried out, in which each predictor was forced to enter the regression equation last. This procedure yields two estimates: the unique amount of variance each variable accounts for, and partial r's with the effect of all other predictors taken out. These conservative estimates are used throughout the chapter. In the text, only those variables accounting for 3% or more of the unique variance are discussed, although all other contributing variables are shown in the tables.

Three models to predict strain at parenthood were constructed: The first uses the subjects' own scores during expectancy as predictors, the second model uses the expectancy scores from the spouses of the subjects, and the third model uses scores from both the subject and his/her spouse during expectancy to predict subsequent strain.

Predicting Women's Strain at Parenthood

The results of the different regression analyses using scores at pregnancy to predict women's strain at parenthood are presented in Table 2.3. The models varied in the amount of variance accounted for, ranging from 26% to 58%. The most successful model (in terms of amount of variance predicted), utilized expectancy scores of both women and men.

The expectancy scores of women, which predicted their subsequent sense of strain at parenthood, included a bad marriage, low instrumentality score, and being responsible for the masculine household tasks during pregnancy. These predictors were uncorrelated with each other.

The model that attempted to predict women's strain at parenthood from their husband's scores during expectancy was not very successful, accounting for only 26% of the variance. The predictors that entered the regression equation included men reporting marital tension, being older in age, and being more instrumental. Among the predictors, marital tension was associated with both the husbands' expectancy experience ($r = -.66, p < .001$), and with his overall stress during expectancy ($r = .46, p < .01$), thus explaining the relatively small amount of variance that each of these variables accounted for when all other variables were partialled out.

From the third model, based on the scores of women and their husbands, women's strain at parenthood was predicted from the wife being low on instrumentality and her husband high in instrumentality and both husband and wife reporting problems in the marriage. The predictors were uncorrelated with each other except for husband's expectancy experience and stressful marriage ($r = -.66, p < .001$).

Predicting Men's Strain at Parenthood

Table 2.4 shows the results of the different regression analyses using scores at expectancy to predict men's strain at parenthood. The different models account for moderate portions of the variance, ranging from 37% to 69%. Similar to the findings for women, men's strain was somewhat more successfully predicted when the wives' scores were included with their own as predictors.

The expectancy scores of men, which predicted their subsequent sense

TABLE 2.3

Results of Stepwise and "Backwards" Regression Equations Predicting Women's Stress at Parenthood from Expectancy Measures of Women, Men, and Jointly from Women and Men

	Stepwise Regression				"Backwards" Regression	
	R^2	Change in R^2	β	r	Change in R^2	Partial r
Predicting from Own Scores						
Good marriage	.25	.25	-.38	-.50	.12	-.41
Instrumentality	.35	.10	-.37	-.42	.13	-.43
Masculine household tasks	.42	.07	.25	.19	.06	.29
Age	.43	.01	.11	.22	.01	.14
Relations with in-laws	.44	.01	-.10	-.21	.01	-.11
Predicting from Husbands' Scores						
Marital tension	.12	.12	.25	.34	.03	.19
Age	.20	.08	.23	.21	.05	.25
Instrumentality	.24	.04	.26	.26	.06	.27
Positive expectancy experience	.26	.02	-.18	-.29	.02	-.14
General stress	.26	.00	.04	.20	.00	.04
Predicting from Own and Husbands' Score						
Wives' instrumentality	.27	.27	-.48	-.42	.21	-.58
Wives' good marriage	.43	.16	-.29	-.50	.07	-.37
Husbands' stressful marriage	.54	.11	.22	.34	.03	.24
Husbands' instrumentality	.56	.02	.19	.26	.03	.26
Husbands' expectancy experience	.58	.02	-.18	-.29	.02	-.19

TABLE 2.4

Results of Stepwise and "Backwards" Regression Equations Predicting Men's Stress at Parenthood from Expectancy Measures of Men, Women, and Jointly from Men and Women.

	Stepwise Regression				"Backwards Regression"	
	R^2	Change in R^2	β	r	Change in R^2	Partial r
Predicting from Own Scores						
General stress	.18	.18	.21	.43	.04	.26
Planned pregnancy	.29	.11	-.50	-.40	.22	-.56
Age	.42	.13	-.38	-.28	.14	-.47
Positive expectancy experience	.52	.10	-.34	-.37	.10	-.40
Marital tension	(did not enter regression equation)					
Predicting from Wive's Scores						
Changed self-concept	.16	.16	.37	.40	.11	.39
Feminine household tasks	.31	.15	-.33	-.31	.09	-.35
Age	.34	.03	-.14	-.40	.01	-.14
General stress	.36	.02	.15	.21	.02	.18
Emotional rehearsal	.37	.01	.10	.30	.01	.12
Predicting from Own and Wives' Scores						
Husbands' general stress	.18	.18	.07	.43	.00	.11
Wives' changed self-concept	.32	.14	.39	.40	.14	.56
Planned pregnancy	.44	.12	-.46	-.40	.19	-.61
Husbands' positive expectancy experience	.58	.14	-.49	-.37	.19	-.61
Wives' age	.69	.11	-.35	-.40	.11	-.51

27

of strain at parenthood, included a high score on general stress, an unplanned pregnancy, being young in age, and a negative expectancy experience. Marital tension did not enter the regression equation. Among the predictors, general stress was inversely correlated with expectancy experience ($r = -.38, p < .05$), and positively correlated with marital tension ($r = .46, p < .01$), while these two variables were inversely related to each other ($r = -.66, p < .001$). This pattern of correlations among the predictors helps explain why general stress, which entered first in the stepwise regression, accounts for only 4% of the unique variance in the backward regression and why marital tension did not enter the regression equation. The backward regression also shows that an unplanned pregnancy is the largest single contributor to men's strain at parenthood, accounting for 22% of the variance.

The expectancy scores of wives modestly predicted their husbands' strain at parenthood, accounting for 37% of the variance. Predictors that entered the regression equation included a changing self-concept among the wives during pregnancy to feeling more motherly, and a low assumption of responsibility for feminine household tasks. Among the potential predictors, the wife's age was correlated with feminine household tasks ($r = .34, p < .05$) and with her emotional rehearsal for parenthood ($r = -.37, p < .05$).

When scores from both men and their wives were used as predictors, men's strain at parenthood was successfully predicted with 69% of the variance accounted for by five predictors. Prenatal predictors included husbands' feeling stressed and a negative expectancy experience, an unplanned pregnancy, and wives who were young, and whose self-concept changed (to being more motherly) during pregnancy. Among the predictors, only the husband's stress and expectancy experience were correlated ($r = -.38, p < .05$), explaining in part why stress, which entered first in the stepwise regression, did not account for any of the unique variance in the backward regression.

DISCUSSION

Strain at parenthood was successfully predicted from measures assessed during expectancy. Somewhat different predictors were effective for men and women, with marital quality and instrumentality salient for women, whereas stress, adjustment to expectancy, and unplanned pregnancy were strong predictors for men. Strain at parenthood was more successfully predicted when the scores of the individual and his spouse were taken into account than when either the husband's or wife's scores alone were used.

The strain that we attempted to predict was not the crippling psychotic depression characteristic of only a tiny percentage of women (Kaij & Nilsson, 1972), nor the widely experienced but highly transient postpartum blues (Pitt, 1973). Instead, we focused on commonly experienced mood changes characterized by fatigue, tension, and a sense that there was more to cope with than could be comfortably handled. A modest degree of strain of this kind was still in evidence in varying degrees 6 months after becoming parents in a sample that primarily described their reaction to parenthood as one of contentment and well-being (Feldman & Nash, 1984). Furthermore, such strain was evident even when the infant was at a relatively easy stage: when his routines had stabilized, he slept through the night, and he was already highly socially responsive to his parents.

Strain at parenthood was assessed by a subjective self-rating, and more properly should be called *perceived strain*. We did not attempt to predict subjective strain from stressors in the contemporaneous situation such as infant characteristics (for example, difficult temperament, poor health, or prematurity), the health of the parents, and their economic, and social situation. Instead, the predictors used in this study were all assessed 6–8 months earlier, during the last trimester of pregnancy. Thus, it is all the more surprising that approximately 50% of the variance in the modest degree of strain experienced at parenthood was predicted successfully from expectancy measures alone.

Two factors limit the generalizability of the findings reported in this chapter. The first is the particular subset of parents studied (namely, highly involved, educated, middle class), and the second is the small sample size. Until comparative data for other socioeconomic groups are available, the applicability of these results should be limited to the advantaged and motivated groups from which the sample is drawn.

When relying on relatively small samples, regression analyses are known to capitalize on chance. Although conservative statistical procedures were used to minimize chance findings, caution is still necessary in interpreting the results. Replication of this study would not be expected to yield precisely the same outcomes in terms of the partial r's or order of entry of the variables into the regression equations. Despite these caveats this exploratory study has identified some important general themes and variables that warrant further consideration.

The model that most successfully predicted strain in new parents used measures from both the husband and the wife. This finding underlines the point that becoming a parent is a couple experience as well as an individual experience, and the characteristics of each member of the couple influence the adjustment of the other. For example, when the husband reported marital tensions and a poor adjustment to expectancy his wife subsequently experienced strain at parenthood. In light of the finding that people under stress are less attuned to and supportive of the needs of others (Belsky,

1984), these fathers, who continued to feel stressed as parents (Feldman & Nash, 1984) were perhaps unable to provide the ongoing support and reassurance needed by their wives to cope with the demands of infant care. In an analogous fashion, the woman's characteristics also influenced her husband's adjustment. For example, an increase in motherly feelings (changed self-concept) at pregnancy predicted more strain for men at parenthood, perhaps because it signaled to the husband his displacement from central focus in his wife's life.

Just as the combined experiences of the the marital dyad provided the best model for predicting individual adjustment, so marital variables were consistently the best predictors of women's strain, regardless of whether the marriage was assessed by the woman herself or by her husband. Although we rated different aspects of the marital relationship, for women these cohered into a single, unified factor labeled *good marriage*. A good marriage during pregnancy gave protection against strain at parenthood. Similar results have been reported by others (Grossman et al., 1980; Nilsson & Almgren, 1970; Russell, 1974). Recent reports suggest that the buffering effects extend even into the second year of motherhood (Cowan & Cowan, 1983). In contrast, marital variables for men were both less cohesive than they were for women (resulting in two independent factors), and, in accord with other studies (Cowan & Cowan, 1983; Grossman et al., 1980) not particularly successful at predicting strain at fatherhood.

Why do marital variables predict better for women than for men? It may be as Gilligan (1982) suggests, that women at all stages of life are more concerned than men with social connection, relationships, and in caring for others. Furthermore, marriage ranks as one of the most important of the interpersonal bonds. Over and beyond this, becoming or anticipating becoming a parent further emphasizes women's familial and social roles. As they give up paid employment and focus their time and energy on the family unit, women become more socially, emotionally, and financially dependent on their husbands, and more of their identity becomes bound up with the caring for and nurturing of family members. In contrast, men's identities are derived in large part from individual achievement (Erikson, 1950). The onset of parenthood almost demands continued occupational involvement as husbands face the need to support an expanding family. Thus, gratifications and stresses come from both the occupational world and marital relations for men, whereas they come primarily from the marriage for women. As a result, marital problems threatened the very foundation of the young women's lives, whereas it played a lesser role in predicting strain in the lives of their husbands.

Although marital relations did not effectively predict men's strain at parenthood it cannot be dismissed as inconsequential in influence. Stressful marriage (at expectancy) correlated significantly with strain at parenthood and failed to enter the regression analyses only because of its substantial correlation with another predictor, namely general stress. It is notable that for men, all the measures of stress correlated with one another: a single stress factor resulted from the factor analysis, which, in turn, was correlated with marital stress and expectancy adjustment. Furthermore, several of the different stress-related measures contributed significantly to the prediction of strain at parenthood. Cowan and Cowan (1983) reported a similar result.

For the man, stress during his wife's pregnancy is an indicator of how he copes with and adapts to change. As such, it is predictive of subsequent coping at parenthood. In contrast, stress for the woman is more differentiated and none of the measures of stress during pregnancy significantly predicted subsequent strain at parenthood. Interview data revealed that women and men experienced stress over different issues. In particular, women were worried about aspects of the pregnancy and the pending labor and delivery, whereas these were minor concerns for the men. Men, in contrast, were more worried about financial obligations and their ability to be sole provider for two dependents. Thus, the content of women's stresses were, in part, stage-of-life specific, whereas men's stresses were more general. It is likely that in a less advantaged sample more general life stresses of women (that are unrelated to pregnancy) would predict strain during parenthood. However in our upper middle-class, highly educated sample, stress during pregnancy and analagously adjustment to pregnancy had little predictive value for subsequent coping.

Somewhat surprisingly, unplanned pregnancy predicted strain for fathers, but not for mothers. In our sample, 35% of the pregnancies were unplanned, but according to parents' self-reports late in pregnancy, more than 95% of them were wanted. Medical records revealed that approximately 20% of this sample had previously used abortion to terminate unwanted pregnancies, and abortion continued to be readily available to these women. Thus, it seems reasonable to accept their statements of wanting the pregnancy at face value. This distinction between planned and wanted pregnancies (Miller, 1978) is important to maintain for it may be that wantedness is a better predictor of strain for stably married couples than is plannedness. For less advantaged, younger, and unmarried samples there may be greater overlap between the planned and wanted dimensions that would account for previously reported findings of unplanned pregnancies predicting strain (Rollins & Galligan, 1978).

Less easy to explain, however, is the finding that in the same advantaged sample unplanned pregnancy was the single best predictor of fathers' strain, accounting for 22% of the variance even after the contribution of other variables were partialled out. In recent reviews, Russell and Radin (1983) and Parke and Tinsley (1983) argue that stressful conditions around the time of the birth of the child results in greater involvement by fathers in childcare. Perhaps unplanned pregnancy should be added to the list of stressors: not only was it psychologically disruptive, but in our previous work (Feldman et al., 1983) it too, predicted increased caregiving by men. Furthermore, the data of this study revealed that observational and self-rating measures of caregiving by men were significantly related to strain, a finding also reported by Atkinson and Rickels (1981). Similar to the correlates of unplanned pregnancy, having a young wife predicted both involvement in child care (Feldman et al., 1983) and increased strain. The additional work of childcare in addition to the full-time employment of men may contribute to a sense of being overburdened, particularly because childcare is traditionally regarded as "women's work."[1]

Other aspects of our data are consonant with the notion that taking on some of the spouse's responsibilities was associated with strain. Thus, men whose wives were low on feminine household tasks (and who therefore had to carry more of the burden of these tasks alone) and women who carried out more of the masculine household tasks during pregnancy experienced more strain at parenthood. It is not known whether strain results from the sheer amount of work (overload), or from the perception of injustice that one's spouse is not contributing appropriately to the demands of housekeeping and parenting. It is striking, however, that strain appears to be related to the performing of cross-sex tasks, and suggests that cultural stereotypes condition the expectations of couples even among those who generally regarded themselves as modern and egalitarian.

Not all aspects of cross-sex typing contribute to strain. In fact, pregnant women who were high in instrumentality—who described themselves in terms such as *independent, assertive,* and *self-sufficient,* who felt satisfied with their autonomy and competence, and whose work was important and salient to them—were less likely to experience strain at parenthood. Successful parenting requires significant competence, autonomy, and decision-making abilities in order to cope with the round-the-clock demands of a dependent infant, the household tasks, and other family relationships. Women who felt effective (instrumental) during pregnancy found they were coping without strain at parenthood despite the change in sphere of competence from workforce to family. In contrast, the husband's instrumentality retained its focus on the workforce, and in our data, highly instrumental

---

[1]To test the interpretation that the influence of unplanned pregnancy on strain was mediated by higher levels of caregiving, we correlated unplanned pregnancy with strain at parenthood, partialling out caretaking. The correlation dropped from $r = .40$ to $r = .30$ ($p < .08$). We also forced caretaking to enter the regression equation first, thus removing all common variance with unplanned pregnancy. The amount of variance accounted for by unplanned pregnancy dropped from 22% to 15%; thus, there is a real albeit small effect of caregiving in mediating between unplanned pregnancy and men's strain.

husbands had wives who showed more strain at parenthood. We suspect that men high on instrumentality focused their energies and commitments more on work than on the family, at a time when social, emotional, and physical support was needed by their wives.

In summary, this research has underscored two important points. First, antecedents of strain differ for fathers and mothers of children. Sex differences in the antecedents of strain are not surprising given the differential impact a baby has on the lives of men and women. Second, prediction of strain is enhanced by knowing information about the spouse as well as about the individual in question. These indirect effects (Lewis, 1984) point to the value of more complex models of influence. Considerable work remains to be done however, in specifying pathways of influence from husband to wife and vice versa. Further, the existence of indirect effects gives added impetus to the study of fathers during the transition to parenthood. Not only are their reactions important for their own sense of well-being and for their fathering behavior, but they also powerfully contribute to their wive's adjustment and mothering.

ACKNOWLEDGMENTS

Special thanks to Sharon C. Nash and Barbara G. Aschenbrenner for their helpful discussions at different stages of this project.

REFERENCES

Abrahams, B., Feldman, S. S., & Nash, S. C. (1978). Sex-role self-concept and sex-role attitudes: Enduring personality characteristics or adaptations to changing life situations. *Developmental Psychology, 14,* 393–400.

Atkinson, A. K., & Rickels, A. V. (1981, April). *Postpartum adjustment in primiparous parents.* Paper presented at the meeting of the Society for Research in Child Development, Boston.

Belsky, J. (1984). The determinants of parenting: A process model. *Child Development, 55,* 83–96.

Belsky, J., Robins, E., & Gamble, W. (1984). Characteristics, consequences and determinants of parental competence: Toward a contextual theory. In M. Lewis & L. Rosenblum (Eds.), *Beyond the dyad* (pp. 251–280). New York: Plenum.

Bem, S. L. (1974). The measurement of psychological androgyny. *Journal of Consulting and Clinical Psychology, 42,* 155–162

Bem, S. L. (1976). *The satisfaction scale.* Unpublished scale, Stanford University.

Benedek, T. (1970). Motherhood and nurturing. In E. J. Anthony & T. Benedek (Eds.), *Parenthood: Its psychology and psychopathology* (pp. 153–166). Boston, MA: Little, Brown.

Bibring, G. L., Dwyer, T. F., Huntington, D., & Valentine, A. F. (1961). A study of the psychological processes in pregnancy and the earliest mother–child relationship. *Psychoanalytic Study of the Child, 16,* 9–44.

Campbell, A. (1975). The American way of mating: Marriage si; children, only maybe. *Psychology Today, 9,* 39–42.

Colman, A. D. (1969). Psychological state during first pregnancy. *American Journal of Orthopsychiatry, 39,* 788–797.

Cowan, P. A., & Cowan, C. P. (1983, April). *Quality of couple relationships and parenting stress in beginning families.* Paper presented at the meeting of Society for Research in Child Development, Detroit.

Curtis, J. A. (1955). A psychiatric study of 55 expectant fathers. *U.S. Armed Forces Medical Journal, 6,* 937–950.

Deutscher, M. (1970). Brief family therapy in the course of first pregnancy: A clinical note. *Contemporary Psychoanalysis, 7,* 21–35.

Duvall, E. M. (1971). *Family development* (4th ed.). Philadelphia, PA: Lippincott.

Erikson, E. (1950). *Childhood and society.* New York: Norton.

Fein, R. A. (1978). Consideration of men's experiences and the birth of a first child. In W. Miller & L. Newman (Eds.), *The first child and family formation* (pp. 327–330). Chapel Hill, NC: Carolina Population Studies.

Feldman, H. (1971). The effects of children on the family. In A. Michel (Ed.), *Family issues of employed women in Europe and America* (pp. 104–125). Leider, The Netherlands: Brill.

Feldman, S. S., Biringen, Z., & Nash, S. C. (1981). Fluctuations of sex-role related self-attributions as a function of stage of family life cycle. *Developmental Psychology, 17,* 24–35.

Feldman, S. S., & Nash, S. C. (1978). Interest in babies during young adulthood. *Child Development, 49,* 617–622.

Feldman, S. S., & Nash, S. C. (1984). The transition from expectancy to parenthood: Impact of the first-born child on men and women. *Sex Roles, 11,* 61–78.

Feldman, S. S., & Nash, S. C., & Aschenbrenner, B. G. (1983). Antecedents of fathering. *Child Development, 54,* 1628–1636.

George, L. (1980). *Role transitions in later life.* Monterey, CA: Brooks/Cole.

Gilligan, C. (1982). *In different voice: Psychological theory in women's development.* Cambridge, MA: Harvard University Press.

Gordon, R. E., & Gordon, K. (1957). Some social-psychiatric aspects of pregnancy and childbearing. *The Journal of the Medical Society of New Jersey, 54,* 569–572.

Grimm, E. R., & Venet, W. R. (1966). The relationship of emotional adjustment and attitudes to the course and outcome of pregnancy. *Psychosomatic Medicine, 28,* 34–49.

Grossman, F. K., Eichler, L. S., & Winickoff, S. A. (1980). *Pregnancy, birth and parenthood.* San Francisco: Jossey-Bass.

Hartman, A., & Nicolay, R. (1966). Sexually deviant behavior in expectant fathers. *Journal of Abnormal and Social Psychology, 71,* 232–234.

Holmes, T. H., & Rahe, R. H. (1967). The social readjustment rating scale. *Journal of Psychosomatic Research, 11,* 213–218.

Kaij, L., & Nilsson, A. (1972). Emotional and psychotic illness following childbirth. In J. Howells (Ed.), *Modern perspectives in psycho-obstetrics* (pp. 364–384). Edinburgh: Oliver & Boyd.

Leifer, M. (1977). Psychological changes accompanying pregnancy and motherhood. *Genetic Psychology Monographs, 95,* 55–96.

LeMasters, E. (1957). Parenthood as crisis. *Marriage and Family Living, 19,* 352–355.

Lewis, M. (1984). *Beyond the dyad.* New York: Plenum.

Lidz, T. (1976). *The person: His development throughout the life cycle* (2nd ed.). New York: Basic Books.

Loesch, J. G., & Greenberg, N. H. (1962). Some specific areas of conflicts observed during pregnancy: A comparative study of married and unmarried pregnant women. *American Journal of Orthopsychiatry, 32,* 624–636.

Lowenthal, M. F., & Chiriboga, D. (1972). Transition to the empty nest: Crisis, change or relief? *Archives of General Psychiatry, 26,* 8–14.

Lowenthal, M. F., Thurnher, M., & Chiriboga, D. (1975). *Four stages of life.* San Francisco: Jossey Bass.

Magnus, E. M. (1980). Sources of maternal stress in the postpartum period: In J. Parsons (Ed.), *The psychobiology of sex differences and sex roles* (pp. 177–208). Washington: Hemisphere.

Myerowitz, J. H., & Feldman, H. (1966). Transition to parenthood. *Psychiatric Research Reports, 20,* p. 78–84.

Miller, W. B. (1978). The intendedness and wantedness of the first child. In W. B. Miller & L. F. Newman (Eds.), *The first child and family formation* (pp. 209–243). Chapel Hill, NC: Carolina Population Center.

Neugarten, B. L. (1968). Adult personality: Toward a psychology of the life cycle. In B. L. Neugarten (Ed.), *Middle age and aging* (pp. 137–147). Chicago: University of Chicago Press.

Nilsson, A., & Almgren, P. (1970). Paranatal emotional adjustment: A prospective investigation of 165 women. *Acta Psychiatic Scandinavica, 220,* 7–140.

Parke, R. D., & O'Leary, S. E. (1976). Family interaction in the newborn period. Some findings, some observations and some unresolved issues. In K. Riegel & J. Meacham (Eds.), *The developing individual in a changing world* (Vol. 2, (pp. 653–663). The Hague. Mouton.

Parke, R. D., & Tinsley, B. R. (1983). Fatherhood: Historical and contemporary perspectives. In K. A. McCluskey & H. W. Reese (Eds.), *Life-span developmental psychology: Historical and generational effects* (pp. 203–248). New York: Academic Press.

Parsons, T., & Bales, R. F. (1955). *Family socialization and interaction process.* New York: Free Press.

Pitt, B. (1973). "Maternity blues". *British Journal of Psychiatry, 122,* 431–433.

Retterstol, N. (1968). Paranoid psychoses associated with impending or newly established fatherhood. *Acta Psychiatic Scandinavica, 44,* 51–61.

Robin, A. A. (1962). The psychological changes of normal parturition. *Psychiatric Quarterly, 36,* 124–130.

Rollins, B., & Galligan, R. (1978). The developing child and marital satisfaction of parents. In R. M. Lerner & G. B. Spanier (Eds.), *Child influences on marital and family interaction: A life span perspective* (pp. 71–105). New York: Academic Press.

Russell, C. S. (1974). Transition to parenthood: Problems and gratifications. *Journal of Marriage and the Family, 36,* 294–301.

Russell, G., & Radin, N. (1983). Increased paternal participation: The fathers' perspective. In M. E. Lamb & A. Sagi (Eds.), *Fatherhood and family policy* (pp. 139–165). Hillsdale, NJ: Lawrence Erlbaum Associates.

Ryder, R. G. (1973). Longitudinal data relating marriage satisfaction and having a child. *Journal of Marriage and the Family, 35,* 604–606.

Senn, M., & Hartford, C. (1968). *The firstborn: Experiences of eight American families.* Cambridge, MA: Harvard University Press.

Shereshefsky, P. M., & Yarrow, L. J. (1974). *Psychological aspects of a first pregnancy and early postnatal adaptation.* New York: Raven Press.

Tasch, R. J. (1952). The role of the father in the family. *Journal of Experimental Education, 20,* 319–361.

Wainwright, W. (1966). Fatherhood as a precipitant of mental illness. *American Journal of Psychiatry, 123,* 40–44.

Mothering, Fathering, and Marital Interaction in the Family Triad During Infancy

Exploring Family System's Processes

Jay Belsky
Brenda L. Volling
The Pennsylvania State University

There was a time when the study of the child in the family seemed simple. Quite probably things never really were simple, although in retrospect the "good old days" often look that way. The times we are referring to were before the "discovery" of the father. For prior to the 1970s, the study of parent–infant relations was synonymous with the study of mother—first maternal deprivation, and then mother-infant interaction and infant-mother attachment. But with the addition of the father to the picture things began to change and became more complex. Although some did not recognize it initially, and treated the father as just another parent in a particular biological suit, inclusion of the father in the study of infancy forced us to come to grips with the family and the different roles that men and women enact in this most important cultural institution. It is by no means clear that developmentalists fully comprehended the nature of the family and what it means for psychologists who typically are concerned with individuals and sometimes with individual relationships, but it is most certainly clear that there is no escaping this new focus.

Interest in the family within the field of developmental psychology developed, to a sizeable degree, in response to the consideration of fathers by infancy researchers. Why such interest did not result 15 to 20 years ago when developmentalists were studying processes of father–child identification and father absence is somewhat difficult to fathom. Undoubtedly it has something to do with the changes that were taking place in the American family during the 1970s when interest in fathering re-emerged. But it is also likely that there was something special about focusing upon the opening years of life when families are forming. For many, the family is not considered to be a reality until the child arrives and the roles of mother and father are generated, complementing those of husband and wife.

One of the major questions that consideration of the father raised for developmentalists had to do with the experiences that infants had with male parents compared with female parents. Much of the initial research on fathering involved comparisons of mothers and fathers in attempts to generate understanding of similarities and differences in the experiences that infants had in the family with the two adults to whom they were probably most exposed. Given the ultimate interest of many developmentalists in the ways fathers influence their infants, this was an appropriate starting point. Research on father absence and maternal deprivation had taught us that understanding parental influence could not be achieved unless we were aware of children's day-to-day experiences. Thus, to understand father influences a descriptive base of father–infant interaction was required.

Characteristics of the Father–Infant Relationship

The early work by Parke and his colleagues (Parke & O'Leary, 1976; Parke, O'Leary, & West, 1972; Parke & Sawin, 1975) revealed that fathers could be just as interested, nurturant, and stimulating interactive partners with their newborn infants as were mothers. Fathers in these studies were as likely as mothers to touch, look at, vocalize to, and kiss their infants. Parke and Sawin (1975) further demonstrated that fathers were not only as competent and successful as mothers with infant feedings, but were also equally sensitive and responsive to infant distress cues such as coughing or spitting-up during feeding.

Further evidence of paternal sensitivity was reported by Phillips and Parke (1981) in their investigation of the quality of language that fathers directed to their infants. As had been chronicled in the case of mothers, fathers were observed to adjust their speech when talking to their newborns in accordance with the infant's perceptual capacities. Thus, fathers, like mothers, used shorter phrases and repeated sounds more frequently when talking to the baby than with another adult. It would seem, then, that the term *motherese* is a potential misnomer for characterizing the kind of speech adults direct toward young babies. The term *fatherese* should be added to our professional vocabulary, or perhaps a less gender-linked term like *parentese*.

Even though, from these studies, fathers appear to be capable, competent, and sensitive parents, other data indicate that actual levels of father involvement and performance in infant caregiving are substantially lower than those displayed by mothers (Pedersen & Robson, 1969; Rendina & Dickersheid, 1976). Although most studies discern considerable variation across families in terms of the amount of time fathers are available to interact with their infants, the general consensus is that fathers are less involved with their infants than are mothers. Pedersen and Robson (1969), for instance, reported fathers of 8- to nine-month-old infants spent an average of 26 hours per week at home when their infants were awake. However, for individual fathers, this range spanned anywhere from 5 to 47 hours per week. The fathers further reported spending between 45 minutes to 26 hours each week in actual interaction with their infants. Similarly, Kotelchuck (1976) reported mothers spent, on the average, 9 waking hours per day with their children, whereas fathers spent just 3.2 hours. These data suggest, then, that although fathers are as competent and capable as mothers in demonstrating nurturant, sensitive, and responsive parenting behaviors, they are generally much less available to their offspring.

The evidence to date indicates not only that fathers are much less available for interaction with their infants, as indicated by these parental-report studies, but also that when they are around they spend far less time engaged in actual interaction with their offspring than do mothers. This con-clusion is based principally upon naturalistic studies of mother–father–infant interaction. For example, in Belsky, Gilstrap, and Rovine's (1984) longitudi-nal investigation of 72 middle- and working-class families that involved observations conducted at 1, 3, and 9 months, mothers were found to respond, stimulate, express positive affection toward, and provide more basic care than fathers did for their infants at all times of measurement; only in the case of the behavioral category of read/watch TV did fathers exceed mothers. The robustness of these results are evident not only in a replication study reported in this chapter, but also in two separate investiga-tions carried out in other nations. In Israel, Greenbaum and Landau (1982) observed 96 middle- and lower class families under naturalistic conditions at 2, 4, 7, and 11 months (cross-sectional design) and found that at every age, mothers greatly exceeded fathers in verbal interactions; in fact, in both social-class groups fathers provided less verbal stimulation than did siblings. In a longitudinal study of traditional and non-traditional families in Sweden, mothers from both kinds of families were observed to be more interactively involved with their infants than fathers were when their infants were 8 and 16 months (Frodi, Lamb, Hwang, & Frodi, 1982).

In summary, it appears that when families are observed in unstructured situations, in which they are permitted to go about their every day household routines, there is very little similarity between mothers and fathers in sheer quantity of involvement. These data thus highlight the need to distinguish between parental competence and performance, that is, between what fathers can do and what they do in fact do on a routine day-to-day basis. Although fathers are able to function quite similarly to mothers when observed in a highly structured situation in which there are few competing demands on their time, when situations are left unstructured, the roles and behaviors of mothers and fathers vary to a sizeable degree.

Additional evidence of differences in maternal and paternal behavior comes from investigations that have examined the quality, not simply the quantity, of parent–infant interaction. Fathers, it seems, participate less in caregiving and engage most often in play with their young infants (A. Clarke-Stewart, 1977, K. A. Clarke-Stewart, 1980; Kotelchuck, 1976; Lamb, 1977). Furthermore, Lamb reported that parents picked their infants up and held them for different reasons: Fathers tended to hold infants in the course of playing with them, whereas, in the case of mothers, holding was most likely to occur during the provision of basic care. There are also distinct differences between mothers' and fathers' styles of play. Specifically, fathers appear more inclined to engage in physically arousing, rough-and-tumble play activities, whereas mothers principally engage their infants in verbally stimulating, visual, and toy-mediated play (K. A. Clarke-Stewart, 1980; Crawley & Sherwood, 1984; Lamb, 1977; Power & Parke, 1982; Weinraub & Frankel, 1977; Yogman, Dixon, & Tronick, 1977). This is not to say, however, that fathers play more with their babies. Although mothers spent a greater amount of time playing, proportionally, more of fathers' time than that of mothers' is spent in play. It is for this reason the role of father as playmate is so frequently underscored.

From a behavioral standpoint, fathers are both like and unlike mothers. Although they can be as sensitive as mothers, and although the behavior they direct toward the infant develops in much the same way as does mothers', it remains true that fathers tend to engage their infants in interaction to a much lesser extent—even when both parents are home—and that they also tend to be more oriented toward highly arousing physical play. Elsewhere we have argued that this portrait of the father represents only one part of the contribution that the study of the father makes to child development (Belsky, 1981). Indeed, we regard this contribution as rather conservative and traditional in its nature and scope because work on similarities and differences in mothering and fathering involved little more initially than the mere application of methods and procedures that had been tried and tested upon mothers to an additional parent, namely, fathers. In our minds, the major contribution that the study of the father could make to the field involved the attention it drew to the family as a system of interdependent relations.

The Father in the Family

The earliest hints of such a contribution came from the discovery that interaction patterns between mothers and their infants were altered when the mother–infant dyad was transformed into the mother-father-infant triad. Parke and O'Leary (1973) were the first to observe such *second-order effects,* as the influence of the father on the mother–infant dyad came to be known. But these effects in which the levels of mother–infant interaction were reduced with the introduction of father were subsequently documented by a host of investigators working in the laboratory and in the home setting with infants of a variety of ages (Belsky, 1979; K. Clarke-Stewart, 1978; Lamb, 1976, 1977, 1978a, 1978b; Lytton, 1979; Pedersen, Yarrow, Anderson, & Cain, 1978).

Evidence of second-order effects in mother–father–infant interaction appears to be of little significance in its own right because similar changes in social interaction had been chronicled in other social groups when the number of individuals available for interaction was modified (Cleaves & Rosenblatt, 1977). What made them so appealing, undoubtedly, was that they hinted at the existence of family system processes that carried great implications for the study of the child in the family.

Evidence that such family system processes were at the heart of these second-order effects was produced by Pedersen et al. (1978) in an effort to account for the actual cause of the reductions in dyadic interaction that were repeatedly discerned when the two-person system was transformed into a three-person system with the addition of the second parent. In the foregoing study, comparisons were made of baby-directed behavior rates between time-sampling intervals when mother and father were conversing with each other and when they were not conversing. This revealed that reductions in parental behavior occurred primarily in intervals in which spouses were talking with one another. Thus, the mere physical presence of the second parent did not seem to be as important in accounting for second-order effects as what that presence afforded—namely, marital interaction.

The implications of these findings to the study of fatherhood and fathering in the family were most significant. As we have argued elsewhere (Belsky, 1981), that which is truly unique about the study of fathering is the demand it places upon investigators to consider other relationships in the family. Inclusion of the father in the study of infancy and child development does more than generate an additional parent–infant relationship; it directs attention to the marital relationship and thus the need to consider husband–wife interaction as well as parent–infant interaction. Moreover, including the father requires that we conceptualize the family as a system of interdependent relationships (Belsky, 1981). Although there are a variety of ways to think about the family as a system, three are of special interest here. One involves examining changes that take place in the marital relationship in response to the birth and rearing of a first child (e.g., Belsky, Lang, & Rovine, 1985; Belsky, Spanier, & Rovine, 1983; Miller & Sollie, 1980; see Cowan & Cowan, this volume). A second approach involves examining the relationship between evaluations of marital functioning and parental functioning (e.g., Easterbrooks & Goldberg, 1984; Feldman, Nash, & Aschenbrenner, 1984); see Belsky and Vondra (in press) for a review of this relationship. And, the third, representing a variant of the second, involves examining the interrelation of ongoing marital and parental behavior in the family triad. Because it is the third approach that characterizes the research reported in this chapter, it is this one to which we pay the most attention. Information pertaining to the other approaches can be found in this volume in chapters by Cowan and Cowan and by Grossman.

Three investigators have looked simultaneously at marital and parent–infant interaction in the mother–father–infant triad in an attempt to illuminate the inner workings of the family system. In two previous studies that we have carried out, it was found that father involvement was more systematically related to marital interaction than was maternal involvement. In our first longitudinal study, for example, we observed that fathers' overall engagement of the infant was reliably and positively related to overall marital engagement at three different times of measurement, whereas maternal engagement was only related to marital engagement at 1-month of age (Belsky et al., 1984). This led us to conclude that for women the roles of parent and spouse are more independent than they are for men, who seem to be either highly involved in the family (via interaction with child and spouse) or not very involved. Indeed, these data suggested to us that one of two processes might be at work in the family system. On the one hand socially oriented, gregarious men might simply choose to be involved in relations with spouses and children, thus generating the relationship between fathering and marital interaction. Or on the other hand, marital communication, especially that which is positive and focused on the infant, might facilitate the father's involvement in parenting. It is this latter hypothesis that we pursue in more detail in the research reported in this chapter.

Lamb and Elster (1985) recently reported results virtually identical to our own regarding the interrelation of parenting and marital interaction using a totally different kind of sample. These investigators observed more than 50 triads composed of teenage mothers and fathers and also found stronger and more systematic contemporaneous correlations between measures of mother–father interaction and fathering than between those of mother–infant interaction and mothering. These findings, coupled with our own and those to be reported, clearly indicate that there is something rather general about the male role that does not seem to be a function principally of stage in the life course. Lamb and Elster were studying men and women who had experienced an "off-time" event, adolescent parenthood, whereas our investigations focused upon couples bearing children at a time consistent with normative cultural expectations and demographic patterns. Similar results have not been reported with parents and much older children, but to our knowledge, such families have simply not been studied with regard to the interrelation of parental and marital behavior.

In this chapter we extend research on similarities and differences in mothering and fathering and on the study of the family as a system. Using data obtained during naturalistic observations of family triads when infants were 1, 3, and 9 months, we compare levels of maternal and paternal behavior and examine the interrelation of parental and marital behavior within each age of assessment. In addition, we extend our past research by conducting longitudinal analyses to see if marital interaction influences father involvement over time and, in addition, whether mothers' interaction with the baby at one age affects or is affected by the fathers' behavior at another age.

METHODS

Subjects

The subjects of this study were 64 white families participating in the second cohort of The Pennsylvania Infant and Family Development Project; the project consists of three longitudinal studies, the first of which has been described in several recent reports (Belsky et al., 1984; Belsky, Hertzog, & Rovine, 1986; Belsky et al., 1983). All participating families were expecting their first child when enrolled in the project during the last trimester of pregnancy and were considered well functioning and principally middle to lower middle class. Annual family income reported during the last trimester of pregnancy averaged $22,475. Couples had been married at the time of this interview an average of 4.2 years. The mean age of mothers and fathers, respectively, was 26.5 and 28.0 years, and the two parents averaged 14.4 and 15.8 years of education. For two of every three couples the first birth was planned. Almost half of the mothers were working outside the home in the first year of their infant's life.

Families were recruited on an individual basis from names provided by a community obstetrical practice. Families were provided with introductory information outlining the project and were later called to determine whether or not they were interested in further information and possible participation in the study. If families did show an interest, a more detailed follow-up letter was sent when mothers were approximately 7 months pregnant. Within a week of mailing the follow-up letters, parents were telephoned and all questions regarding the study were answered. Those families interested in participating were scheduled for a 1½ hour prenatal interview in order to enroll them in the study and to collect background information. With respect to enrollment, there was a 40% rate of participation.

Procedure

The focus of this report is behavioral data obtained on mother–infant, father–infant, and husband–wife interaction during three separate, naturalistic, 1-hour home observations carried out when infants were 1, 3, and 9 months of age.

For 64 minutes an observer recorded mother–infant, father–infant, and husband–wife interactions using a 31-item pre-coded behavioral checklist employed on a 15-second observe, 5-second record, time-sampling basis (total time-sampling periods = 192). Time-sampling periods were identified via a portable cassette recorder that emitted an "observe" or "record" message to the observer through an inconspicuous ear phone. For each parent–infant dyad, five behavioral functions were coded; these included contingently responding to some aspect of the infant's behavior (Respond); focusing the child's attention on some object or event in the environment and/or arousing the attentional state of the infant (Stimulate/Arouse); diapering, wiping, washing, or grooming the baby or engaging in some other activity focused upon basic physical care (Caregiving); expressing positive emotional feeling toward baby by hugging, kissing, smiling at, or verbalizing endearments (Positive Affection); and engaging in personal leisure activity involving reading or watching television (Read/Watch TV). Husband–wife interaction was recorded in terms of whether, during each time-sampling period, spousal communication focused upon baby-related (Baby-Related) and/or non-baby-related topics (NonBaby-Related); whether both husband and wife were jointly attending to the infant (Joint-Attention) and/or sharing pleasure (e.g., smiling at one another or laughing together) from the baby's activities (Share Pleasure); and whether non-baby-related interaction between spouses was positively affectionate (e.g., spouses kiss, hug, or praise one another, smile at each other, affectionately touch each other) (Positive). Finally, five infant behaviors were also coded, but are not the subject of this report (see Belsky et al. 1984).

Immediately following each 15-second time-sampling period in which these parenting and marital behaviors were coded, each parent-infant dyad and the spousal dyad were rated on a global 4-point scale of reciprocal engagement that assessed the extent and intensity of the observed interactions between members of a given dyad within the preceding time sampling period. These ratings ranged from no interaction (0) and minimal interaction (1), as when a parent merely held or looked at the baby, to intense engagement (3), as frequently evident in face-to-face play or other social and object-mediated games that involve repeated turn-taking. In order to create an overall engagement score for each dyad, individual 15-second-period engagement scores were summed. Periods of highest engagement received

3 points, those of moderate engagement 2 points, and those of limited engagement 1 point; periods of no dyadic engagement received a score of zero, and thus contributed nothing to the overall engagement score.

All observers were trained intensively over a period lasting no less than 2 months, first using videotapes, then during actual home observations. During the course of the study, more than 25 formal reliability assessments were conducted during home observations. Intercorrelation of total frequency scores for each of the discrete behaviors and for the reciprocal engagement categories ranged from .76 to .98 with a mean of .87.

RESULTS AND DISCUSSION

Three sets of analyses are presented in this chapter. In the first we examine basic similarities and differences in mothering and fathering by comparing mean levels of maternal and paternal behavior within and across time. In the second set of analyses we attempt to illuminate the influence of each parent on the other by examining the interrelation of mother's and father's behavior both within and across time. Finally, in a third set of analyses the interrelation of marital and parental behavior is examined as part of an effort to further illuminate similarities and differences in the behavioral implementation of the maternal and paternal roles in the family.

Development of Mothering and Fathering: Similarities and Differences

In order to examine developmental changes in maternal and paternal behavior, as well as parental differences in observed parenting behavior, the observational data gathered at 1, 3, and 9 months were subjected to a 3 (Time) $\times$ 2 (Parents' Gender) $\times$ 2 (Infants' Gender) repeated measures multivariate analysis of variance, in which time and parent were treated as repeated measures. Significant multivariate effects for age (F 12,49 = 7.72, $p < .001$) and parent (F 6,55 = 17.00 $p < .001$) led us to conduct univariate follow-up analyses using the same statistical model. The results of these analyses are presented in Table 3.1.

Developmental Changes.   With respect to developmental change, the data reveal similar trends for fathers and mothers, as evidenced by the absence of significant interactions between the parent factor and the other two factors in the model. More specifically, overall engagement of the infant declined significantly from 3 to 9 months (F 1,124 = 4.52, $p < .05$), as did positive interaction (F 1,124 = 14.11, $p < .01$), read/watch TV (F 1,124 = 7.23, $p < .01$), and responsiveness (F 1,124 = 7.24, $p < .05$). These

TABLE 3.1
Mean Levels of Parental Behavior as a Function of Age, Parent, and Child Gender

Parental Behavior	Age				Parent			Gender		
	1	3	9	F (2,120)	Mother	Father	F (1,60)	Boy	Girl	F (1,60)
Total	136.7	1.45.5	130.0	2.42#	168.7	106.1	38.43***	139.1	135.4	0.19
Respond	14.9	13.4	9.0	5.56**	15.0	9.8	18.80***	13.6	11.1	1.48
Stimulate	41.3	48.6	44.4	2.13	51.6	37.9	12.18***	45.7	43.7	0.23
Caregive	42.9	32.2	22.9	18.00***	47.4	18.0	68.8***	32.6	32.8	0.01
TV/Read	48.8	44.5	32.4	6.10**	29.8	54.1	35.2***	39.2	45.0	0.65
Positive	5.2	6.3	3.9	5.33	6.7	3.5	22.2***	5.4	4.7	0.60

#$p < .10$
**$p < .01$
***$p < .001$

results replicate similar patterns of change discerned for primiparious parents participating in the first cohort of our three cohort longitudinal study of infant and family development. Also replicating the results of our first study is the linear decline in basic caregiving evident in Table 3.1 (F 1,124 = 39.26, $p < .001$).

The fact that patterns of mothering and fathering changed in much the same way highlights a basic similarity in the ways in which men and women care for their infants. Such similarities in the face of striking differences in the overall amount of time that our mostly primary caretaker mothers and secondary caretaker fathers are exposed to their infants underscore the powerful influence of the changing baby on the care she/he receives. In the analysis of data on infant behavior in the second cohort as well as the first, it was found that frequency of fussing and crying decreased linearly over time, whereas frequency of smiling and exploration increased. These patterns underscore the increasing behavioral maturity of the infant that undoubtedly permits his/her parents to spend less time providing basic care and responding to the infant. This would seem particularly true in the face of the decreased time spent crying and the increased exploration the baby displays by 9 months of age. In summary, both men and women appear equally responsive to the developmental changes of their babies, as evidenced by the comparable changes observed in their mean levels of behavior.

Mother-Father Differences.   Despite similar patterns of developmental change in their observed parenting, mothers and fathers differed dramatically in their overall levels of interactive involvement. As we found in our first longitudinal investigation (Belsky et al., 1984), mothers exceeded fathers to a highly significant extent ($p < .001$) in every behavior observed except read/watch TV; in the case of the latter measure, fathers exceeded mothers. It should be noted that these differences in parental behavior existed at all times of measurement, as demonstrated by the absence of any statistical interactions between the parent and time factors in the statistical model.

These findings are completely consistent with those we reported for parents of both first- and laterborn children in our first longitudinal study (Belsky, Gilstrap, & Rovine, 1984). Moreover, virtually identical results have been reported in two naturalistic observational studies carried out in Israel—at 2, 4, 7, and 11 months (Greenbaum & Landau, 1982)—and in Sweden—at 3, 8, and 16 months (Frodi, Lamb, Hwang, & Frodi, 1982). The fact also that comparable mother–father differences were evident in both traditional and non-traditional (i.e., father as primary caregiver) families in the Swedish investigation provides strong evidence that, across quite diverse contexts, the experience that infants have with their two parents on a day-to-day basis are quite different, even if in some ways similar (i.e., developmental change in mothering and fathering).

In summary, our results underscore once again the need to distinguish between parental competence and performance. What fathers can do does not necessarily reflect what they actually do. Despite the fact that in over half of the families under study mothers were not working outside the home and so had been home with their infants all day at the time of observation, and fathers had recently arrived in the home after work, fathers interacted with their children far less than did mothers.

It does not seem to be the case that gender of the child exerted any influence on parents—at least insofar as the behaviors we coded are concerned. As in our first longitudinal study (Belsky et al., 1984), no differences were discerned at any age, for either parent, in the way in which sons and daughters were treated. The possibility remains, however, that had a more refined, microanalytic measurement system been employed, that subtle gender-based difference might have emerged from our analyses. Indeed, R. D. Parke (personal communication, May 31, 1984) suggests that gender differences in parental treatment are discerned primarily when styles of play are differentiated. In such investigations, boys are routinely observed to be handled in a more "rough and tumble" manner than girls are. Our study focused on the study of the family triad, and particularly the marital subsystem as well as the two parent–child subsystems in the family, and we were thus unable to examine parent–child interactions in great depth.

The Interrelation of Mothering and Fathering

The second set of analyses reported in this chapter characterized the functioning of mothering and fathering within the family, and pursued one particular process of influence within the family system—namely, the potential influence of one parent's behavior upon the parenting of his/her spouse. As a first step toward these goals, the behavior of each parent was correlated with those of his/her spouse within each time of measurement. On the bases of the results of these analyses, a series of cross-lag panel analyses was implemented in search of evidence that might substantiate the contention that the functioning of one parent influenced that of the other.

Cross-Sectional Analyses.   The results of the within-time correlation of maternal and paternal behavior scores at 1, 3, and 9 months are displayed in Table 3.2. Throughout this chapter we considered meaningful patterns, trends, and consistencies, rather than addressing each and every significant or near significant correlation. Two general sets of findings seem noteworthy in the data presented in Table 3.2.

TABLE 3.2
Intercorrelation of Maternal and Paternal Behavior at 1, 3, and 9 Months

Mother Behavior	Father Behavior				
1 Month (n = 59)	Respond	Positive	Stimulate	Read/TV	Caregive
Respond	.47***	−.18	−.36**	.26*	.61
Positive	.03	.17	−.10	−.01	−.14
Stimulate	−.33**	−.22	.15	−.18	−.36**
Read/TV	.12	.00	−.25	.56***	.25*
Caregive	−.08	.06	−.35**	.12	−.12
3 Month (n = 62)					
Respond	.54***	.17	−.19	.15	.23
Positive	.15	.46***	−.10	.14	.18
Stimulate	−.25*	−.15	.03	−.03	−.17
Read/TV	−.08	−.08	.02	.40***	.14
Caregive	−.06	.19	−.05	−.01	−.06
9 Month (n = 58)					
Respond	.54***	.28*	−.11	.28*	.00
Positive	.12	.26*	−.17	.15	−.22
Stimulate	−.31*	−.05	−.06	.19	−.30*
Read/TV	−.11	−.06	−.21	.43***	−.21
Caregive	−.04	−.03	−.24	.09	−.04

Underlined coefficients indicate interparent correlations for each variable.
*$p < .05$
**$p < .01$
***$p < .001$

The first, at all three times of measurement a pattern of positive covariation can be discerned between maternal and paternal responsiveness. This can be seen by examining the same behavior categories for each parent, such as maternal and paternal positive affection (except at 1 month), and maternal and paternal read/watch TV. Note the coefficients underlined in Table 3.2 that indicate interparent relationships for each variable. From a substantive standpoint, these data show that in homes in which mothers are frequently responding to their infants' behavior, displaying positive affection and infrequently reading or watching television, fathers tend to be doing much of the same. Although such contemporaneous correlations of frequency data do not enable us to determine whether mothers are influencing fathers or vice versa, it is clear that in many households babies get a great deal from both parents or very little from each, at least during periods of time when both parents are home with the child. Indeed, there is nothing about these findings to suggest that the behavior of one parent precludes the involvement of the other or compensates for the lack of involvement on the part of the other parent.

The second trend to emerge from an inspection of the data in Table 3.2 concerns relationships between parents across different categories of behavior. These results tell a somewhat different story, one that may be interpreted in terms of compensatory or exclusionary involvement on the part of one parent. At all three times of measurement, consistent negative correlations emerge between the stimulation offered by one parent and the behavior of the other parent. The consistency of this trend is most evident when one examines the correlations between maternal stimulation and father responsiveness and caregiving. Thus, it seems that the more mothers stimulated and aroused their infants in the triad, the less involved fathers were or, conversely, the less fathers responded to and provided basic care for their babies, the more mothers were inclined to stimulate their infants. Given the contemporaneous correlational nature of the data at hand, it is, of course, impossible to distinguish between these or other explanations of these statistical relationships.

The two trends highlighted by this discussion of the data in Table 3.2 raise the distinct possibility that two family processes may take place within the family system; alternatively, these data may indicate that there are two types of triadic family systems. On the one hand, one may be seeing evidence of triadic interaction patterns in which mothers and fathers jointly respond to the baby's behavior, display positive affection, or watch TV, and another in which the stimulating involvement of one parent precludes the participation of the other (or the uninvolvement of one parent leads to the compensatory involvement of the other). At different times during an observation the processes responsible for both the positive and negative correlations between maternal and paternal behavior could characterize the family triad. But the possibility also remains that these data reflect two kinds of families—one in which parents conjointly interact with the baby (resulting in positive correlations) and another in which they trade off involvement (resulting in negative correlations). Teasing apart these two possibilities would require a larger sample than we currently have and thus remains beyond the scope of this chapter. Worth noting at this point, however, is the fact that the two trends emerging from Table 3.2, and the different interpretations they suggest, foreshadow similar results that will emerge when we examine the interrelation of marriage and parenting.

Longitudinal Analysis.   Select results from the cross-sectional analysis raised the possibility that the behavior of one/parent might actually be influencing the behavior of the other. We can think about such a process using both a short- and long-term perspective. A short-term perspective would raise the possibility of parent-to-parent influence transpiring within each observation; to make the most convincing case for such influence, sequential strategies of analysis would be employed. Because our data were not gathered with such analyses in mind, we are forced to forego the pursuit of such processes of influence within the family triad. But another, less microanalytic way of pursuing parent-to-parent influence is available—by examining the interrelation of maternal and paternal behavior across the 1-, 3-, and 9-month observation periods. Toward this end, we proceeded to carry out a series of cross-lag panel analyses in an effort to further illuminate select relationships between mother and father behaviors that emerged from the within-time analyses. Although the bases of inferring causal influence from cross-lag analyses has been criticized in recent years (Rogosa, 1979), we proceed in this manner, nevertheless, for heuristic reasons. Caution must obviously be exercised when drawing causative interpretations from any essentially nonexperimental data base.

The cross-lag analyses, carried out in an effort to determine whether the behavior of one parent affected that of his/her spouse over time, are depicted in Fig. 3.1. As can be seen in this diagram, we sought to determine whether there existed any evidence that the responsiveness, positive affection, and reading/television watching of one parent affected the same behavior of the other parent (Panels A, B, & C), and whether maternal stimulation affected paternal responsiveness or vice versa (Panel D). The most important features of all the panels in the figure are the diagonals linking the behavior of one parent at 1 or 3 months with the behavior of the spouse at 3 and 9 months, respectively. In the logic of cross-lag analysis, evidence of causation would emerge if, within the left-and/or right-hand side of any panel, the coefficient of one of the two diagonals achieved statistical significance whereas that of the other did not. From a methodological standpoint it is also helpful if the autocorrelations (within time) do not show evidence of substantial decline over time (Cook & Campbell, 1979).

Of the four cross-lag analyses carried out, and of the eight pairs of correlation coefficients compared, findings consistent with causal influence emerged in two cases. Inspection of Panel A of Fig. 3.1 reveals that maternal responsiveness at 1 month was a reliable predictor of paternal responsiveness at 3 months, whereas paternal responsiveness did not forecast maternal responsiveness. When interpreted in the context of cross-lag analyses, these data suggest that the responsiveness of mothers at 1 month promoted paternal responsiveness at 3 months. We can think of two basic reasons why such a process of influence might occur. On the one hand,

FIG. 3.1   Cross-lag analyses of the influence of one parent's behavior on that of the other parent.

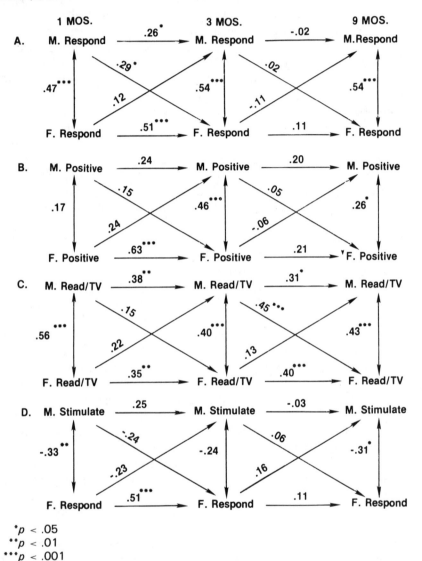

*p < .05
**p < .01
***p < .001

fathers may simply be learning from mothers how to relate to their infants through a simple process of modeling or imitation. On the other hand, a more transactional process might account for these data. The responsiveness of the mother in the infant's life might well promote the alert, responsiveness of the baby which, in turn, eventually fosters increased responsiveness on the part of the father. Thus, more responsive babies, who became that way as a function of their mothers' behavior, may well elicit greater responsiveness from their fathers. At this point in our analyses, we are unable to tease these alternative, but by no means mutually exclusive, explanations apart.

The second place in Fig. 3.1 in which we find results consistent with the proposition that the functioning of one parent influences that of the other is in the right-hand side of Panel C. These data reveal that extensive reading and/or television watching by mothers at 3 months promoted similar behavior on the part of fathers at 9 months. From one vantage point, it seems as if fathers learn directly from mothers to pursue personal interests (reading, TV watching) at the probable expense of involvement with the infant. On the other hand, however, a more transactional explanation of these findings may be appropriate. Infants whose mothers spend more time in personal leisure activities may simply become less effective in eliciting involvement from either of their parents. And this dampened social attractiveness may well be responsible for the increased time fathers spend reading and watching TV at 9 months if their spouses engaged in this activity frequently at 3 months.

As inspection of the remaining two panels reveals, we find no evidence that the positive affection displayed by either parent toward the baby affects that of the other parent, or that maternal stimulation leads fathers to be unresponsive or is promoted by fathers' unresponsiveness. The possibility exists, of course, that such influence processes do take place, but simply cannot be detected at the level of analysis at which we are pursuing it in these cross-lag analyses. Conceivably, a microanalytical sequential analysis might reveal more parent-to-parent influence within an observation session even when we cannot find evidence of such a process across observation sessions. In summary, the results of the cross-lag analyses provide some evidence that the behavior of mothers influences that of fathers—both from 1 to 3, as well as from 3 to 9 months.

The Interrelation of Marital and Parental Interaction

The third and final set of analyses reported in this chapter was intended to illuminate the interrelation of marital and parental behavior in the family triad. As a first step toward this goal, a simple correlational analysis was undertaken linking observed marital behavior scores with maternal and paternal behavior scores within a family, within each time of measurement. Then, upon reducing the number of variables through factor analyses to produce single composite measures of marriage, mothering, and fathering at each age of measurement, we proceeded to implement a cross-lag panel analysis to illuminate potential pathways of influence over time.

Cross-Sectional Analysis.   The results of the intercorrelation of parental and marital behaviors, within each time of measurement, are displayed in Tables 3.3 and 3.4. Inspection of these tables reveals that there is a greater degree of relationship between fathering and marital interaction than there is between mothering and marital interaction. Although 6 of 25 correlations are statistically significant for mothers at the 1-month observation in comparison to 4 of 25 for fathers, by 3 months, 10 of 25 are reliable for fathers, with mothers achieving 7 of 25, and by 9 months 14 of 25 are significant for fathers whereas only 5 of 25 achieve statistical significance in the case of mothers. Moreover, it is generally the case that the magnitude of the significant associations is greater for fathers than for mothers—even at the first time of measurement when the absolute number of significant mothering–marriage correlations exceed those involving fathers.

As we have seen in our previous work using just the global parental and marital engagement indices (Belsky et al., 1984), the roles of mother and wife, at least behaviorally, appear more independent than those of father and husband. Fathers who are involved with their children tend to come from families in which marital interaction is frequent. And although a similar trend is evident in the case of women, it is by no means as strong as in the case of men—as revealed here by the intercorrelation, at three different ages, of discrete parental and marital behaviors.

A closer examination of the data in Tables 3.3 and 3.4 reveals some substantively interesting patterns of covariation that enhance our understanding of the interrelation of marriage and parenting and, thereby, of the father in the family. First, for both men and women, at most times of measurement, high levels of positive marital interaction (share pleasure, positive) occur in families in which parents are responsive to their offspring and, with the exception of mothering at 3 months, also occur in the context of positive parent–child exchanges. Another pattern that is consistent across time and across parent is that frequent stimulation of the baby seems to occur in the context of spouses jointly attending to the child. When one considers these patterns of intercorrelation across time and parent, the sense emerges of a truly interactive triad in which positive marital communication and stimulating, positive and responsive mothering and fathering co-occur. Observations of such truly reciprocal and triadic interchanges are particularly pleasurable but such naturally occurring triadic exchanges tend to be relatively rare in occurrence. They tend to figure prominently in the observer's mind and it is possible that they hold a special place in the family and are experienced in a particular way by the baby and are particularly influential.

It is also evident from the data displayed in Tables 3.3 and 3.4 that marital interaction concerning the baby tends to be strongly related to all kinds of father involvement, especially at 3 and 9 months. Because our data

TABLE 3.3
Intercorrelation of Maternal and Marital Behavior at 1, 3, and 9 Months

	Marital Behavior				
1 Month (n = 59)	Baby-Related	Share Pleasure	Joint Attention	Non-Baby Related	Positive
Respond	.04	.19	−.09	−.17	.25*
Positive	.22	.38**	.17	−.02	.25*
Stimulate	.00	−.08	.32**	−.19	−.36**
Read/TV	−.19	.04	−.19	−.11	.12
Caregive	.3	.09	.14	.12	.19
3 Months (n = 62)					
Respond	.27*	.28	.09	−.15	.29*
Positive	.31*	.25*	.21	−.14	.05
Stimulate	−.11	−.17	.28*	−.37**	−.25*
Read/TV	−.14	−.15	−.22	−.08	−.12
Caregive	.09	−.01	.09	−.14	−.05
9 Months (n = 62)					
Respond	.25*	.14	−.13	−.13	.41***
Positive	.11	.11	.13	−.11	.60***
Stimulate	−.14	.04	.30*	−.37**	−.05
Read/TV	−.21	−.10	−.05	−.19	−.09
Caregive	.13	−.05	−.09	−.00	.14

$*p < .05$
$**p < .01$
$***p < .001$

represent frequency counts and are not quickly amenable to sequential analysis, it is impossible to determine whether these contemporaneous correlations reflect a process whereby fathering fuels marital communication or the other way around. Our suspicions are, of course, that the processes of influence are bidirectional in nature with father involvement encouraging talk about the baby, and baby-related communication encouraging father involvement. When the results of our longitudinal analyses are considered we can speak more definitively about this issue.

One other trend that emerges from these data involves the negative association between non-baby-related communication and mothering and

TABLE 3.4
Intercorrelation of Paternal and Marital Behavior at 1, 3, and 9 Months

1 Month (n = 59)	Marital Behavior				
	Baby-Related	Share Pleasure	Joint Attention	Non-Baby-Related	Positive
Respond	.06	.26*	−.05	−.03	.36**
Positive	.15	.21	.08	.04	.50***
Stimulate	.09	−.03	.33*	−.11	−.18
Read/TV	−.18	.04	−.14	−.08	−.02
Caregive	.08	.05	.00	.02	.07
3 Month (n = 62)					
Respond	.52***	.47***	.26*	.00	.51*
Positive	.58***	.49***	.35**	−.17	.05
Stimulate	.25*	.19	.25*	−.15	−.08
Read/TV	−.21	−.14	−.14	−.15	−.09
Caregive	.34**	.15	.03	.04	.14
9 Month (n = 58)					
Respond	.50***	.37**	−.07	.07	.26*
Positive	.35**	.30*	.33*	−.17	.44**
Stimulate	.39**	.30*	.40***	−.20	−.06
Read/TV	−.28*	−.00	−.10	−.37**	.02
Caregive	.34**	.27*	.15	.04	.04

*$p < .05$
**$p < .01$
***$p < .001$

fathering in general, and stimulating maternal behavior in particular (at 3 and 9 months). Although this pattern is neither as strong nor as consistent as those others already mentioned, it is clearly worth noting. Obviously, it is not always the case that marital interaction and parental behavior reciprocally foster each other. As the consistent negative coefficients in the second to last column in Tables 3.3 and 3.4 make clear, under some conditions parental involvement and marital interaction seem mutually exclusive. Of special interest is the fact that it is the same kind of maternal behavior that also was negatively correlated with father involvement—namely, maternal stimulation.

It is conceivable that the data under consideration reflect two distinct interactive processes, and even possibly two distinct family types. In one, mother/wife, father/husband, and infant interact with one another, creating an interactively rich and pleasurable triadic context. In the other, either marital communication or parental involvement takes precedence, thereby limiting the other type of family participation.

Longitudinal Analysis. The goal of our final analysis was to determine whether we could further illuminate processes of influence between marriage and parenting by examining the interrelation of marital and parental behavior across time. In order to make this task more manageable the number of variables that would be linked across time was reduced. Toward this end, a series of three separate factor analyses was carried out one on marital data, one on paternal data, and one on maternal data—at each time of measurement. Thus, each data set was subjected to a principal axis analysis, with factors obliquely rotated to produce a promax solution consisting of no more than two factors. Because so few variables were available for each factor analysis, a decision was made before the analyses to consider only the first factor. The results of these analyses, that is, the weightings of each variable on the first factor to emerge from each analysis, are presented in Table 3.5.

With the results of the factor analyses in hand, summary scores of maternal and paternal involvement and marital interaction at each time of measurement were created by summing all variables with weightings in excess of .30 on any individual factor. In the case of the marital interaction factors, this meant simply excluding the non-baby-related variables at all three ages of measurement. In the case of both mothering and fathering at 1 month, this meant summing the following scores: Respond, Caregive, and Positive; and at 3 months it meant replacing Caregive with Stimulate. Finally, in the case of fathering at 9 months, both the scores Caregive and Stimulate were summed along with Respond and Positive, whereas in the case of mothering, Stimulation was excluded. Thus, at 1 and 3 months the variables comprising the mothering and fathering composites were identical, although at 9 months a slight difference characterized the two parental composite variables.

Having generated three summary scores for each age of measurement, we proceeded to carry out two parallel cross-lag panel analyses, the results of which are integrated in a single figure (see Fig. 3.2). The top half of Fig. 3.2 depicts within and across time relations between maternal involvement and marital interaction, whereas the bottom half depicts the identical relationships between paternal involvement and marital interaction.

The most important findings to emerge from the two cross-lag analyses is the evidence, in the left-hand side of the bottom panel, of the "influence"

TABLE 3.5
Weightings of Individual Mothering, Fathering, and Marriage Variables
on First Maternal, Paternal, and Marital Factors: 1, 3, and 9 Months

Mothering	One Month	Three Months	Nine Months
Respond	.66	.42	.51
Caregive	.50	.27	.45
Stimulate	– .08	.33	.27
Positive Affection	.55	.43	.51
Read/Watch TV	– .08	– .27	.28
Eigenvalue	1.00	.62	.87
Fathering			
Respond	.69	.60	.44
Caregive	.34	.23	.65
Stimulate	–.05	.41	.75
Positive Affection	.52	.49	.54
Read/Watch TV	.26	– .13	– .26
Eigenvalue	.92	.84	1.53
Marriage			
Baby-related	.88	.86	.66
Joint Attention	.68	.58	.49
Share Pleasure	.54	.73	.51
Non-baby-related	.21	.14	– .11
Positive Affection	.33	.37	.39
Eigenvalue	1.60	1.77	1.10

of marital interaction at 1 month on father involvement at 3 months in the absence of any significant relationship between fathering at 1 month and marital interaction at 3 months. Thus, from this standpoint of cross-lag analyses, these data indicate that positive communication between husband and wife about the baby at 1 month promotes stimulating, responsive, and positively affectionate father involvement at 3 months. Beyond this one set of findings, we find no evidence that marital communication fosters father involvement at 9 months or maternal involvement at any time.

FIG. 3.2   Cross-lag analysis of the influence of marital interaction on parenting and parenting on marital interaction.

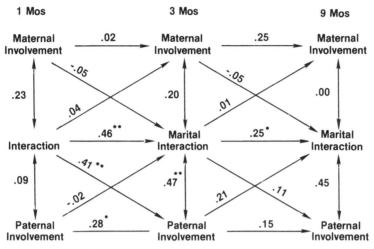

*p < .05
**p < .01

CONCLUSIONS

We have sought in this chapter to do two things—examine once more similarities and differences in mothering and fathering in the family triad and extend inquiry into family system processes in the triad. With respect to the former goal we have once again found that the behavioral roles of mothers and fathers are both similar and different. Although the parenting behavior of mothers and fathers develops in much the same way in the family triad, with overall engagement, as well as responsiveness, the display of positive affection and the provision of basic care declining in absolute frequency of occurrence over time, it remains true that mothers are more involved with the baby than are fathers. Recall that the only thing that fathers do more frequently than mothers, on average, is read and watch television.

In addition to the longitudinal analyses of mean levels of parenting behavior, evidence of similarity and differences in mothering and fathering can also be found in the results of the factor analyses. These analyses of maternal and paternal data painted much the same picture of the two parental roles. At both 1 and 3 months the variables with high loadings were virtually identical. But especially intriguing was the similar change in the "organization" of parenting from 1 to 3 months, with the weighting of stimulation increasing at the expense of that of caregiving. Only at 9 months did a major difference in variable weightings emerge. Recall that stimulation loaded much more heavily on the fathering than mothering factor. It seems conceivable that this difference is a result of the emerging emphasis in the paternal role of father as playmate because then the "stimulate" code would have been recorded if the father was arousing the infant as would be likely in social, and especially vigorous motor play, or drawing his attention to objects as would be likely in play with toys. On the basis of the factor analytic data, we can certainly conclude that at least at 1 and 3 months mothering and fathering in the triad, at least as coded in this study, are organized in much the same way. This result seems particularly important in view of the striking differences in the mean values of all maternal and paternal behaviors.

As we turn to the second focus of this chapter, the family as a system, we need to consider two system processes that have been illuminated. The first involves the influence of the parenting of one parent on that of the other. In two instances we provided evidence that maternal behavior influenced paternal behavior. In no case, however, was a reverse process discerned. We find no evidence, then, of bidirectionality in the system, although it is by no means appropriate to accept the null hypothesis and claim that such bidirectionality does not exist. But it is safe to say that although such reciprocal influence remains theoretically attractive, it also remains empirically undocumented in the current data set.

When we searched for processes of influence across relational subsystems, that is, between marriage and parenting, we again found evidence of influence being exerted on the father. These results importantly extend the cross-sectional correlations that have now been reported in several studies by showing that child-oriented marital communication seems to foster father involvement. Exactly how this process works remains unclear at present. Do wives essentially interest husbands in fathering by talking about the baby, or are fathers literally imitating and modeling the behavior of mothers over time? More careful study is obviously called for before such alternative, but not necessarily mutually exclusive, explanations can be teased apart.

What stands out of all the family system findings is the fact that wherever longitudinal pathways of influence were uncovered, they involved the father rather than the mother being influenced. These data, then, are consistent with a notion that men, because their socialization to parenthood has been less extensive, and because their role is less well defined by the community—especially in this day and age and during the infancy period—are more susceptible to influence. This finding may well highlight the most important and distinctive difference between fathers and mothers of all those discussed so far.

The behavior patterns of fathers may simply be more plastic and it is for this reason that we probably see evidence of them being influenced by the parenting of their partner and by the spousal relationship. The care that mothers offer babies, on the other hand, may be too highly canalized—by biological imperatives (e.g., breastfeeding), by a lifetime of anticipatory socialization for motherhood and, of course, by contemporary expectations. Such processes would obviously work against the father, of all people, exerting a great deal of influence on how mother handles the baby. This is the arena in which she is the expert, and in which he is assumed to be the novice, however well or ill prepared either is for the role. It would be interesting to know whether, as the child develops, influence begins to flow the other way in the family system. Quite likely the answer to this query will depend on the nature and extent of father's involvement up to that point in the child's subsequent development.

ACKNOWLEDGMENTS

Work on this paper and the research reported herein were supported by grants from the National Science Foundation (No. SES-8108886), the National Institute of Child Health and Human Development (No. R01HD15496-01A1), the Division of Maternal and Child Health of the Public Health Service (No. MC-R-424067-02-0), and the March of Dimes Birth Defects Foundation (Social and Behavioral Sciences Branch, No. 12-64), and by a National Institute of Mental Health Research Scientist Development Award (MH 00486-01A1) to Jay Belsky, Principal Investigator.

REFERENCES

Belsky, J. (1979). Mother-father-infant interaction: A naturalistic observational study. *Developmental Psychology, 15,* 601–607.
Belsky, J. (1981). Early human experience: A family perspective. *Developmental Psychology, 17,* 3–23.
Belsky, J., Gilstrap, B., & Rovine, M. (1984). The Pennsylvania Infant and Family Development Project I: Stability and change in mother-infant and father-infant interaction in a family setting at 1-to-3-to-9 months. *Child Development, 55,* 692–705.
Belsky, J., Hertzog, C., & Rovine, M. (1986). The multiple determinants of parenting: A structural equations approach. In M. Lamb, A. Brown, & B. Rogoff (Eds.), *Advances in developmental psychology* (Vol. IV, pp. 153–202). Hillsdale, NJ: Lawrence Erlbaum Associates.
Belsky, J., Lang, M., & Rovine, M. (1985). Stability and change in marriage: A second study. *Journal of Marriage and the Family, 47,* 855–866.
Belsky, J., Spanier, G. B., & Rovine, M. (1983). Stability and change in marriage across the transition to parenthood. *Journal of Marriage and the Family, 45,* 553–556.
Belsky, J., & Vondra, J. (in press). Lessons from child abuse: The determinants of parenting. In

D. Cicchetti & V. Carlson (Eds.), *New theoretical and research perspectives on child maltreatment.* Boston, MA: Cambridge University Press.

Clarke-Stewart, A. (1977). *The father's contribution to family interaction and the child's early development.* Unpublished manuscript, University of Chicago.

Clarke-Stewart, K. (1978). And daddy makes three: The father's impact on mother and young child. *Child Development, 44,* 466–478.

Clarke-Stwart, K. A. (1980). The father's contribution to children's cognitive and social development in early childhood. In F. Pedersen (Ed.), *The father-infant relationship* (pp. 111–146). New York: Praeger.

Cleaves, W. T., & Rosenblatt, P. C. (1977, March). *Intimacy between adults and children in public places.* Paper presented at the Biennial Meeting of the Society for Research in Child Development, New Orleans.

Cook, T. D., & Campbell, D. T. (1979). *Quasi-experiementation: Design and Analysis issues for filed Settings.* Chicago: Rand McNally.

Crawley, S., & Sherwood, K. (1984). Parent-infant play during the first year of life. *Infant Behavior and Development, 7,* 65–75.

Easterbrooks, M., & Goldberg, W. (1984). Toddler development in the family: Impact of fathers involvement and parenting characteristics. *Child Development, 55,* 740–752.

Feldman, S. S., Nash, S. C., & Aschenbrenner, B. (1984). Antecedents of fathering. *Child Development, 54,* 1628–1636.

Frodi, A. M., Lamb, M. E., Hwang, C., & Frodi, M. (1982, March). "Increased paternal involvement and family relationships." Paper presented at the International Conference on Infant Studies, Austin, TX.

Greenbaum, C. W., & Landau, R. (1982). The infants exposure to talk by familiar people: Mothers, fathers and siblings in different environments. In M. Lewis & L. Rosenblum (Eds.), *The social network of the developing infant* (pp. 229–247). New York: Plenum.

Kotelchuck, M. (1976). The infant's relationship to the father: Experimental evidence. In M. Lamb (Ed.), *The role of the father in child development* (pp. 123–157). New York: Wiley.

Lamb, M. (Ed.). (1976). *The role of the father in child development.* New York: Wiley.

Lamb, M. (1977). Father–infant and mother-infant interaction in the first year of life. *Child Development, 48,* 167–181.

Lamb, M. (1978a). The effects of social context on dyadic social interaction. In M. Lamb, S. Suomi, & G. R. Stephenson (Eds.), *Social interaction analysis: Methodological issues* (pp. 106–131). Madison, WI: University of Wisconsin Press.

Lamb, M. (1978b). Infant social cognition and "second order" effects. *Infant Behavior and Development, 1,* 1–11.

Lamb, M., & Elster, A. (1985). Adolescent mother–infant–father interaction. *Developmental Psychology, 21,* 768–773.

Lytton, H. (1979). Disciplinary encounters between young boys and their mothers and fathers: Is there a contingency system? *Developmental Psychology, 15,* 256–268.

Miller, B., & Sollie, D. (1980). Normal stresses during the transition to parenthood. *Family Relations, 29;* 459–465.

Parke, R., & O'Leary, S. (1973, August). *Family interaction in the newborn period: Some findings, some observations, and some unresolved issues.* Paper presented at the Biennial Meeting of the International Society for the Study of Behavioral Development, Ann Arbor, MI.

Parke, R. D., & O'Leary, S. (1976). Family interaction in the newborn period: Some findings, some observations, and some unresolved issues. In K. Riegel & J. Meacham (Eds.), *The developing individual in a changing world. Vol. 2. Social and environmental issues* (pp. 49–62). The Hague: Mouton.

Parke, R. D., O'Leary, S. E., & West, S. (1972, August). Mother-father-newborn interaction:

Effects of maternal medication, labor, and sex of infant. Paper presented at the annual convention of the American Psychological Association, Washington, DC.

Parke, R., & Sawin, D. (1975, April). *Infant characteristics and behavior as elicitors of maternal and paternal responsivity in the newborn period.* Paper presented at the biennial meeting of the Society for the Research in Child Development, Denver.

Pedersen, F. A., & Robson, K. S. (1969). Father participation in infancy. *American Journal of Orthopsychiatry, 39,* 466–472.

Pedersen, F., Yarrow, L., Anderson, B., & Cain, R. (1978). Conceptualization of father influences in the infancy period. In M. Lewis & L. Rosenblum (Eds.), *The social network of the developing infant* (pp. 267–289). New York: Plenum.

Phillips, D., & Parke, R. D. (1981). *Father and mother speech to prelinguistic infants.* Unpublished manuscript, University of Illinois.

Power, T. G., & Parke, R. D. (1982). Play as a context for early learning: Lab and home analyses. In T. E. Sigel & L. M. Lasoa (Eds.), *The family as a learning environment* (pp. 157–175). New York: Plenum.

Rendina, I., & Dickersheid, J. (1976). Father involvement with first-born infants. *Family Coordinator, 25,* 373–379.

Rogosa, D. (1979). Causal models in Longitudinal research: Rationale, formulation, and estimation. In J. R. Nesselroade & P. B. Baltes (Eds.), *Longitudinal research in the study of behavior and development* (pp. 111–156). New York: Academic Press.

Weinraub, M., & Frankel, J. (1977). Sex differences in parent-infant interaction during free play, departure, and separation. *Child Development, 48,* 1240–1249.

Yogman, M. W., Dixon, S., & Tronick, E. (1977, April). *The goals and structure of face-to-face interaction between infants and fathers.* Paper presented at the Biennial Meeting of the Society for Research in Child Development, New Orleans.

Father-Infant Interaction Among Men Who Had Contrasting Affective Responses During Early Infancy

Follow-up Observations at 1 Year

Frank A. Pedersen, Martha J. Zaslow, Richard L. Cain,
Joan T. D. Suwalsky, Beth Rabinovich
National Institute of Child Health and Human Development

In a previous study (Zaslow, Pedersen, Cain, Suwalsky, & Kramer, 1985), observations of 3-month parent–infant interaction in the home were compared for men who had experienced contrasting affective responses during the first months of parenthood. The present report addresses 1-year follow-up observations of these men, asking whether individual differences in early adaptational patterns tend to persist or whether they are relatively transient and unpredictive of later behavior involving the baby. Our interest in the affective domain and associated parental behavior partially overlaps with research reported by Feldman (this volume), who addressed the subjective sense of strain parents experienced during their infants' first 6 months of life. Research of this nature provides a fuller understanding of adaptational processes by expanding our knowledge of parents to include their subjective feeling states. Much of past research on fathers has had a behavioral bias with very little focus on affective dimensions that might covary with behavioral patterns. Affective states in the parent also may contribute to defining an emotional climate that modifies the meaning of overt behavior involving the baby.

Research on affective response to parenthood, as is true for most research in the infancy period, has been vastly more extensive for mothers than for fathers. For mothers, three differentiations in depressive emotional response following childbirth have been made: the "maternity blues," postpartum psychosis, and mild postpartum depression (Hopkins, Marcus, & Campbell, 1984). *Maternity blues* refer to an apparently transient alteration in mood characterized by tearfulness and depression that frequently occurs in the first few postpartum days. Estimates of the prevalence of this short-lived reaction range from 50% to 80%, and it has usually has been attributed in part to the major hormonal changes that occur in the mother following childbirth (Yalom, Lunde, Moos, & Hamburg, 1968). Prevalence estimates for *postpartum psychosis* are very low, on the order of .01% to .02% of all births (Herzog & Detre, 1976), and it is usually understood and treated as similar to other psychotic reactions. Between these extremes is a broad range of affective responses that has been called *mild postpartum depression,* characterized by dysphoric mood, sleep problems, despondency, tearfulness, and feelings of inadequacy with regard to caring for the baby. Using standard psychometric measures of depression, such as elevated scores on the Beck Depression Inventory (BDI; Beck, Ward, Mendelson, Mock, & Erbaugh, 1961), prevalence estimates range from about 10% to 30% between the first and third month postpartum (Hopkins et al., 1984).

A large amount of psychological research has been conducted on mild postpartum depression among mothers, especially studies attempting to identify factors that contribute to depression. One important issue that has received surprisingly little research attention is the manner in which the mother's affective response to parenthood influences her interaction with her infant. A relevant investigation by Field and her colleagues (Field et al., 1985) compared video records of two groups of mother–infant pairs during brief face-to-face interaction in a laboratory setting at age 4 months. One group had elevated depression (BDI) and anxiety scores, the other was a normal control matched on background characteristics. The results indicated that depressed and anxious mothers showed less activity, fewer imitative behaviors, fewer contingent responses, and less frequent playful behavior during their interactions than the control mothers. The infants of the depressed mothers were more frequently drowsy, showed less relaxed activity (frequent squirming and arching of the back), fewer contented expressions, and more fussiness. This study provides evidence that mild postpartum depression affects the mother–infant adaptation, resulting in lowered rates of focused interaction, but there is need for more research on this problem. Although the groups were matched on background characteristics, participants were of low socioeconomic levels and had a mean of only 11 years of education; similar studies of middle-class samples would be desirable. Further follow-up was not reported, so it is not known whether these initial adaptations tended to persist or whether they were relatively transitory.

The affective state in fathers that is a counterpart to mild postpartum depression among mothers rarely has been studied. More frequently, the literature on fathers' difficulties associated with the transition to parenthood has focused on clinical studies of severe psychological reactions (Lacoursiere, 1972; Wainwright, 1966). At the same time, there appears to be some appreciation that all fathers must make several adjustments in family relationships and role behavior with the birth of a baby and that this process can be psychologically taxing even if not sufficient to precipitate psychiatric illness (Shereshefsky & Yarrow, 1973).

The only investigation that has attempted to link men's affective response in the early postnatal months and their interactions involving babies was conducted by Zaslow et al. (1985). This study was based on an interview measure of depression and dysphoria conducted when the infant was 4 months old. The father was questioned whether he had experienced periods of "blues" during the period from the baby's birth to age 4 months. Comparison groups were created by restricting the analysis to approximately the upper and lower thirds of the distribution of scores of dysphoric mood. This division of the sample yielded 11 men who experienced relatively long periods of blues (8 or more days), and a comparison group of 14 men who said that they never experienced periods of blues. Observations at 3 months in the home environment indicated that whether or not the fathers reported dysphoric mood was associated with distinctive patterns of behavior involving the baby. Men who experienced relatively prolonged blues were observed to spend longer periods physically remote from the baby compared to men who reported no blues. Men with blues also touched the baby less frequently, and they provided less frequent caregiving and affection. In complementary fashion, mothers whose spouses experienced more prolonged blues showed higher rates of behavior in areas where the men showed lower rates. This pattern suggested the possibility that wives of dysphoric men either were compensating for their husband's lower involvement with the child or that the fathers themselves withdrew from the baby in the face of their wives' higher rates of involvement.[1] In any case, the father's report of experiencing more prolonged blues was accompanied by some disengagement from the baby. Because one of the distinguishing behavioral manisfestations of depressed mood often is behavioral inhibition and social withdrawal (Beck, 1967), the results of the Zaslow et al. investigation are of considerable conceptual interest.

An important question is whether these inital patterns of behavior tend to persist. Some inferences may be drawn from research on mothers' affective response to parenthood. In one study based on interview measures alone, not including direct assessment of mother–infant interaction (Pitt, 1968), it was found that 12 out of 28 mothers (43%) who were mildly depressed at 2 months postpartum (out of a total sample of 305) were also

---

[1]The inference of complementary involvement with the baby was based on group summaries alone. A more precise test of the complementarity of mothers' and fathers' behaviors would be reflected in inter-parent correlations, an analysis at the level of individual families. Negative correlations would suggest that parents are compensating for or reactive to their spouses' rates of behavior with the baby.

depressed at the end of the first year. Stated in reverse, the majority of mothers who experienced mild postpartum depression tended to recover within the first year. This suggests that for mothers, mild depression on the whole is a relatively self-limited phenomena, but it also can persist in some cases. There are no data on mild depression for fathers from which one can make such extrapolations. On the other hand, one study of the continuity of individual differences in fathers' behaviors over the first year, independently of fathers' affective states, show consistency roughly comparable to that of mothers (Belsky, Gilstrap, & Rovine, 1984).

Among factors that have been implicated with mild postpartum depression for mothers are problems in the marital relationship. For example, Tod (1964) found that 55% of mothers with mild postpartum depression reported marital problems compared with 7% of undepressed controls. Another study (Paykel, Emms, Fletcher, & Rassaby, 1980) reported that marital problems have a significant impact on postpartum depression, even when controlling for other stressful life events and the mother's previous psychiatric history. In an investigation that attempted to identify empirical predictors of postpartum depression for mothers (Braverman & Roux, 1978), three out of seven items that had predictive validity involved the marital relationship. Similarly, Feldman (this volume) found that the quality of the marital relationship was significantly related to the mother's subjective sense of strain at 6 months postpartum. Feldman suggested, however, that the marital relationship had a more critical influence for mothers than it did for fathers.

Zaslow et al. (1985) reported significant findings that implicated problems in the marital relationship for fathers who had experienced blues in the early months of parenthood. Two out of four interview items that discriminated the prolonged blues and no blues groups of fathers dealt with the marital relationship. The group of men who experienced blues, compared to the no blues group, reported experiencing relatively more problems since the birth of the baby in the spouse relationship and in the time they had with their spouses. When men who had experienced blues were asked of their own perception of contributing factors, 8 out of 11 saw problems in the marriage relationship as relevant. In examining the persistence of initial adaptations of men to parenthood, a relevant question is whether the quality of the marital relationship also remains stable.

The examination of the constancy of behaviors associated with early dysphoric mood is itself an instance of a much larger conceptual issue regarding the nature of early experience and our theoretical models of development. Two contrasting positions have been identified: The linear effects model and the transactional model. The linear effects model (Reese & Overton, 1970) involves a strategy of focusing on the early identification of behavior directly predictive of important later outcomes. This quest has been expressed in the pursuit of predictors of later intelligence in infants (Bornstein & Sigman, 1986), or, for example, child abuse by the parent (Spinetta & Rigler, 1972). The clinical urgency of such research is predicated on the belief that an intervention program might avert a negative outcome that otherwise has a high probability of occurrence. The linear effects model is optimistic as science in the expectation of relatively high continuity between early events and later outcome, but it is pessimistic regarding human adaptability; that is, the assumption is made that early problems will persist unless interventions are provided. Statistically, the linear effects model attempts to identify main effects that are strong enough to emerge independently of potentially modifying circumstances.

In contrast to the linear effects model, the transactional model of development (Sameroff & Chandler, 1975) has emphasized the "self-righting" nature of developmental adaptations. The transactional model proposes that often compensating features of the environment come into play when deviant patterns of development emerge. The transactional model is pessimistic regarding the direct predictability of later outcomes from early events, but it is optimistic regarding human adaptability. Statistically, transactional models usually postulate interactions between two or more variables on the outcome rather than a simple main effect of a single variable. An example of a transactional hypothesis, cited by Sameroff and Chandler (1975), is that a high-risk neonate is likely to show an impaired developmental outcome only if it is reared in an adverse environment.

In the present investigation, the degree of continuity found for the interactional patterns associated with dysphoric mood may be viewed in relation to these two models of development. If the men who experienced early blues and exhibited a more withdrawn style of relating to their 3-month-old infants showed some consistency in this pattern over time, the data would fit with the linear effects model. Lack of consistency, however, does not necessarily support the transactional model. A failure to find patterns of father–infant interaction that are conceptually congruent with an earlier withdrawn style may obtain merely because of unreliability of measurement or because the initial differences were truly ephimeral. More compelling evidence for the transactional model would require signs of some compensatory process that actively conteracts the earlier withdrawal from the infant. The data on consistency of men's early adaptations are examined with an eye toward their relevance to these two models of early experience.

METHODS

Sample.   The sample on which the follow-up analyses at age 1 year were conducted consisted of 25 families. This is the subset of 37 families, each with a first-born infant, originally described by Zaslow et al. (1985) at age 3 months. The subset consists of approximately the upper and lower thirds of the original sample, selected on the basis of fathers' scores on an interview measure of duration of blues or dysphoric mood experienced during the first 4 months of the baby's life. There were 14 families in which fathers reported no periods of blues (designated Group N, for "no" dysphoric mood) and there were 11 families in which fathers reported 8 or more days of dysphoric mood (designated Group P, for "prolonged" dysphoric mood) during the early months of parenthood. The original pool of participants was recruited from childbirth education groups in the metropolitan Washington, DC area. As in many samples of families that elect involvement in childbirth education groups, the parents were predominantly of nonminority background, well educated, and they had deferred childbearing. The mean age of the fathers and mothers was 32 and 30 years respectively. All the couples were married, with the average duration of marriage 4 years at the birth of their first child. Eighty-nine percent of the fathers and 84% of the mothers had college level (or more) education. At the 1-year follow-up, 44% of the mothers were employed 20 or more hours per week. There were no significant differences between the two groups on any background characteristics. Group N had 7 male and 7 female infants, while Group P had 5 male and 6 female infants. All the infants were medically normal at birth and were considered to be developing normally throughout the period of the study. Caesarean-delivered infants (and infants with medical complications) were excluded from the sample because of the possibility that birth complications might influence the parents' adaptations.

Observational Procedures.   There were two home observations conducted when the infant was 1-year-old, usually 1 week apart, and each observation was 1 hour in duration. They were scheduled usually in the early evening on a weekday when mother and father were typically together in the home and the infant was expected to be awake. This time period appeared to have "ecological validity" for most fathers (i.e., it was representative of their day-to-day experiences with their infants). Families were encouraged to go about their normal routines, ignoring the observer to the extent that this was possible. The observer remained in the same room with the infant, but the parents were free to use the physical space of the residence according to their preferences.

The observational procedure was essentially identical to the procedures employed at 3 months, involving time sampling of preselected behaviors of mother, father, and infant. Ten-second observation periods were followed by 20-second recording periods, a cycle repeated througout the observation. The occurrence of a particular behavior was coded once for each 10-second episode. The scores for behavior had a potential range of 0 to 120 for each observation; analyses were based on the mean of the two observations.

There were 14 categories of parental behavior (parallel measures were used for mothers and fathers) that sampled five conceptual areas and five categories of infant behavior that sampled two areas. The parental measures were: (a) *distal communication* (mutual visual regard; verbalizations, i.e., meaningful words; vocalizations, i.e., nonword utterances like humming, and playful sounds like clucking); (b) *physical contact* (hold at a distance, i.e., without trunk to trunk contact; hold close with trunk to trunk contact; touching, such as patting, stroking and caressing; and vigorous tactile-kinesthetic stimulation); (c) *expression of positive affect* (smile or laugh; expression of affection, i.e., hugging, praise or verbal endearments); (d) *play* (focused social play; encouraging the child's attention to objects; presenting and manipulating objects); and (e) *caregiving* (feeding; all other caregiving, including cleaning, changing diapers, and grooming). In addition, it was noted whether the parent was out of the room in which the baby was located.

The infant measures were: (a) *social signals* (fret or cry; smile or laugh; positive vocalizations), and (b) *exploratory behavior* (look at object; manipulate object).

Reliability data were established with observations of 11 families with two observers present. Median reliability on behavior categories was .92 (range of .52 to .99) based on product-moment correlations of the frequency scores. The three observers were blind in regard to the hypotheses of this study, and for each family a different person conducted the 12-month observation than did the 3-month observation.

Interview Measures at 1 Year.   The follow-up assessments on the families at 1 year did not include direct inquiry into whether there were further periods of blues. On the other hand, efforts were made to probe the parent's sense of the kinds of changes that had occurred in their lives since the 3-month home observations were conducted. Mothers and fathers were each asked individually to make judgments on 5-point rating scales for 12 areas of experience. Items included the amount of sleep they were getting, amount of housework they were doing, the spouse relationship, and contacts with friends and relatives, and so on. These scales were designed to determine whether changes had occurred that might bear upon the parents' sense of well-being, and it was recognized that either positive or negative changes might occur. A score of 3 implied, on balance, no change; scores of 4 and 5 implied some change and substantial change, respectively, in a positive direction; scores of 2 and 1 represented some change and substantial change, respectively, in a negative direction. The reference point for reporting a sense of change was the parent's own definition of how he or she felt when the baby was 3-months old in each of the 12 areas.

RESULTS

The central question of this report, whether early adaptational patterns of contrasting groups of fathers tended to persist, was examined with repeated-measure analyses of variance.[2] Analyses were done at the level of discrete, individual measures of paternal behavior and at a more global level with a composite score derived from the individual measures. First, ANOVAs were computed for the 14 separate measures of paternal behavior and for the measure Out of Room. Although seemingly a diffuse attack on the problem, in fact the primary interest was upon a limited number of measures in which the groups differed at age 3 months. As Zaslow et al. (1985) reported, three measures, Touch, Caregiving other than Feeding, and Out of Room, were significantly ($p < .05$) related to whether or not fathers experienced periods of blues. Another measure, Affection and Positive Evaluation, was of borderline significance ($p < .10$) at 3 months. The nature of these findings was that fathers in Group P showed lower behavior rates than those in Group N (except for Out of Room, which was, of course, in the opposite direction). If initial patterns tended to persist, the inclusion of the 12-month data would lead one to expect significant main effects for group on the selected measures; this would imply that differences at 3 months were basically replicated at age 12 months.

A second level of analysis was based upon a composite variable, Variety of Stimulation. This summary measure, recomputed with Zaslow et al.'s (1985) original data at 3 months, complements the analyses of discrete measures, asking whether there is a general pattern to paternal behavior reflected in the 14 measures as a whole.[3] Variety of Stimulation was calculated by counting the number of *measures* (of the 14) on which a subject scored above the median. A high score implies relatively a large

---

[2] A secondary question, how mothers were observed to behave in families where fathers had contrasting affective reactions, was analyzed separately. It was felt that 3-factor ANOVAs, with group, sex of parent, and age as the comparisons, tended to obscure the central interest in the father's adaptational patterns. This is because a 3-factor statistical design brings maternal behavior into various permutations of comparisons whether or not it is conceptually meaningful to consider these data concurrently.

[3] A traditional method of pooling variables, computation of a MANOVA, did not lead to statistically significant findings. Stevens (1980) noted that the power of a MANOVA in small samples is dependent on the number of variables and their intercorrelations, implying that the meaning of negative results sometimes may be moot.

breadth in ways of actively engaging the child, whereas a low score suggests more selective ways of interacting with the child. A repeated-measures ANOVA was then calculated for the composite measure, Variety of Stimulation.

Paternal Behavior.   Table 4.1 summarizes the means and tests of sigificance for rates of paternal behavior. Neither the individual measures nor the composite measure, Variety, shows significant main effects for group. There is absolutely no evidence to support continuity over the first year in father–infant interaction patterns for the two groups of men who at age 3 months showed differential behaviors associated with contrasting affective responses.

Table 4.1 also reports tests of significance for differences in paternal behavior associated with maturation of the child, main effects of age. There are several findings that, in general, reflect a shift from proximal to distal modes of communication. Compared with fathers' behavior when the infant was 3 months old, at 12 months physical contact with the child was lower, verbalizations to the child were more frequent, and exploratory behavior was fostered more frequently by directing children's attention to inanimate objects such as toys. These results are similar to other normative developmental studies (Belsky et al., 1984), although they are not the primary focus of this report.

Of greatest interest in Table 4.1 are the findings that among the individual measures there are three significant interactions of group by age. The measures, Touch, Affection and Positive Evaluation, and Caregiving other than Feeding, all show a similar pattern: At age 3 months, Group N fathers scored higher than Group P fathers, whereas at 12 months the reverse was found. One other discrete behavior, Verbalize, followed this same pattern, but was of borderline statistical significance ($p < .10$). Out of Room, which reflects upon a father's more global readiness to engage the child, showed a pattern ($p < .10$) of similar psychological meaning but numerically opposite the behavioral measures. The composite measure, Variety of Stimulation, yielded a significant interaction of group by age that paralleled the pattern found with the discrete behaviors. The significant interactions of group by age are presented graphically in Fig. 4.1.

Infant Behavior.   Infant-behavior rates were compared at ages 3 and 12 months for the two groups. There were no significant findings related to group or group by age interactions. Each of the five measures was significantly related to age in a manner consistent with maturational changes of the child expected in the first year. Children showed a decrease in crying and increases in smiling, vocalizations and exploratory behavior. Details of these results are omitted for brevity of reporting.

TABLE 4.1
Mean 3- and 12-Month Behavior Rates for Fathers Who Had Contrasting Affective Responses During Early Infancy

Behavior	No Dysphoric Mood (N = 14)		Eight or More Days of Dysphoric Mood (N = 11)		F-ratios		
	3 Mo	12 Mo	3 Mo	12 Mo	Group	Age	Group × Age
Distal							
Eye-to-Eye	13.9 (6.8)	7.9 (5.3)	11.1 (8.3)	8.9 (7.7)	—	6.4*	—
Verbalize	30.1 (9.0)	30.6 (12.9)	22.8 (17.2)	33.0 (16.6)	—	4.7*	3.5†
Vocalize	10.5 (7.3)	9.9 (6.8)	5.2 (3.5)	9.4 (5.7)	—	—	—
Contact							
Hold	15.0 (14.7)	3.5 (2.5)	10.6 (7.1)	4.2 (2.3)	—	11.9**	—
Hold Close	21.4 (15.7)	7.5 (8.4)	15.6 (11.5)	8.8 (4.9)	—	13.2**	—
Touch	32.7 (9.5)	12.6 (5.3)	22.7 (19.7)	16.3 (8.0)	—	25.3**	6.8*
Vigorous Tactile/ Kinesthetic	1.8 (1.4)	2.6 (1.8)	2.4 (2.4)	3.8 (4.6)	—	—	—
Positive Affect							
Smile	8.9 (9.1)	10.5 (9.5)	6.1 (4.3)	11.0 (10.8)	—	—	—
Affection/Pos. Evaluation	3.0 (2.3)	1.6 (1.8)	1.3 (1.9)	2.1 (2.1)	—	—	8.3**

Play							
Social Play	6.7 (4.0)	4.9 (4.0)	6.1 (4.4)	5.0 (5.2)	—	—	—
Enc. Attn. to Objects	1.8 (1.0)	4.7 (5.2)	2.2 (1.8)	9.4 (9.0)	—	15.2**	—
Present/Manipulate Objects	7.5 (7.2)	7.1 (6.9)	5.8 (5.4)	8.9 (7.0)	—	—	—
Caregiving							
Feed	5.6 (9.3)	3.5 (3.2)	5.6 (13.5)	2.9 (3.1)	—	—	—
Other Caregiving	7.8 (3.8)	3.4 (3.3)	4.6 (4.4)	7.7 (4.9)	—	—	13.8**
Out of Room	17.4 (.1)	20.4 (12.8)	29.7 (22.9)	20.4 (18.4)	—	—	3.3†
Variety of Stimulation (Composite Score)	6.9 (2.4)	6.1 (2.8)	5.5 (3.7)	7.8 (4.3)	—	—	4.4*

†p < .10; *p < .05; **p < .01
Standard Deviations in parentheses

FIG. 4.1   Developmental course in selected behaviors for fathers who had contrasting affective responses in early infancy.

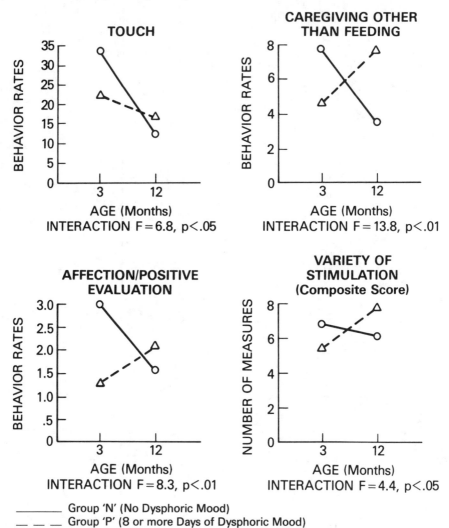

_____ Group 'N' (No Dysphoric Mood)
_ _ _ _ Group 'P' (8 or more Days of Dysphoric Mood)

Maternal Behavior.   Table 4.2 reports means and tests of significance for maternal behaviors in the groups defined by the contrasting affective responses of the fathers. As was the case for paternal behaviors, there are no significant main effects for group and there are several areas where maternal behavior shows changes with the age of the child, changes consistent with the child's maturation and greater autonomy. In addition, comparisons between mothers in the two groups revealed three significant interactions of group by age. In each case, the pattern of the results was in a general sense opposite to that of the fathers in the same groups. That is, mothers in families where fathers had prolonged blues showed, relative to mothers in families where fathers did not experience blues, higher rates of involvement with the baby at 3 months and numerically lower rates at 12 months. This pattern held for the discrete behavior, Caregiving other than Feeding, and the more general measure, Variety. The measure, Out of Room, was psychologically comparable though the numbers were in the opposite direction.

Inter-parent Correlations.   As noted, the findings at age 3 months suggested a complimentary pattern for mothers and fathers in Group P (i.e., that fathers' low behavior rates were accompanied by higher behavior rates on the part of mothers in these families). A more direct test of this hypothesis, however, would involve an analysis at the level of individual families rather than comparisons based on group summaries. Negative correlations between scores for mothers and fathers on each category of parental behavior would suggest one parent is either compensating for or reacting to the behavior rate of the other parent; positive correlations between mothers' and fathers' behavior rates, on the other hand, suggests an additive style in which the behavior of one parent tends to parallel the rates of the other.

Table 4.3 reports the directionality of inter-parent correlations for the 14 discrete behaviors.[4] In Group P, at both ages, only 5 out of 14 correlations were positive. Correlations in Group N were predominantly positive in sign at both ages. Because of the indeterminate interdependencies of the measures, conventional tests of significance for the differences between the groups in prevalence of sign are of questionable meaning. If one is flexible about such concerns, it may be noted that a Fisher Exact Probability test indicates that the proportion of positive correlations is significantly different for the two groups at 3 months ($p < .05$) and at 12 months ($p < .01$).

Interview Measures.   Table 4.4 reports tests of significance on interview items administered to mothers and fathers after the 12-month observations were completed. Parents were asked to evaluate on 5-point rating scales their sense of change in 12 areas of their lives since their baby was 3 months old. Scores above 3.0 reflect positive change. Results indicate that, of the five significant differences found, four of these reflect more positive changes in the families where the fathers reported prolonged blues at the earlier assessment. Three of these four significant items indicated improvement in the quality of the spouse relationship or in the time available to be

---

[4]The magnitudes of the relationships were not reported because of the instability of correlation coefficients based on small samples.

TABLE 4.2
Mean 3- and 12-Month Behavior Rates for Mothers in Families Where Fathers Had Contrasting Affective Responses

Behavior	No Dysphoric Mood (N = 14)		Eight or More Days of Dysphoric Mood (N = 11)		F-ratios		
	3 Mo	12 Mo	3 Mo	12 Mo	Group	Age	Group × Age
Distal							
Eye-to-Eye	10.2 (5.3)	8.9 (4.5)	11.7 (5.1)	6.8 (5.7)	—	5.1*	—
Verbalize	33.1 (14.5)	41.3 (14.3)	30.3 (17.2)	33.7 (15.4)	—	4.9*	—
Vocalize	7.1 (5.9)	11.6 (5.7)	4.5 (2.9)	7.8 (9.0)	—	6.0*	—
Contact							
Hold	8.7 (6.6)	3.0 (2.4)	12.6 (9.9)	3.3 (2.4)	—	21.5**	—
Hold Close	27.5 (19.4)	6.5 (4.2)	33.5 (21.4)	9.3 (10.6)	—	30.7***	—
Touch	22.2 (9.3)	13.9 (6.3)	32.1 (14.2)	15.1 (10.5)	—	29.7**	3.5†
Vigorous Tactile/Kinesthetic	1.5 (4.1)	1.7 (1.5)	2.0 (2.4)	2.9 (3.9)	—	—	—
Positive Affect							
Smile	10.1 (7.8)	14.2 (6.3)	9.5 (6.4)	10.3 (10.5)	—	—	—
Affection/Pos. Evaluation	2.6 (3.2)	2.7 (1.8)	3.2 (2.3)	3.5 (2.9)	—	—	—

Play

Social Play	3.8 (4.9)	3.6 (3.0)	3.5 (3.2)	4.8 (5.9)	—	—	—	—
Enc. Attn. to Objects	1.9 (2.6)	6.3 (5.0)	2.6 (2.7)	5.7 (4.0)	—	—	16.2**	—
Present/Manipulate Objects	3.9 (4.8)	5.3 (2.9)	5.5 (3.6)	6.9 (4.6)	—	—	—	—

Caregiving

Feed	14.6 (13.9)	3.7 (4.5)	21.3 (16.3)	4.3 (5.9)	—	—	23.4**	—
Other Caregiving	4.8 (3.8)	5.9 (4.4)	9.0 (7.3)	5.6 (5.2)	—	—	—	4.8*
Out of Room	25.4 (14.7)	21.4 (14.6)	14.0 (8.9)	24.2 (8.2)	—	—	—	8.3**

Variety of Stimulation (Composite Score) | 6.0 (2.9) | 7.8 (3.4) | 8.1 (2.6) | 6.4 (4.8) | — | — | — | 5.4* |

†$p < .01$; *$p < .05$; **$p < .01$
Standard Deviations in parentheses

79

TABLE 4.3
Directionality of Inter-Parent Correlations for Behaviors at 3-Months and 12-Months
in Families Where Fathers Had Contrasting Affective Reactions

	No Dysphoric Mood	Eight or More Days of Dysphoric Mood
3 Months		
Positive/Negative Correlations	11/3	5/9
12 Months		
Positive/Negative Correlations	13/1	5/9

with the spouse. The fourth significant finding of improved circumstances for the blues group was that these fathers reported an improved energy level, a finding that on face value suggests diminished dysphoric feelings. One area of change was more positive for the no blues group; mothers in these families reported an improved quality in their contact with relatives.

DISCUSSION

The data on which this report is based speak to an interesting problem that has not been examined before, follow-up observations of father–infant interaction for groups of men that evidenced contrasting affective responses during the early months of parenthood. We recognize from the outset, however, that some caveats must be stated that may qualify our conclusions. Our sample size was quite small; the statistical comparisons were made on groups of 14 and 11 subjects. On the other hand, such findings as were uncovered probably represent relatively robust phenomena to emerge from so small a sample.

The sample, in addition to being small, was not broadly representative. Participants, as a group, were well-educated, non-minority families that had married somewhat later and had deferred childbearing as compared to normative patterns for middle-class families. Clearly, there is need for investigation with samples of differing background characteristics. One might speculate that our investigation with families that were educationally and socioeconomically advantaged yields a conservative estimate of the impact of mild depression in fathers, but more satisfying conclusions would be based on empirical studies with broader samples.

These reservations notwithstanding, there are several positive conclusions that may be drawn from our findings.

First, it seems safe to conclude that there is no evidence at all that

TABLE 4.4
12 Month Areas of Change:
Comparisons of Mothers and Fathers in Families
Where Fathers had Contrasting Affective Reactions[a]

AREA	MOTHERS			FATHERS		
	Prolonged Blues	No Blues	t	Prolonged Blues	No Blues	t
Sleep	4.4 (.9)	4.2 (.8)	—	4.0 (.8)	4.0 (.7)	—
Housework	3.2 (1.1)	3.3 (1.0)	—	2.9 (.5)	2.6 (.9)	—
Energy Level	4.3 (.6)	3.7 (1.1)	—	3.5 (.8)	2.9 (.6)	2.1*
Relationship with Spouse	4.0 (.6)	3.4 (.6)	2.5*	3.8 (.6)	3.2 (.7)	2.3*
Sexual Relations	3.4 (1.1)	3.4 (1.0)	—	3.5 (1.1)	3.5 (.9)	—
Time with Spouse	3.8 (.9)	2.8 (1.0)	2.7**	3.5 (1.1)	3.1 (1.1)	—
Contact with Friends	3.8 (1.1)	3.1 (1.3)	—	3.1 (.9)	2.9 (1.1)	—
Contact with Relatives	3.4 (.7)	4.1 (.7)	2.5*	3.5 (.9)	3.9 (.7)	—
Time for Self	3.5 (1.6)	2.9 (1.3)	—	3.0 (1.1)	2.4 (.6)	—
Emotions and Feelings	4.2 (.6)	3.7 (.6)	1.9†	3.7 (.8)	3.2 (.8)	—
Need for Support	3.3 (.9)	3.0 (1.0)	—	3.5 (.5)	3.1 (.5)	—
Finances	2.8 (1.0)	3.3 (.8)	—	3.0 (1.1)	3.1 (.9)	—

$†p < .10; *p < .05; **p < .01$
[a]Entries are means of 5-point ratings; scores above 3.0 reflect positive change.
Standard deviations in parentheses.

fathers' early behavioral adaptations associated with contrasting affective states tend to persist. Within the range of severity encountered in our sample (which is unlikely to include anyone considered clinically depressed), the lower rates of interaction with the infant at age 3 months that distinguished men who reported more prevalent blues was in itself not a long-lived phenomenon. This suggests that the blues response identified by Zaslow et al. (1985) is primarily of conceptual interest but that there is no special need to sound the clarion call for intervention programs. Follow-up studies of this nature are important in order to recognize that there may be "blips" in men's transition to parenthood that do not necessarily presage long-term problems or deviant adaptations.

A second conclusion from our findings relates to their distinctive and recurring pattern: In every instance of a statistically significant result involving the father's affective state, we found an interaction of group by age in which the pattern of early group differences was reversed at the follow-up period. This suggests to us that there may be a conceptually interesting dynamic at work, an active compensatory process. The data suggest a "catch-up" phenomena in the fathers with the initial prolonged blues experience. Areas of behavior that were earlier linked to a subjective sense of dysphoria and at age 3 months expressed at low rates were at age 12 months being engaged in more actively relative to the men in the no blues comparison group. This pattern to the results suggests that a more complex psychological process is occurring than merely the waning of initial differences between the groups.

We are unable to discern a meaningful pattern in the specific paternal behavioral areas that were implicated with dysphoric mood at 3 months and showed recovery, relative to the comparison group, at 12 months. That is, the variables significantly related to mood appeared to cut across different stimulus modalities for engaging the infant, involved affective elements of interaction, and included relatively mundane matters such as caregiving in contexts other than feeding. There does not seem to be a single conceptual dimension that was particularly sensitive to differences in early dysphoric mood. The more general variable, Variety of Stimulation, may be the best marker event to tell the basic story of these findings. That is, many aspects of paternal behavior showed some connection with dysphoric mood (though only a limited number of measures were statistically significant) so that the main influence of dysphoric mood at 3 months was to depress interaction along a broad spectrum of behavior; moreover, at 12 months, recovery encompassed a range of behavior. The measure, Out of Room, similarly may reflect upon a generalized tendency to be uninvolved with the baby at 3 months and more actively involved at 12 months.

The results for behaviors of mothers in families where the fathers experienced contrasting affective reactions also are of interest. Although mothers in both groups, as a whole, showed conspicuous changes in their behavior that were appropriate to the developmental maturation of the child, there were a few measures for which significant interactions of group by age were found. This means that usual maternal accommodation to the child's developmental change was modified, depending on the father's early affective state and his accompanying behavior. The pattern of these differences was generally opposite to that of these fathers. Our data show that maternal behavior is therefore systematically connected with the father's affective state and his parental behavior. These results provide further evidence to that in other chapters of this volume that the adaptations to parenthood of mothers and fathers are psychologically linked with one another.

A second line of evidence regarding the interconnectedness of maternal and paternal behavior is based on the inter-parent correlations for the two groups. Two somewhat different patterns were tentatively identified. In the group where fathers reported no blues, correlations between maternal and paternal behavior rates were almost all positive. This suggests a model of additive experience in which mothers and fathers may learn from or model one another. This pattern is conceptually similar to results reported by Belsky and Volling (this volume) for the measure, Respond, and for ignoring the baby (Read/Watch TV) in their sample as a whole. In the group of families where fathers experienced dysphoric mood, inter-parent correlations were more likely negative in direction (9 of 14 comparisons at each age). This suggests that these families have somewhat more of a compensatory model of experience in which mother and father may be reactive to each other's patterns of involvement. It is possible that different family dynamics (i.e., different influences of mother and father on each other's relationship with the child) are being played out in the groups identified by the presence or absence of the father's early dysphoric mood.

We do not know the causal factors that may underlie the onset of dysphoric mood early in men's parenthood nor what may be behind their apparent "catch up" evident at age 12 months. Zaslow et al., however, reported exploratory findings that men who experienced prolonged blues often perceived problems in the spouse relationship as having a contributory effect. In addition, significantly more men in the blues group reported negative changes in the marital area than did men in the no blues group. The series of interview items addressing areas of change in mothers' and fathers' lives between 3 and 12 months are extremely interesting in this regard. On the whole, the prolonged blues group at 12 months appears to show more positive changes (four significant items and one item of borderline significance) than the no blues group (one significant item). Especially interesting, three of the four items reflecting positive change for mothers and fathers in the blues group are related to the marital relationship. These results, as well as other findings reported in this volume (Feldman; Cowan & Cowan) suggest that variation in equilibrium in the marital relationship may be especially critical in explaining the onset of fathers' dysphoric mood as well as, at 12 months, the recovery in those behaviors that had been associated with early dysphoric mood.

The interrelations of the marital and parental subsystems that are highlighted in the aforementioned findings do not, of course, indicate the family dynamics that may be influencing fathers' adaptational patterns. Nor do they speak to possible causal chains of influence among the different subsystems. Two different (but not necessarily exclusive) processes may be at play. One possibility is that the fathers who experienced early dysphoric mood did so because they first encountered a sense of loss of the spouse as she became absorbed in the care of the infant. According to this perspective, the fathers' problems in the marital realm were primarily because his needs for emotional closeness with his wife were thwarted as a consequence of her more exclusive interest in nurturing the infant. His low rates of involvement with the infant at 3 months might even have been due to being "crowded out" by the mother. At 12 months, as the child became more autonomous, some improvement in the marital realm might occur. This change might also provide a greater sense of emotional support to these men, and their improved sense of well-being could express itself in greater involvement with the child.

An alternative explanation to our findings is that the father's sense of competence or self-efficacy in his nurturing role is central to whether or not he experienced blues, and his evaluation of the marital relationship may have been secondary to feelings about his nurturing skills. This interpretation places more emphasis on the possibility that the very young infant was something of a conundrum to the father, but as the child matured and its need for nurturance changed, the father may have become more skilled and comfortable. As his dysphoria lifted, a sense of an improved marriage relationship might also occur. According to this possibility, the mother's earlier high rates of involvement with the infant were merely picking up the slack for the father's disengagement.

It is interesting to note that theoretical speculations in sociobiology have yielded two somewhat similar views to explain in evolutionary terms the human male's investment in the care of the young. A widely held position (Fisher, 1982) is that a major evolutionary change was the female's loss of estrus. This resulted in the formation of a relatively monogamous bond between males and females, and a secondary benefit to the female of the male being "kept guessing" was that he invested more in the care of the young. Roughly restated, the bond between the parents led to a secondary increase in the father's parenting investment. An opposing interpretation (Lancaster, 1985) is that the primary evolutionary development was the long period of juvenile dependence; this necessiated a contribution of both male and female parent toward juvenile survival expressed in the division of labor between male hunting and female gathering. The female's loss of estrus was a secondary "favor" that relieved the male of constantly having to fight off potential consorts. This perspective posits a basic tie between the male and his progeny, and, in a sense, makes the union between the parents secondary. Although such evolutionary speculations go far afield from our data, they encourage conceptualization of the family dynamics that may underlie the statistical connections established between the marital and parental subsystems.

Finally, it is appropriate to evaluate our results in relation to the linear effects and transactional models of early experience. Because on none of the measures did we find that initial patterns of paternal behavior were maintained through the end of the baby's first year of life, there is no support in our data for the linear effects model. Furthermore, there does appear to be a compensatory process at work on selected parental behaviors as well as within the marital relationship among the men who reported early dysphoric mood. Although we do not know much about the dynamics of these changes, still, the fact that a compensatory process is evident is consistent with a transactional model.

SUMMARY

We have reported follow-up observations of father-infant interaction at 1 year for men who evidenced contrasting affective reactions during the early months of parenthood. Men who reported in interviews that they had experienced periods of blues or dysphoric mood, as contrasted to men who did not report such feeling states, were found in home observations at 3 months to have a more disengaged style of relating to their babies. They spent more time physically remote from the baby, touched their babies less frequently, and they provided less frequent caregiving and affection than did the comparison group. At age 12 months, statistically significant interactions of group by age were found on these measures. The nature of the interactions was that the areas of behavior that were sensitive to dysphoric mood and were engaged in at rates lower than the comparison group at 3 months were, at 12 months, engaged in at rates higher than the comparison group. In addition, a factor that was associated with experiencing dysphoric mood at 3 months, problems in the marital relationship, was reported by the men and their wives as significantly improved at age 12 months. These findings provide evidence of a compensatory process at work in men who had initial adaptational difficulties. The pattern to the findings is consistent with a transactional model of early experience that emphasizes the "self-righting" potential in human adaptations.

REFERENCES

Beck, A. T. (1967). *Depression: Clinical, experimental, and theoretical aspects.* New York: Harper & Row.

Beck, A. T., Ward, C. H., Mendelson, M., Mock, J. E., & Erbaugh, J. (1961). An inventory for measuring depression. *Archives of General Psychiatry, 4,* 561–571.

Belsky, J., Gilstrap, B., & Rovine, M. (1984). The Pennsylvania infant and family development project, I: Stability and change in mother-infant interaction in a family setting at one, three, and nine months. *Child Development, 55,* 692–705.

Bornstein, M. H., & Sigman, M. D. (1986). Continuity of mental development from infancy. *Child Development, 57,* 251–274.

Braverman, J., & Roux, J. F. (1978). Screening for the patient at risk for postpartum depression. *Obstetrics and Gynecology, 52* (6), 731–736.

Field, T., Sandberg, D., Garcia, R., Vega-Lahr, N., Goldstein, S., & Gay, L. (1985). Pregnancy problems, postpartum depression and early mother–infant interactions. *Developmental Psychology, 21*(6), 1152–1156.

Fisher, H. E. (1982). *The sex contract.* New York: Morrow.

Herzog, A., & Detre, T. (1976). Psychotic reactions associated with childbirth. *Diseases of the Nervous System, 37,* 229–235.

Hopkins, J., Marcus, M., & Campbell, S. B. (1984). Pospartum depression: A critical review. *Psychological Bulletin, 95*(3), 498–515.

Lacoursiere, R. B. (1972). Fatherhood and mental illness: A review and new material. *Psychiatric Quarterly, 46,* 109–124.

Lancaster, J. B. (1985). Evolutionary perspectives on sex differences in the higher primates. In A. S. Rossi (Ed.), *Gender and the life course* (pp. 3–27). New York: Aldine.

Paykel, E. S., Emms, E. M., Fletcher, J., & Rassaby, E. S. (1980). Life events and social support in puerperal depression. *British Journal of Psychology, 136,* 339–346.

Pitt, B. (1968). "Atypical" depression following childbirth. *British Journal of Psychiatry. 114,* 1325–1335.

Reese, H. W., & Overton, W. F. (1970). Models of development and theories of development. In L. R. Goulet & P. B. Baltes (Eds.), *Life span developmental psychology: Research and theory* (pp. 115–145). New York: Academic Press.

Sameroff, A. J., & Chandler, M. J. (1975). Reproductive risk and the continuum of caretaking casualty. In F. D. Horowitz (Ed.), *Review of child development research* (Vol. 4, pp. 187–244). Chicago: University of Chicago Press.

Shereshefsky, P. M., & Yarrow, L. J. (1973). *Psychological aspects of a first pregnancy and early postnatal adaptation.* New York: Raven Press.

Spinetta, J. J., & Rigler, D. (1972). The child-abusing parent: A psychological review. *Psychological Bulletin, 77,* 296–304.

Stevens, J. P. (1980). Power of multivariate analysis of variance tests. *Psychological Bulletin, 88*(3), 728–737.

Tod, E. D. M. (1964). Puerperal depression: A prospective epidemiological study. *The Lancet, 2,* 1264–1266.

Wainwright, W. H. (1966). Fatherhood as a percipitant of mental illness. *American Journal of Psychiatry, 123,* 40–44.

Yalom, J. D., Lunde, D. T., Moos, R. H., & Hamburg, D. A. (1968). "Postpartum blues" syndrome. *Archives of General Psychiatry, 18,* 16–27.

Zaslow, M. J., Pedersen, F. A., Cain, R. L., Suwalsky, J. T. D., & Kramer, E. L. (1985). Depressed mood in new fathers: Associations with parent-infant interaction. *Psychology Monographs, 111*(2), 135–150.

Separate and Together:
Men's Autonomy and Affiliation in the Transition to Parenthood

Frances Kaplan Grossman
Boston University

Separate and together. Can young fathers be both? Although the examples given below may not answer the question, they do illustrate the relevance of these dimensions to early fatherhood.

One young father from the Pregnancy and Parenthood Project (Grossman et al., 1980) was pleased but surprised and very anxious. During his wife's pregnancy, he had not anticipated any great feelings of involvement with his baby, but at the end of her first year, he found himself hooked: attached, involved, occupied, and preoccupied with his daughter.

> It's been a lot of fun to watch her grow. . . . But at the same time, it's a lot of responsibility. Like this Saturday, I babysitted all day, and, like I was a nervous wreck by the end of the day. I just had never been around babies, and I didn't know. . . . I just didn't have any idea of what being a father was all about. . . . And, I'm really attached. I find myself thinking about her at work, rushing to the day care center to pick her up, just because every day she learns something new and you just want to see it and kind of share it with her.

He thought he had changed, as do we. "My personality has changed a lot. I take things a little slower. I think about her more. I guess when you decide to have a baby, you don't think about those things. You don't think your life is really going to change. All of a sudden, you gotta be somebody's *father!* It's different, but it's fun."

Listening to this man's unanticipated involvement with his infant, we thought the experience of having a child was effecting his interest in, and maybe capacity for, closeness with another person. He seemed more affiliative than he had been before, and we thought it boded well for his relationship with his daughter.

There were other tapes in which the men seemed, by virtue of personality and circumstance, unable to be close. At times, their separate, independent activities seemed pitted against their relationships. In one such instance, in the pregnancy interview, the man seemed notably lacking in what we would call "intimate"—or he would call "satisfying"—relationships with anyone, although he seemed to do well in his career, in which he functioned separately, independently. At the 5-year followup, we found he had not been able to use the opportunity of his relationship with his child to develop closer, more empathic bonds, but instead had become more invested in his job and was increasingly isolated from the warm, related, and somewhat exclusive unit made up of his wife and several children. He was also dissatisfied and lonely, but had no idea what was wrong. Thus, he responded to the stress of the early phases of family development by becoming more separate, more independent, and also less affiliative, and this augered poorly for his feelings about himself, his relationship with his wife, and his parenting.

Over the years of listening to many tapes of men and women in the early stages of building their families, we began to focus on their connection to other people and also their investment in separate and independent ideas and activities. Many seemed to experience pressures both to be more related, more empathic and responsive, and also to develop aspects of their own personal and separate lives. They came to early parenthood with different capacities in these areas, and some were able to use the stresses of this period in their lives to develop new abilities in one or both of these dimensions.

Variations on this set of issues have emerged recently as an important topic in the literature on individual and family development. For example, within an object relations framework, Kohut (1980) proposed the existence of dual parallel lines of development, in contrast to the earlier psychoanalytic view of one strand, going from symbiosis to individuation (e.g., Mahler, 1968). Kohut's position is consistent with increasing evidence from research on young children (e.g., Stechler & Kaplan, 1980; reviewed in Pollack, 1981), suggesting that even infants need and develop an aspect of themselves separate from relationships, alternating in an internally determined rhythm with their need for attachment. Further, this literature suggests, as Pollack (1981) found, that children whose parents can support both their relatedness and their separateness develop in more healthy ways than children whose parents are just empathic and warm, or just supportive of their autonomy.

Similarly, but on the basis of different kinds of data, Gilligan (1982) described two contrasting ways of understanding the world. One, which she called *intimacy,* focuses on relationships and connectedness; the other, which she termed *identity,* on separateness and differentiation. Gilligan tied these two modes to gender differences, arguing that women tend to experience themselves as essentially connected, and are comfortable with and good at, intimacy, but fearful of separateness and identity. Men, on the other hand, are good at identity but have difficulties with intimacy.

Other closely related concepts include Bakan's (1966) agency and communion, Gutman's (1970) autocentric and allocentric domains, Kegan's (1982) inclusion and differentiation, and before all of that, of course, Freud's dictum that healthy adults can love and can work.

Aspects of these dimensions have been central in theories of adult development. Some writers, such as Erikson (1982), Levinson (1978), and Vaillant (1977) posited individuation and separateness, best reflected in (men's) capacity to work, as most important for healthy adult identity (discussed in Fedele, 1983).

Others question whether this is even true for men. Fasteau (1974) wrote compellingly of the sterility of men's lives when they are focused so predominantly on independent, separate, usually career-related activities. Biller (1982) interpreted the literature as indicating that the quality of a man's relationship with his children has a significant impact on his life satisfaction. Haward (1973, in Rapoport, Rapoport, & Strelitz, 1977) found that airline pilots made fewer errors on the job and were less dangerous to others when they felt more connected with their families. It seems likely that at this point in time in American culture, both autonomy and affiliation are important, and may be vital to healthy, satisfying adult functioning for men and women.

Another question revolves around the degree of interrelationship between autonomy and affiliation. Although data exist suggesting some degree of congruence (e.g., Valliant, 1981), it seems clear from the literature (e.g., Gilligan, 1982) and our own clinical judgments from our sample, that above a certain basic level of functioning, adults can vary significantly in their levels on each. On the other hand, we do not see them usually as antagonistic, either, necessarily opposed to one another, although an extreme exmphasis on autonomous activities does seem inevitably to interfere with affiliation.

The literature as well as our clinical experiences with the men and women in our longitudinal study suggest that how adults deal with closeness and separateness during early parenthood might be an important factor in how well they relate to their child or children and to their spouse, and in how they feel about themselves.

Similar concepts have been considered with regard to adults' adaptation to pregnancy and early parenting. As long ago as 1967, Benson argued for the importance of the expressive function of fathers in modern families. Cowan, Cowan, Coie, and Coie (1983) described one of the tasks of couples during pregnancy as that of finding a balance between what they call *individuality* and *coupleness*. They also found the time the men in their longitudinal sample spent with their infant during the baby's first year was related to their lesser involvement with their jobs during pregnancy (Cowan & Cowan, 1984).

Rapoport, Rapoport, and Strelitz (1977) presented compellingly the thesis that "a continuous set of challenges [that] confront parents . . . centre on the question of how much of themselves to give to parenting and how much to other interests—friendships, community involvements, leisure interests and work" (p. 19). They suggest that a particularly important problematic aspect of achieving this balance for men is to integrate work demands and the family. Otherwise, the man and his wife find themselves on increasingly divergent pathways, and the wife can feel "entrapped" by home demands. These authors did not emphasize the distress of the man in this scenario, which is not an unimportant omission, given the thoughtfulness of their discussion. When they were formulating the problem, the extent to which the arrangement of men's lives was not satisfactory for their wives was clear, but not (at least for many) the extent to which the traditional role was also unsatisfying for the man as well.

Feldman, Nash, and Ashenbrenner (1983) found that low job salience for men during their wives' pregnancies predicted playfulness and caregiving with their 6- to 8-month-old baby. And Feldman (1984) reported that a strong career focus in men during pregnancy leads to stressed wives in the first postpartum year. Pruett (1983) reminded us that the traditional view of fathering is that it helps develop the child's autonomy and individuation. He refered to this view as an "unattachment theory," and pointed out that it says little about the other side of father–child relationships, which have varying degrees of intimacy and relatedness.

From this literature, and our clinical understanding of the men in the Pregnancy and Parenting Project, we began to think men's capacity for attachment was very important to their parenting. We hypothesized that men's capacity to relate empathically, and to value such relationships would make them better able to respond to the tasks of early parenting. We also speculated that some men who did not relate in this way might learn to as they, with their wives, went through the experiences of pregnancy, childbirth, and early parenting. As Jessner, Weigert, and Foy (1970) suggested, "Pregnancy is an opening-out experience and a commencement, which powerfully stimulates the potentialities for mutual concern, intimacy and tenderness" (p. 241).

However, something else that is known about men in their 20s and 30s, which is the age most men have children, is that they are in a stage where career development is extremely salient (Levinson, 1978; Rapoport & Rapoport, 1975). They often feel this is the time, and possibly the only chance, for them to get established, and for some careers, this is undoubtedly true. For many men, realizing career aspirations seems closely allied at this stage in their development with feeling comfortable with their masculinity, and so has even more heightened importance.

Furthermore, as in our data (Grossman et al., 1980), the imminent birth of at least a first child arouses anxieties in men about their capacity to provide. Many told us that their first response to learning of their wives' pregnancies was to feel an increased sense of responsibility. In this context, some began putting in more hours at work, in order to bring home more money, in order to be a better father–provider (as others have found in their studies, e.g., Liebenberg, 1973; also discussed in Hoffman & Manis, 1978). Benedek (1970) argued that what interferes with good fatherliness is excessive career activity, related to the basic wish to be a good, providing father. So men's needs, coming from both inside and out, to build their careers at this stage of their lives, to emphasize the autonomous dimension of their lives, clash with their equally real needs to relate to their growing families.

Finally, a discussion of factors interfering with men's involvement in early childrearing is incomplete without mentioning the reluctance or unwillingness of many women to relinquish their role as the only major caretaker, particularly with a first born child (e.g., Grossman et al., 1980). Noted by many authors, (e.g., Paloma & Garland, 1971; Pressman, 1980; Weingarten, 1978), this reluctance can be expressed openly and unambivalently or more covertly and in conflict with consciously held values. However it is manifest, it has been shown to interfere with men's involvement with their young children.

One result of these several converging sets of pressures is some tendency for men to become less affiliative and more extremely focused on independent activities around the crisis of the birth of a child to the family, at the same time as their wives are becoming less autonomous and more extremely caught up in intimate, empathic relationships (also noted by Feldman & Nash, 1984). To clinicians, this seems less than optimal. Some men we talked with sounded lonely, alienated, interpersonally deprived, and devoid of values to support them in their work (also Fasteau, 1974). We hypothesized that men who were more involved in relationships and committed to such closeness, would feel better about themselves at the end of the first year of parenting. We also thought they would be more satisfied with their marriages, and would be more able to support the healthy development of their child then men who did not have that connectedness.

Conceptually, it also seemed as though fathers of first and later borns might have different experiences around these issues. The birth of a first child undoubtedly provides much more of an impetus to change, for the family system and also for men intrapsychically, and thus creates more of a developmental crisis. In fact, in our research, it has seemed that the birth of a second or third child creates a crisis in a different way, putting particular pressures on these issues of men's affiliation and autonomy. Perhaps, as Lamb (1978) argued, the later born child tends to pull the man more into the family because of the manifest need for his involvement. If so, fathers of later borns who are unwilling or unable to reinvest in the family, and become more involved in childcare are more problematic for themselves and their families than fathers of first borns who stay uninvolved. Yet Robinson's (1977) time survey data indicate that men do progressively less childcare with each additional child in the family. Possibly there are different ways in which fathers of first and later born children become involved. Clearly the existing literature does not answer the question of the relative importance of autonomy and affiliation to fathers of first and later born children.

With these interests in mind, we came to define *autonomy* primarily from the object relations perspective (e.g., Kohut, 1977) and related infant research, drawing particularly on Stechler and Kaplan's (1980) concepts. *Autonomy,* as we define it, refers to a view of oneself as separate or distinct from others, to a participation in and enjoyment of activities carried out alone, or at least separate from important personal relationships, and to a sense of valuing that individual and separate part of the self as important to one's development. Autonomy, then, is related to, but not defined solely by, participation in separate activities.

Affiliation refers to a view of oneself as importantly connected to others, to participation in and enjoyment of empathic, responsive relationships, in which one retains a sense of a separate identity, and to a sense of valuing that related part of the self as important to one's development. Just as autonomy is not defined simply behaviorally, so *affiliation* is related to, but not defined solely by, participation in relationships.

In this project, then, we looked at men's autonomy and affiliation as reflected in the interview in early pregnancy, and then again at 1 year postpartum. We thought we would find differences between fathers of first and later born children, and differences from pregnancy to the 1-year visit. We hypothesized that men who were more affiliative would feel better about themselves at 1 year, would feel more satisfied with their marriages, and would be interacting more skillfully and responsively to their child when that child was 1, 2, and 5.

Although we had no specific hypotheses about autonomy, we did not think that very autonomous men would be advantaged in early parenting. In fact, we suspected there would be a curvilinear relationship between autonomy and affiliation.

Finally, because Gilligan (1982) and others (e.g., Gutmann, 1970) linked affiliation and autonomy, and gender differences and gender identity, we also wanted to explore the relation of these concepts to traditional measures of masculinity and femininity.

METHOD

Sample

The sample consisted of men and their wives and children who have been part of the Boston University Pregnancy and Parenthood Project (Grossman et al., 1980). This project is a longitudinal study of normal families from early in the woman's pregnancy; at the most recent data collection, the child from that pregnancy was 5 years old. For the purposes of this chapter, the focus is on the men early in pregnancy and at 1 year postpartum. Several scores from the 2- and 5-year follow-up are also considered.

Included in the sample during that time period were 42 white men and their families. They ranged from working class to upper middle class (Coleman & Neugarten, 1971) and are primarily middle to lower middle class (the mean score was 3.08, on their 7-point scale, on which 1 is upper class). The men's average age was 30.0 for the total sample (28.4 for the fathers of the first born children and 31.8 for the fathers of later born children). The average age for wives was 28. Most were in relatively traditional marriages, with the husband considered the primary breadwinner and the wife primarily responsible for childcare. Twenty-one were studied when the couples were pregnant with their first child, 21 with their second through fourth. Seventeen of this latter group had one other child. Nineteen had girls and 23 boys.

Procedure

The essential goal of the research method of the project has always been to combine sophisticated, clinical understanding and scientific credibility. Toward that goal, we have seen families in their own environments and interacting with one another and have asked them to describe their experiences from their point of view and in their own words. (The research method is described in detail in Grossman et al., 1980). We have utilized a variety of measures, ranging from highly structured to open-ended, assessing feelings and functioning at different levels on a variety of tasks and problems. We listen to what individuals say about their lives, but also pay careful attention to what we as clinicians hear beyond the manifest content.

For the visits described here, two or three researchers visited the families. The husband and wife were interviewed individually in a semistructured interview, and given numerous paper and pencil scales to complete. At the

1-, 2-, and 5-year followup, within 2 weeks of the child's birthday, the child was also assessed on a variety of measures, and parent–child interactions observed. At the visit around the second and fifth birthdays, the parents and children were observed and videotaped in dyadic and triadic interactions.

Measures

The scales for autonomy and affiliation were developed for this project, and consisted of two 6-point scales, one for each concept.[1] Once adequate interscorer reliability was established scorers listened to the first five consecutive 5-minute segments of the pregnancy interview or the 1-year interview and assigned each segment a score on each scale. The final scores for each subject were the averages of the five scores on each dimension. When two scorers rated the same interview, either the scores were averaged across scorers, or when great differences occurred, a negotiated score was arrived at.

Affiliation.   The Affiliation scale was designed to measure the extent to which, in a 5-minute interview segment, the individual expressed a view of him or herself as importantly connected to others, as participating in and enjoying empathic relationships, in which he or she retained a sense of separate identity, and indicated a sense of valuing that related part of the self as important to their self-development.

The justification for using one important relationship to generalize about a person's general capacity for affiliation comes partly from clinical lore that suggests people relate at a similar level to others in their lives. It also is supported by Vaillant's (1977) clinical finding from his longitudinal study of successful college males. For those men, their object relationships tended to be the same across domains.

Interscorer reliability overall was based on the total score for Affiliation. With an N of 21, the r was .78.

Autonomy.   The Autonomy scale was designed to measure the extent to which an individual expressed a view of him/herself as separate and distinct from others, indicated a sense of felt efficacy of that self, described participation in, and enjoyment of, activities carried out alone, or at least separate from important personal relationships, and indicated that he/she valued that individual and separate part of the self as important to their own development. Interscorer reliability overall based on 10 cases was .69.

In addition to these measures, developed for this project, relevant vari-

---

[1] Copies of the scoring code can be obtained by writing Frances K. Grossman, Department of Psychology, Boston University, 64 Cummington Street, Boston, MA 02215.

ables from the longitudinal study were included. They are described briefly in the order of data collection. Means and standard deviations for all variables are in Table 5.1.

Early Pregnancy Visit

Life Adaptation. The Life Adaptation score was assessed by the Cox Adaptation Scale (Cox, 1970). This score, obtained from ratings made from a semistructured interview, reflects the extent to which an individual is coping with some of the major tasks of adulthood. The subscales we used included Adaptation to Work, Marriage, Relation to Own Parents, and Freedom from Symptoms.

Each area of functioning was scored with the rater blind as to other information about the individual, and independently of scoring the other area of adaptation. Interscorer reliability was .90 for the total score.

Anxiety. The State Anxiety Scale (Speilberger, Gorsuch, & Lushene, 1968) was given.

Masculinity and Femininity. The Bem scales (1974) were used. These assess the extent to which an individual's self-perception is stereotypically masculine or feminine.

Marital Adjustment. The revised Locke–Wallace Marital Adjustment Inventory (Kimmel & Vanderveen, 1974; Locke & Wallace, 1959) was used.

Socioeconomic Status. The measure of socioeconomic status (SES) was Coleman and Neugarten's (1971), which places families on a 7-point scale, based on separate ratings of the husband's and wife's education and occupation. Low scores indicate higher social class.

Number of children. This score was the number of living children at the time of the pregnancy visit.

Age. This score was the man's age at the time of the pregnancy visit.

One-Year Postpartum Visit

Emotional Well-Being. This variable was developed for the study (Grossman et al., 1980). It is made up of three subscales, each with 5 points: comfort in caring for the baby, acceptance of own needs, and mood, scored from tapes of a semistructured interview. Interscorer reliability was .86.

TABLE 5.1
Means and Standard Deviations

	First time		Experienced	
	X	SD	X	SD
Sociocultural				
Pregnancy				
SES	3.02	.80	3.17	10.11
Number of children			1.35	.74
Paternal age	28.38	2.29	31.77	2.94
Individual				
Pregnancy				
Life Adaptation	4.85	.34	4.71	.42
State Anxiety	34.08	10.99	35.71	9.67
Masculinity	103.71	20.42	110.35	11.73
Femininity	97.86	10.28	93.33	11.21
Affiliation	4.52	.74	4.64	.51
Autonomy	4.98	.71	5.15	.55
One year				
Emotional Well-being	4.10	.70	4.16	.59
State Anxiety	35.04	9.64	34.86	7.86
Affiliation	4.60	.78	4.51	.70
Autonomy	4.71	.51	4.64	1.32
Marital				
Pregnancy				
Marital Adjustment	112.44	13.71	108.15	13.06
One Year				
Marital Adjustment	114.65	10.64	112.73	11.19
Parental				
One Year				
Paternal Adaptation	4.29	.48	4.25	.49
Two Years				
Observed Nurturance	24.65	5.04	25.02	4.79
Observed Physical Stimulation	24.77	5.23	26.30	5.26
Five Years				
Support for Autonomy	4.15	.52	3.89	.73
Support for Affiliation	4.36	.45	4.20	.50

Anxiety.   Same as previously described.

Marital Adjustment.   The Dyadic Adjustment Scale (Spanier, 1976), was given. This scale has been found to correlate .93 with the revised Locke–Wallace.

Parental Adaptation from Interview.   This measure, developed for this project (Grossman et al., 1980), was designed to reflect the adequacy of parents' interactions with their infants, based on judgments made from taped interviews of the parents' descriptions of the infants and their relationships with them. Subscales, each of 5 points, included acceptance, feelings of competence with the child, awareness of child's needs, emotional involvement, and degree of differentiation. Interscorer reliability on the summary score was .91.

Two-Year Visit

Observed Nurturance.   This score was derived from the Father Behavior Rating Scale (Keylor, 1978), based on a 15-minute observation of a free-play situation between the father and toddler. The measure of Nurturance, based on Radin's (1972, 1973) definition of nurturance, was an average of subscale scores on expression of positive affect, sensitivity to the child's implicit and explicit needs, and inquiries about child's thoughts, feelings, and wishes. Interscorer reliability on the summary score was .89.

Observed Physical Stimulation.   This measure, also derived from the Father Behavior Rating Scale (Keylor, 1978) and based on the 15-minute observation period just described, included the subscales: activity level of father, amount of physical contact with the child, and level of stimulation of body contact. Interscorer reliability on the summary score was .85.

Five-Year Visit

Support for the Child's Affiliation.   This score, developed by Pollack and others for this project, was based on structured dyadic interactions (see Pollack, 1981). Mother–child and father–child dyads were each asked to perform two tasks. One task was for the parent to help the child carry out a moderately difficult physical activity (e.g., balancing a box of marbles on his or her head). The other was to play store, using props we provided. The order of parents were counterbalanced, as was the match between parent and child gender. Each part of the interactions was observed and scored in six 50-second-observe, 50-second-score intervals. Subscales of this score included Attention, Appropriate Mirroring, and Responsiveness. Interscorer reliability for the summary score was .87.

Support for the Child's Autonomy.   This score has a similar basis to the one just described, and includes the subscales: Toleration of Child's Distress, and Allowing Self-Direction. Interscorer reliability for this summary score was .81.

Results and Discussion

Overall, in this nonclinical sample, men's scores on Autonomy and Affiliation were toward the high end of our scale (Table 5.1). However, there was a moderately wide range, on Autonomy from 3.00 to 6.00, and on Affiliation from 2.60 to 5.83.

The following excerpt illustrates a 6.00 on Autonomy. In this pregnancy interview, the man was asked about his job.

A: I'm my own boss. . . . The job is exciting. It changes all the time. You get to meet a lot of people. I really enjoy it.

In contrast, the following man received a 3.00 on this segment for Autonomy. He was also talking about his job, which was as a sales person.

A: I don't have feelings about the job.
Q: What do you like best and least about it?
A: I really don't have any feelings. It's a job that pays the rent.
Q: Is it important to you to be good at what you do?
A: It's important that I'm adequate at it.

The same man quoted with a 6.00 on Autonomy received a 6.00 on Affiliation for the following segment of the pregnancy interview. He had been asked about his marriage.

A: It's really great. My wife is probably smarter than I am, really warm. She can handle herself really well, which I really like. . . . She's a great girl, I really love her.

Another high-affiliation father had this to say about the baby at the 1-year interview:

A: Having him (the baby) has been wonderful. He's been awfully much fun, more than I ever could have imagined.
Q: Who does he resemble in the family?
A: He's his own person. We've had that feeling, practically from the day he was born.

In contrast, the man in the following segment received a 3.00 on affiliation:

Q: Tell me about your marriage.
A: It's good.
Q: What's your wife like?
A: Boy, you're getting personal! She's somewhat typically Jewish, if you know what that means. She comes from a fairly wealthy family. She can be pretty difficult. She's pleasant, good looking. She doesn't have a hell of a lot of patience. She's basically a good mother, a good cook.

This last segment was also scored 3.00 on Affiliation. The man is the father of three children, the youngest is the 1-year-old.

Q: What do you do with the children?
A: I play with the kids once in a while. Mostly kids don't want to be with their parents. . . . It's pretty easy being a father.

Autonomy and Affiliation correlated significantly (Table 5.2), but this relationship never accounted for more than a relatively small proportion of the variance of each score. In this essentially healthy sample, these dimensions are only somewhat related. (Presumably, in a more pathological population, the correlation would be much higher. Without basic ties, genuinely autonomous development is unlikely.)

Repeated measures analyses of variance showed no significant differences on Autonomy or Affiliation between first-time fathers and experienced fathers, or between fathers early in pregnancy and fathers at 1 year postpartum, and no interaction. Although clearly some men changed in the degree to which they manifest these characteristics, they did not change in a systematic way related to the number of children they had or the time relative to the birth of the target child. By and large, we were impressed with the relative stability of the scores across this period of time and assessed by rather different interview contents.

We next looked at how these scores related to four domains of adult functioning: sociocultural, individual psychological, marital, and parental. Inititally, Pearson correlations were computed (Tables 5.2 and 5.3).[2] Correlations were considered significant when they were at the .05 level or better. All p values are for two-tailed tests of significance. Because of the possibility that Affiliation and Autonomy scores might be interdependent, two-way analyses of variance were carried out on all dependent variables, using a median split to dichotomize these two variables. None of the

---

[2]The nature of the data made it impossible to carry out tests for curvilinearity. Visual scanning of scatter plots of the relationships between autonomy and affiliation with the dependent variables did not suggest such a function.

TABLE 5.2
Corelates of Men's Autonomy

	Autonomy—Pregnancy			Autonomy—1 Year			Autonomy—Total		
	First Time[a]	Experienced[b]	Total[c]	First Time[a]	Experienced[b]	Total[c]	First Time[a]	Experienced[b]	Total[c]
Sociocultural									
Pregnancy									
SES	-.59**	-.24	-.37*	-.10	-.32	-.21	-.43*	-.27	-.32*
Number of Children		-.54*	.15		.11	-.10		.22	.07
Age	.22	-.14	.03	-.06	-.07	.02	.02	-.13	.00
Individual									
Pregnancy									
Life Adaptation	.52*	.43	.48**	.41	-.01	.13	.59**	.22	.38*
State Anxiety	-.05	.20	.08	-.46	.34	.03	-.24	.33	.07
Masculinity	-.10	.36	.10	.14	.49*	.29	.16	.43*	.25
Femininity	-.13	-.20	-.16	.33	-.45	-.22	.11	-.41	-.21
One Year									
Emotional Well-being	.32	.02	.18	-.09	.11	.06	.18	.14	.16
State Anxiety	-.28	.22	-.05	-.30	-.08	-.18	-.31	.09	-.11
Marital									
Pregnancy									
Marital Adjustment	-.25	.33	.08	.36	.13	.18	.06	.28	.17
One Year									
Marital Adjustment	-.50*	.11	-.20	-.31	-.12	-.20	-.51*	.03	-.21

Parental

One Year									
Paternal Adaptation	−.14	.45	.16	.41	.47*	.40*	.10	.53*	.31*
Two Year									
Observed Nurturance	.29	.05	.18	.06	.22	.13	.25	.17	.22
Observed Physical Stim	.03	.09	.02	.55*	.01	.26	.31	.17	.22
Five Year									
Support for Autonomy	.60*	−.37	.09	.29	−.19	−.04	.57*	−.28	.08
Support for Affiliation	.10	.08	.09	.09	−.27	−.07	.14	−.06	.06
Affiliation									
Pregnancy	.38								
One Year		.38	.38*						
Total				.45*	.52*	.45**	.60**	.44*	.49***

aThe *N*'s range from 17 to 21
bThe *N*'s range from 10 to 21
cThe *N*'s range from 27 to 40
*p < .05, 2-tailed
**p < .01, 2-tailed
***p < .001, 2-tailed

interactions reached acceptable levels of statistical significance, and so are not presented.

Sociocultural Domain

The sociocultural dimension included men's age, social class, and number of children. Social class related significantly to Autonomy; men rated more autonomous were from higher socioeconomic groups. More educated men have the concepts and vocabulary to think and talk about self-development, and often also the opportunities to develop this aspect of themselves. It is not surprising that there was such a relationship.

However, to assure that this correlation was not an artifact responsible for many other statistical relationships, SES was partialed from all correlations involving the three autonomy scores. In only three did this reanalysis make a significant difference and these are described here.

Looking at men's age, for fathers of later borns only, the younger they were, the more affiliative they were in pregnancy. This is undoubtedly related to the finding that the more children these experienced fathers had, the less affiliative—enthusiastic?—they sounded in the interview. The older men in our sample were not less competent with their children; there was no relationship between the men's age and their paternal adaptation on the measures considered here. It is likely, then, that these results relate to the meaning of pregnancy and also of the pregnancy interview, to experienced fathers. This topic is discussed further later.

Individual Psychological Domain

The scores reflecting aspects of men's individual psychological adaptation include their Life Adaptation (measured in pregnancy), Emotional Well-Being (measured at 1 year), their Anxiety (from pregnancy and 1 year postpartum), and their Masculinity and Femininity (measured in pregnancy).

Several strong and significant relationships appear. Fathers of first borns who were judged to be more autonomous and more affiliative had significantly higher life adaptation overall; they were doing better in their lives. This was true only for first-time fathers: There were no significant relatonships between these scores for fathers of later borns.

The finding that high life adaptation, and high affiliation and autonomy go together for fathers of first borns is consistent with Valliant's (1978) finding that object relationships correlated strongly with mental health and maturity for the men in his study. It is also consistent with views such as those of Freud, with his emphasis on love and work.

More puzzling is the lack of such findings for experienced fathers. On the one hand, the two groups of men appear similar on virtually all

TABLE 5.3
Correlates for Men's Affiliation

	Affiliation—Pregnancy			Affiliation—1 Year			Affiliation—Total		
	First Time[a]	Experienced[b]	Total[c]	First Time[a]	Experienced[b]	Total[c]	First Time[a]	Experienced[b]	Total[c]
Sociocultural									
Pregnancy									
SES	-.16	.26	.03	-.19	-.23	-.22	-.26	.11	-.11
Number of Children		-.54*	.01		-.11	-.10		-.43*	.00
Age	-.32	-.44*	-.32*	-.34	-.05	-.19	-.38	-.36	-.29*
Individual									
Pregnancy									
Life Adaptation	.48*	-.05	.25	.65**	.19	.43**	.54**	.12	.37*
State Anxiety	-.32	-.09	-.23	-.26	.42	.01	-.20	.23	-.07
Masculinity	.02	.03	.01	.25	.32	.21	.28	.24	.25
Femininity	.21	.13	.18	.27	.00	.13	.28	.10	.20
One Year									
Emotional Well-being	.37	-.07	.24	.49*	-.11	.21	.42	-.03	.25
State Anxiety	-.18	-.16	-.17	-.13	-.12	-.13	-.10	-.19	-.12

Marital

Pregnancy Marital Adjustment	.55*	-.09	.36*	.15	.08	.12	.32	.15	.26
One Year Marital Adjustment	-.37	.15	-.10	-.03	-.14	-.05	-.17	.04	-.09

Parental

One Year Paternal Adaptation	.33	.11	.22	.52*	.13	.34*	.44	.16	.32*
Two Year Observed Nurturance	.37	.13	.28	.37	.59*	.42	.44*	.45	.42*
Observed Physical Stim	.48*	.61*	.50**	.36	.52	.39*	.41	.67**	.44***
Five Year Support for Autonomy	.47	-.11	.21	.22	-.22	.07	.40	-.19	.20
Support for Affiliation	.19	.45	.26	.37	-.12	.28	.31	.28	.30

[a]The N's range from 17 to 21
[b]The N's range from 10 to 21
[c]The N's range from 27 to 40
*$p < .05$, 2-tailed
**$p < .01$, 2-tailed
***$p < .001$, 2-tailed

measures. However, the study findings have always showed different patterns of correlations for the two groups of men around issues related to the birth of the new baby and parenting. For first-time fathers, pregnancy often represents a powerful psychological event, marking an important change point in their lives and requiring intense psychological work (e.g., Rapoport, Rapoport, & Strelitz, 1977). In that context, their feelings about themselves and about the pregnancy (i.e., how they are dealing with this developmental crisis) have important implications for their mental health. In contrast, for men who have been through it before, it does not constitute a developmental crisis or task of the same proportions, even though there are some distinctive stresses associated with it. The pregnancy, and their reactions to it, are relatively unimportant, both experientially and in how they predict to the men's later adaptation (Grossman et al., 1980).

As we predicted, fathers of first borns who were more affiliative at 1 year were also feeling better about themselves, as reflected in higher scores on Emotional Well-Being. Sometimes the literature appears to suggest that it is for women's sake that men need to expand their capacity for intimacy. (e.g., Bernard, 1981). These data suggest that it is also for the health of the man. Separateness and individuation are not sufficient for men's well-being; they need connections as well.

Men's anxiety had no relationships with autonomy and affiliation. Anxiety, which is such a strong predictor of aspects of women's functioning (e.g., Grossman et al., 1980), does not appear to be a good predictor for men. The strong cultural prohibition against men's expression of anxiety changes the meaning of responses to such a scale.

Finally, for fathers of later born children only, the higher their judged autonomy, the more masculine they had appeared on the Bem in pregnancy. This significant correlation disappeared with SES partialed out. However, partialing SES out led to statistical significance between first-time fathers' affiliation at 1-year and their Femininity scores. This finding is consistent with Feldman and Ashenbrenner's (1983) conclusion that men increase their feminine role behaviors with the transition to parenthood, in order to meet the needs of their changing families. These results also explain some of the difficulty men have allowing themselves to feel and be nurturant because these feelings and behaviors are so tied to the feminine sex-role stereotypes in this culture (see also Chodorow, 1978; Gaiter & Johnson, 1983.)

Marital Domain

Turning to findings regarding the marriage, by and large, more affiliative men were more satisfied with their marriages, whereas men high on autonomy tended not to express as much satisfaction with their marriages. In all cases, this was true for fathers of first borns only. It is particularly of interest because our Autonomy scores were not based on separateness within a relationship, as some conceptions of autonomy are (e.g., Chodorow, 1978), but simply other areas of interest and involvement. Furthermore, men could express a high valuation of intimate relationships, despite lack of time to enjoy them, and receive high scores on Affiliation, so the correlation does not reflect simply the limitations of time to do everything one wants.

It certainly makes sense in a common sense way, and is supported by writers such as Fasteau (1974) and others (e.g., Bailyn, 1970; Rapoport, Rapoport, & Strelitz, 1977), who emphasize the problems for marital relationships of men's extreme independence and separateness.

This issue was clearly discernible in the tapes. The following excerpt was from the pregnancy interview with a man who already had one child. He was asked about his marriage.

A: Well, it's difficult for me to live with anyone. I don't know if this has anything to do with my being an only child, but . . . I could spend a great deal of time alone—without having a wife, without having a sexual partner, and also without having children. But, at the same time, all these things are very important to me. If I could be 100% selfish and just have my wife when I wanted her and just have my kids when I wanted to, that would suit me. But I can see that that marriage wouldn't last. So it becomes a balancing act, a constant balancing act.

The issue of striking a workable balance between autonomy and affiliation is an ongoing developmental task for all adult men and women. For men with strong inclinations toward separateness and autonomy, marriage and parenting heighten inevitable and probably insoluable stresses. As the man just quoted suggests, the best that such men can likely do is to balance their own and their families' conflicting needs. Less extreme autonomy seems to create less of a conflict.

Parental Domain

Finally, we looked at men's relationship to their children, as this dimension of their lives related to autonomy and affiliation. Our hypothesis about the importance of affiliation for parenting was strongly supported. Looking at the interview score of adaptation to the infant at 1 year, more affiliative fathers of first borns were rated as higher on adaptation to the child at 1 year. With SES statistically controlled, more autonomous first-time fathers were also doing better with their children. These findings underline the importance of both separateness and togetherness for healthy parental functioning. Adult men need to be both autonomous and affiliative to do well at the important adult task of fathering.

More affiliative first-time and experienced fathers were more nurturant and provided more physical stimulation to their 2-year-olds than less affiliative men. For fathers of first borns only, men who were more autonomous at 1 year also were more nurturant and provided more physical stimulation to their 2-year-olds in the observed interaction. These dimensions of personality, examined in the context of a particular stage in a man's life, and of his family system, seem to be important ones, carrying over several years and manifesting themselves in several ways.

We then turned to the two interaction scores from the 5-year-follow up. Although a father's support for his child's affiliation at age 5 was not significantly related to his level of autonomy or affiliation (although the latter correlations approached significance), for fathers of first borns, the higher their autonomy during their wives' pregnancies, the more support they provided for their child's autonomy at 5 years. Thus a characteristic measured in an interview more than 5 years before predicted something important about how the father would respond in interaction with his offspring. Once we recovered from our surprise at the finding, we were impressed with the apparent importance of these dimensions of autonomy and affiliation to early fatherhood.

Finally, because issues of affiliation and autonomy seem importantly related to sex-role socialization, we looked at relatonships of men's autonomy and affiliation as these predicted differentially to aspects of their parenting of girls and boys. When the sample was divided both by birth order and child gender, each subgroup was too small for the findings to be more than suggestive. This being said, some intriguing differences did appear, and even reached statistical significance. For example, men's autonomy in pregnancy predicted to higher paternal adaptation at 1 year with their first-born daughters, but it was their affiliation that predicted significantly the quality of their relationship with their first-born sons.

In one other provacative difference, the greater the men's autonomy in pregnancy, the more support they provided for the affiliation of their 5-year-old sons, but not their daughters.

The findings are tantalizing in their hint at ever more complex systemic relationships between aspects of men's sense of self and capacity for intimacy and how that influences their relationships differentially with sons and daughters, which in turn must play a part in the sex-role socialization of these children.

CONCLUSIONS

Separate and together, autonomy and affiliation—men are usually good at the separate part. Relatively recently in this culture, we have begun to realize that the together part is also vital to men, as well as to their families. Men, as women, need both dimensions to feel good about themselves, to live comfortably within enduring relatonships, and to be good fathers to their children. The cultural definition of masculinity, and its harsh training of boys to fit that model, needs to be broadened to allow the softer, more expressive, and more vulnerable feelings to emerge and effect men's behavior.

In this study, we found compelling evidence for the wideranging importance of autonomy and affiliation for young fathers, in at least three areas of adaptation: in their internal sense of comfort and satisfaction, in their marriages, and in their parenting. These concepts—autonomy and affiliation—are not only important in general, they are important for the study of adult development in parenthood.

We think we have the data to argue that these concepts must be incorporated into family systems' and family interaction views of family development, as well as continued and researched in theories of individual adult development. Early parenthood brings together a perfect convergence of crises for both individuals and for their family systems, and thus creates the ideal context for examining how conflicting demands—on separate, individuated growth and on relationships—are negotiated and with what consequences. We found that men's autonomy and affiliation during pregnancy indeed had an impact not only on their own development but on the marriage and on the children as old as age 5.

ACKNOWLEDGMENTS

I want to express my appreciation to past and current members of the Pregnancy and Parenthood Project, who have helped with this chapter. In particular, Ellen Golding, and William Pollack made useful comments on the chapter. I also want to thank Anne Copeland, Abigail Stewart, and Henry Grossman for their ideas and assistance.

REFERENCES

Bailyn, L. (1970). Career and family orientations of husbands and wives in relation to marital happiness. *Human Relations, 23*(12), 97–113.

Bakan, D. (1966). *Duality of human existence.* Chicago: Rand McNally.

Bem, S. L. (1974). The measurement of psychological androgeny. *Journal of Consulting and Clinical Psychology, 42,* 155–162.

Benedek, T. (1970). Fatherhood and providing. In E. J. Anthony & T. Benedek (Eds.), *Parenthood: Its psychology and psychopathology* (pp. 167-184). Boston: Little, Brown.

Benson, L. (1967). *Fatherhood: A sociological perspective.* New York: Random House.

Bernard, J. (1981). The good-provider role: Its rise and fall. *American Psychologist, 36,* 1-12.

Biller, H.B. (1982). Fatherhood: Implications for child and adult development. In B.B. Wolman & G. Stricker (Eds.), *Handbook of developmental psychology* (pp. 702-725). Englewood Cliffs, NJ: Prentice-Hall.

Chodorow, N. (1978). *The reproduction of mothering.* Berkeley, CA: University of California Press.

Coleman, R.P., & Neugarten, B.L. (1971). *Social status in the city.* San Francisco: Jossey-Bass.

Cowan, C.P., & Cowan, P.A. (1984, May). *Becoming a father: Changes in self, roles and marriage.* Paper presented at National Institute of Child Health and Development meeting on Transition to Fatherhood. Bethesda, MD.

Cowan, C.P., Cowan, P.A., Coie, L., & Coie, J.D. (1983). Becoming a family: The impact of a first child's birth on the couple's relationship. In W. Miller & L. Newman, L. (Eds.), *The first child and family formation* (pp. 46-78). Chapel Hill, NC: Carolina Population Center.

Cox, R. (1970). *Youth into maturity.* New York: Mental Health Materials Center.

Erikson, E.H. (1982). *The life cycle completed.* New York: Norton.

Fasteau, M.F. (1974). *The male machine.* New York: McGraw Hill.

Fedele, N.M. (1983). *The developing parent: The impact of life span development upon the quality of parenting.* Unpublished doctoral thesis, Boston University.

Feldman, S.S. (1984, May). *Predicting strain in fathers of infants.* Paper presented at National Institute for Child Health and Development Conference on Transition to Fatherhood. Bethesda, MD.

Feldman, S.S., & Ashenbrenner, B. (1983). Impact of parenthood on various aspects of masculinity and femininity: A short-term longitudinal study. *Developmental Psychology, 19,* 278-289.

Feldman, S.S., & Nash, S. C. (1984). The transition from expectancy to parenthood—impact of the first-born child on men and women. *Sex Roles, 11,* 61-78.

Feldman, S.S., Nash, S.C., & Aschenbrenner, B.G. (1983). Antecedents of fathering. *Child Development, 54,* 1628-1636.

Gaiter, J.L., & Johnson, A.A.S. (1983, March). *Contact with intensive care infants: Father's sex-type, infant preference and frequency of visits.* Presented at Second World Conference on Infant Psychiatry. Cannes, France.

Gilligan, C. (1982) *In a different voice.* Cambridge, MA: Harvard University Press.

Grossman, F.K., Eichler, L.S., Winickoff, S.A., Anzalone, M.K., Gofseyeff, M., & Sargent, S.P. (1980). *Pregnancy, birth and parenthood.* San Francisco: Jossey-Bass.

Gutmann, D. (1970). Female ego styles and generational conflict. In E. Walker (Ed.), *Feminine personality and conflict* (pp. 77-96). Belmont, CA: Brookes-Cole.

Hoffman, L.W., & Manis, J.D. (1978). Influences of children on marital interaction and parental satisfactions and dissatisfactions. In R.M. Lerner & G.S. Spanier (Eds.), *Child influences on marital and family interaction: A life span perspective* (pp. 165-214). New York: Academic Press.

Jessner, L., Weigert, E., & Foy, J.L. (1970). The development of parental attitudes during pregnancy. In E.S. Anthony & T. Benedek (Eds.), *Psychology and psychopathology of parenthood* (pp. 209-244). Boston: Little, Brown.

Kegan, R. (1982). *The evolving self: Problem and process in human development.* Cambridge, MA: Harvard University Press.

Keylor, R.G. (1978). *Paternal interaction with two-year-olds.* Unpublished doctoral dissertation, Boston University.

Kimmel, D., & Vanderveen, F. (1974). Factors of marital adjustment in Locke's Marital Adjustment Test. *Journal of Marriage and the Family, 36,* 57-63.

Kohut, H. (1977). *The restoration of the self.* New York: International Universities Press.

Kohut, H. (1980). From a letter and summarizing reflections. In A. Goldberg (Ed.), *Advances in self-psychology* (pp. 46-63). New York: International Universities Press.

Lamb, M.E. (1978). Influence of the child on marital quality and family interaction during the prenatal, perinatal and infancy periods. In M. Lerner & G.B. Spanier (Eds.), *Child influences on marital and family interaction: A life span perspective* (pp. 137-164). New York: Academic Press.

Levinson, D. (1978). *Seasons of a man's life.* New York: Knopf.

Liebenberg, B. (1973). Expectant fathers. In P.M. Shereshefsky & R.F. Yarrow (Eds.), *Psychological aspects of a first pregnancy and early postnatal adaptation* (pp. 103-114). New York: Raven Press.

Locke, H.J., & Wallace, K.M. (1959). Short marital-adjustment and prediction tests: Their reliability and validity. *Marriage and Family Living, 21,* 251-255.

Mahler, M.S. (1968). *On human symbiosis and the vicissitues of individuation.* New York: International Universities Press.

Pollack, W.S. (1981). *"I"ness and "We"ness: Parallel lines of development.* Unpublished doctoral dissertation, Boston University.

Paloma, M.M., & Garland, T.N. (1971). The myth of the egalitarian family: Familial roles and the professionally employed woman. In H. Theodore (Ed.), *The professional woman* (pp. 741-761). Boston: Schenkman.

Pressman, R.A. (1980). *Father participation in child care: An exploratory study of factors associated with father participation in child care among fathers with working wives and young children.* Unpublished doctoral dissertation, Boston University.

Pruett, K. (1983). Infants of primary nurturing fathers. *Psychoanalytic Study of the Child, 38,* 257-276.

Radin, N. (1972). Father-child interaction and the intellectual functioning of four-year-old boys. *Developmental Psychology, 6,* 353-361.

Radin, N. (1973). Observing paternal behavior as an antecedent to intellectual functioning in pre-school boys. *Developmental Psychology, 8,* 369-376.

Rapoport, R., & Rapoport, R.N. (1975). *Leisure and the family life cycle.* London: Routledge & Kegan Paul.

Rapoport, R., Rapoport, R.N., & Strelitz, Z. (1977). *Fathers, mothers and society.* New York: Basic Books.

Robinson, J. (1977). *How Americans use time: A sociological analysis of everyday behavior.* New York: Basic Books.

Spanier, G.B. (1976). Measuring dyadic adjustment: New scale for assessing the quality of marriage and similar dyads. *Journal of Marriage and the Family, 38,* 15-28.

Speilberger, C.D., Gorsuch, R.L., & Lushene, R.E. (1968). *The state-trait anxiety inventory.* Palo Alto, CA: Consulting Psychologist Press.

Stechler, G., & Kaplan, S. (1980). The development of the self: A psychoanalytic perspective. *The Psychoanalytic Study of the Child, 35,* 85-106.

Vaillant, G. (1977). *Adaptation to life.* Boston: Little, Brown.

Vaillant, G. (1978). Natural history of male psychological health. *American Journal of Psychiatry, 135,* 653-659.

Vaillant, G. & Vaillant, C. (1981). Natural history of male psychological health: Work as a predictor of positive mental health, *American Journal of Psychiatry, 138,* 1433-1440.

Weingarten, K. (1978). The employment pattern of professional couples and their distribution of involvement in the family. In J. Bryson & R. Bryson (Eds.), *Dual-career couples* (pp. 43-52). New York: Human Sciences Press.

Interrelationships Within the Mother-Father-Infant Triad

Jane R. Dickie
Hope College

A family's transition from the husband-wife dyad to a mother-father-infant triad precipitates new role definitions and introduces complex new relationships (Gutmann, 1975). Even in egalitarian marriages or marriages in which both husband and wife are employed, having a baby tends to be a force for more traditional role divisions (Bernard, 1974; Hoffman, 1978). Women especially may experience more role disruptions than anticipated (Feldman & Nash, 1984). Sleep, recreation time, sexual intimacy, time with friends, and time with spouse are all affected by the transition (Feldman & Nash, 1984; Hobbs & Cole, 1976). It seems little wonder that decreases in marital satisfaction (Spanier & Lewis, 1980) and increases in marital stress and individual stress accompany the birth of a baby (Russell, 1974; Weinberg & Richardson, 1981). New expectations about the role of the father may contribute additional stress (Bloom-Feshbach, 1981). Today's cohort of fathers enters parenthood with 1980s demands and an upbringing that reflects values of the 1950s or 1960s. Current research emphasizes the importance of the father's role in child development (see Biller, 1981; Hoffman, 1981; Pedersen, 1981; Radin, 1981; Sagi & Sharon, 1983 for reviews), but social and work structures sometimes push fathers out of the picture at a time when fathers and mothers are anticipating greater father participation (Levine, Pleck, & Lamb, 1983). Even psychologists' past research strategies, which ignored fathers (Lamb, 1981), may have aggravated this problem. Finally, the infants' qualities, such as irritability, may add additional burdens. Parents need to respond to the individuality of their infants. However, whether parents plan to react flexibly to their infant or not, the infant's unique qualities have an impact on them (Lewis & Rosenblum, 1974).

113

The transition to parenthood is a time when parents feel fatigued, when their role expectations are being challenged, their marriage is being changed, and they must adjust to the uniqueness of their infant. It requires knowledge to understand these processes and to promote optimal adaptation. As background for a study focusing on the mother–father–infant triad, results from two types of investigations are reviewed: intervention studies and correlational, descriptive studies.

Intervention Studies

Parenting interventions before 1975 focused exclusively on the mother–infant dyad. Most current intervention projects continue this focus. Folk wisdom as well as the reality that most mothers hold primary responsibility for infant care contributed to this approach. Even though mothers, on average, spend more time with their infants than do fathers, 102 hours versus 16 hours per week (Yarrow et al., 1984), women's roles are changing and fathers are needed in childcare (Levine et al., 1983). Despite fathers' comparatively lower levels of participation, their influence on children's development can be significant (Lamb, 1981), and research efforts should include fathers. Another reason for assessing fathers is that the mother–infant dyad exists within a family context (Bronfenbrenner, 1977) and the marriage relationship is linked in complex ways to maternal and paternal adaptation to parenthood (Grossman, Eichler, & Winickoff, 1980; Shereshefsky & Yarrow, 1973).

Intervention studies focusing on fathers have taught us two important lessons: (a) there are significant interrelationships between parenting roles and spousal roles and hence, there is need to examine each individual's and each relationship's contribution to triadic functioning, and (b) methodological factors affect results and, hence, there is need for both self-report and observational measures of marriage and parenting variables. Some father-intervention studies that relied heavily on fathers' self-reports show that intervention had little effect. Wente and Crockenberg (1976) found that Lamaze training for childbirth had no effect on the father's self-reported adjustment to his child. Wandersman (1980) found that fathers participating in a support group reported a lower sense of well-being and perceived their infants as more fussy. However, because there were no observations of the father–infant interaction, we do not know if fathers merely felt less capable or if they behaved less capably with their infants.

In the most extensive intervention project so far, Cowan and Cowan (1983) focused almost entirely on the husband–wife relationship. The design included support groups that met weekly from 3 months prior to the birth of the infant to 3 months postpartum. Self-reports of adjustment were collected including depression, marriage satisfaction, and parenting stress. Only minimal effects of group participation were obtained at follow-up sessions when the infants were 6 months and 18 months old. Participants and nonparticipants did not differ in reported marriage satisfaction, role arrangements, or parenting stress. However, perceptions of the interconnections of parenting and role satisfactions did differ, as indicated by different patterns of correlations. At 6 months, fathers with the intervention experience reported less satisfaction with their roles than those without intervention; mothers with the intervention experience were more satisfied and reported fewer conflicts. By 18 months, both mothers and fathers in the intervention group reported more satisfaction with their role arrangements, although the actual role divisions were the same as that of the nonintervention participants. The intervention fostered discussion among parents that may have clarified fathers' feelings about parenting and marriage issues. For fathers who received the intervention, marital satisfaction was positively correlated with parenting stress, husband–wife problem solving, and mutual role arrangement. For fathers in the control group, marriage satisfaction was unrelated to these variables. Mothers with and without intervention were more similar than the two groups of fathers were. For both groups of mothers, marriage satisfaction was related to satisfaction with role arrangements and low parenting stress. However, amount of reported husband–wife conflict was correlated negatively with marriage satisfaction for mothers in the control group. Participation in the intervention experience thus may have provided a mechanism for diffusing the consequences, although not decreasing, conflict.

Cowan and Cowan are continuing to examine the marital relationship and the self-reported feelings of these parents. Their work provides important information about the transition to parenthood. However, their data so far provide only limited evidence that support-group intervention improves the marriage relationship or improves parenting skills, at least for these relatively low risk parents. Participation in the intervention experiences did appear to help clarify how parents felt, although it did not necessarily make them feel better. It is possible that there were improvements, both in the marriage and in parenting, but measures in the study have not captured them.

Myers (1980) combined a cognitive intervention approach with self-report assessment. He trained groups of new fathers and new mothers to play simple games and exercises designed to increase their familiarity with their infants. The games were based on Brazelton's Neonatal Behavioral Assessment Scale (1973). Myers then compared the intervention groups with a control group of untrained parents, using self-report measures of parenting. The trained groups reported greater knowledge of their infants than the comparison group, as well as more confidence and satisfaction in parenting. In addition, when the infants were 4 weeks old, the trained fathers were more involved with their infants than were the untrained fathers. Although this study demonstrates that parents' sense of competence is greater following intervention, it would have been helpful to have observations confirming greater parenting skill as well.

Other intervention programs have included observations of the father–infant relationship. Generally, these programs have shown significant effects of the intervention. Parke, Hymel, Power, and Tinsley (1980) had new fathers observe a brief videotape describing cognitive and social competence of infants and play techniques, and demonstrated fathers engaging in caregiving tasks. Assessment 3 months later showed that fathers with this intervention knew more about their infants than did fathers in a control group. The intervention showed more efficacy for fathers of sons than fathers of daughters; these fathers were more involved in caregiving and provided more responses that were contingent on the infants' behaviors. Perhaps it was the brevity of the intervention that limited the effects to fathers of sons. Other research has suggested that fathers generally are more involved with their sons (Parke, 1979) and intervention may have served to strengthen this already existing tendency.

Zelazo, Kotelchuck, Barber, and David (1977) also capitalized on the potential for a close father–son bond. Using a social learning approach, they taught 20 low-interacting fathers how to play games with their 12-month-old sons. The fathers and sons then played 30 minutes per day for 4 weeks. Laboratory observations of father–infant interaction (outside of the assigned play sessions) showed that the intervention group infants interacted more with their fathers, looked at them more, and initiated more contact with them than did those in a control group. This study's focus on infants shows the importance of observing both members of the parent-child dyad to assess intervention effects.

An intervention study in which all dyadic relations (mother–infant, father–infant, husband–wife) were assumed to be important (Dickie & Gerber, 1980) further illustrates both the need to examine each individual's contribution to triadic functioning as well as the methodological distinction between observational and self-report measures. This intervention sought to improve the social competence of mother, father, and infant. Comparisons of families randomly assigned to an intervention or a control group showed that all three members of the triad were affected by the intervention. Infants of trained parents were observed to be more predictable and responsive than controls and sought interactions more often with their fathers, whereas infants of parents without training sought interactions more often with their mothers. The intervention also was successful in increasing the competence of both mothers and fathers. The trained parents more often anticipated infant needs and responded contingently to their infants than the control parents did. Most important, a reciprocal pattern was evident, such that increases in the trained fathers' interactions were accompanied by decreases in the trained mothers' interaction. The reciprocal nature of the mother, father, and infant interactions illustrates why it is so important to look at all members of the family to understand these adaptational processes.

Trained fathers and mothers received the highest competency ratings from an observer and trained couples rated their spouses' parental competence higher than did the control couples, but self-report measures showed no indication that trained parents felt more competent than non-trained parents. Apparently behaving more competently (as rated by one's spouse and an outside observer) and feeling more competent are independent of each other. Such findings reaffirm that observational and self-report measures yield different information.

Correlational Studies

Correlational studies reveal three areas of potential significance for understanding adaptations by mother, father, and infant. These are (a) parental role expectations, (b) the marriage relationship, and (c) characteristics of the infant.

Role Expectations.   As sex-role expectations change, the cultural definitions and proscriptions of what it means to be a "good" mother or "good" father also change. Current conceptions of mothers' and fathers' roles show a great deal of diversity; additionally, men and women differ in their expectations. Because of lack of definite cultural role descriptions, parents may also experience great discrepancies between their role preferences and what they actually experience in their parenting behaviors.

Diversity in role definitions and the different perspectives of men and women are illustrated in a study of the transition to parenthood conducted by Entwisle and Doering (1981). New parents were asked to define *motherliness* and *fatherliness* with three adjectives. The responses ranged from no similarity between each parent's definitions (6% of wives, 10% of husbands), indicative of stereotypic sex-role divisions, to complete congruence between each's definitions (55% of wives, 38% of husbands), indicative of similar expectations for parents to be nurturant regardless of gender. The definitions were important in that the mothers' and fathers' nurturant definition of fatherliness was correlated with the fathers' actual interest in their babies.

Discrepancies between women's and men's definitions of appropriate parenting roles can contribute to conflict. Cowan et al. (1983) reported that 92% of parents in their study reported more conflict after the birth of a baby than before, and that most of this conflict revolved around the division of labor for household and child-care tasks. Mothers performed more baby-related tasks than either husbands or wives expected during pregnancy. Women tended to underestimate the extent to which their lives were arranged around an infant, whereas men estimated more closely what they came to experience as fathers (Entwistle & Doering, 1981; Feldman & Nash, 1984).

Parents' expectations and performance of child-care and household tasks can have a significant impact on marriage satisfaction Chadwick, Albrecht, & Kunz, 1976; Frank, Anderson, & Rubenstein, 1980). However, parents' satisfaction with roles appears to be more important than the actual arrangements. Cowan et al. (1983) found that women's satisfaction with roles such as parent, spousal, and work roles, was positively correlated with self-esteem and marriage satisfaction. Men's role satisfaction was associated with higher self-esteem and higher marriage satisfaction, but this was true only for the men who were in a parent support group. Couples who were satisfied with their roles were also more satisfied with their ability to discuss issues of division of labor.

Parents' concepts of their roles also are reflected in their sense of identity in being a parent. In our culture, women are socialized to invest much of their identity in parenting. Until recently, men's identities were expected to evolve around work (Gilligan, 1982). Dickie, Van Gent, Hoogerwerf, Martinez, and Dieterman (1981) and Cowan et al. (1983) found that mothers attribute more of their identity to parenting. But, interestingly, mothers who report less parental identity than the average, and fathers who report more parental identity than the average, report greater life satisfaction (Dickie et al., 1981) and higher self-esteem and happiness with themselves (Cowan et al., 1983). Perhaps men and women have similar needs to nurture their children, but in our culture women may be in this role too much and men, too little.

Although the aforementioned studies relied heavily on self-reports of marriage satisfaction and role expectations, other research has examined the relationships between expectations and observed parenting skill and behavioral measures of husband–wife interaction. Dickie et al. (1981) conducted an intervention study with 38 parents of 4- to 12-month-old infants. Parents were asked to what extent they assumed responsibility for child-care tasks, including diapering, bathing, feeding, and playing with the infant. They were then asked to what extent should they ideally assume responsibility. Mothers and fathers were found to express discrepancies between their actual and ideal child-care responsibilities, but the content and direction of their discrepancies differed. Mothers expressed greatest discrepancies in diapering and bathing: They felt they did too much. Fathers expressed greatest discrepancy in playing with their infants: They felt they did too little.

An important question is whether these discrepancies in expectations were related to husband–wife interaction and parenting skill. Discrepancies between actual and ideal responsibility for childcare were related to the observed marital relationship and to observed parenting skill based on observers' ratings of husband–wife emotional support and parental competence. Both mothers and fathers who reported less discrepancy between their actual and ideal responsibilities for childcare were rated more emotionally supportive in their interactions than were parents who reported greater discrepancies. Likewise, the most competent parents were those who reported less discrepancy between actual and ideal time spent in childcare.

Parental role expectations thus appear important both for the marriage relationship and for parenting. However, different aspects of the parental role appear more salient for mothers and fathers. Direct physical care of the infant is obviously a major part of the parental role for mothers, but what are the expectations for fathers? Research should consider direct care such as feeding, diapering, bathing, tending the infant at night, and taking the infant to the doctor. Playing, however, appears to be more a special province of fathers (Parke, 1979), and this is a conception that both parents may or may not share. Some important aspects of the parental role do not involve direct interaction with the infant. Some investigators have suggested that indirect effects are the most important part of the father's effect on his infant (Bronfenbrenner, 1977). One aspect of indirect parental influence is decision making regarding the infant, in which preferences may be expressed regarding medical care, the child's safety needs, sleep schedules, clothing, toys, and furniture.

The Marriage Relationship.   A second important aspect of the context for parenting is the marriage relationship. Bronfenbrenner (1977) has particularly stressed the possible indirect or second order effects of the marital relationship on child development. Most speculation about indirect effects on parenting has focused on the father as the individual who indirectly affects the infant by influencing the mother in the marriage relationship (Lewis & Weinraub, 1976). In this view, the father's role is one of providing emotional support for his wife. There is evidence that fathers not only do assume this supportive role, but that it is important for the mother's adaptation to parenthood (Shereshefsky & Yarrow, 1973), her marital satisfaction (Barry, 1970), and her psychological adjustment through the first year after the infant is born (Grossman et al., 1980).

The importance of the father's support for his wife, thereby influencing their children, seems clear. A problem with this perspective is that the father's need for his wife's support has been ignored. As Pedersen (1981) has suggested, this oversight may be due to sex-role stereotypes that define the father as the strong supportive parent and the mother as weak, and in need of support. At the same time, this perspective reinforces the role of wife as mother, and husband as breadwinner. Indeed, fathers may need more support than mothers for direct interaction with infants because our culture is more likely to recognize the primacy of the mother–infant relationship and less likely to recognize the importance of the father.

There is evidence that the mother's support for her husband may be just as important for his functioning as husband and father as his support is for her functioning as wife and mother. Correlations between ratings of marital adjustment and ease in adjusting to parenthood are higher for fathers than for mothers (Hobbs, 1968; Russell, 1974). Fathers' sense of parental competence and their general sense of well-being are associated with positive perceptions of their marriage (Wandersman, 1980). Fathers who have experienced "blues" after the birth of their infants reported experiencing problems finding time to be with their wives and problems with the quality of the marriage (Zaslow, Pedersen, Kramer, & Cain, 1981). Finally, the quality of marriage, whether reported by the husband or wife, is a powerful predictor of subsequent father involvement and satisfaction with the child (Feldman, Nash, & Aschenbrenner, 1983).

Global measures of the marriage relationship restrict analyses to a unidimensional construct, and studies have suggested a uniformly positive relationship between marriage and parenting. However, as the parental role has different dimensions, so too does the marriage relationship. We need to recognize that some aspects of the marriage relationship may enhance the parental role, whereas other aspects of the marriage may compete with the parental role. For example, rates of interaction between one parent and the infant are reduced when the other parent is present (Clarke-Stewart, 1978; Pedersen, Zaslow, Cain, & Anderson, 1980), although lower rates of interaction do not necessarily imply diminished quality (Dickie & Gerber, 1980). When mother, father, and infant are all present, husband–wife communication may either conflict with parent–infant communication or enhance it. Belsky (1979), in an observational study in the home, found that whether there was a conflicting or enhancing effect depended on the content of husband–wife verbal exchanges. Conversation between parents about their toddler was positively associated with rates of father–child interaction, but other husband–wife conversation was either unrelated or negatively related to the father–infant interaction, and parental communication about the child was unrelated to the mother–infant interaction. These findings suggest that we must not only assess the impact of different aspects of the marriage on parenting, but that we need to recognize different patterns for mothers and fathers. This is especially important because husbands' and wives' perceptions of the marriage may be quite different (Feldman, Nash, & Aschenbrenner, 1983).

Belsky (1979) found that husband and wife communication about the infant had an enhancing effect for their father–infant interaction, but we do not know whether the parents agreed about childcare in their conversations. The importance of parental agreement is illustrated by Entwisle and Doering's (1981) report that although new parents reported little "quarreling," 52% said that they had "disagreements about the baby." Folk wisdom suggests that it is important for husbands and wives to present a "united front" to their children, and there is some support for this view. When parents disagree over child rearing, children may be exposed to confusing and contradictory messages. The child's attempt to discern order may be thwarted. Block and Morrison (1981) gave this interpretation to their finding that parental agreement in child rearing was more important in predicting the child's competence than the particular rearing values that were endorsed.

Husbands and wives support one another by agreeing, or at least by dealing with parenting issues. Grossman et al. (1980) reported that husband–wife discussion dealing well with parenting issues was positively related to how well fathers related to the family. In our studies, agreement about goals and techniques of child rearing, which we termed *cognitive support,* appeared important not only for parents feelings of competence but also for their observed competence. The distinction between competent feelings and competent actions is important, because the two are not necessarily related (Dickie & Gerber, 1980). Parents who felt supported by spouses also felt more competent and confident in their parental role. However, parents' agreement about child rearing was much more important for their competence than parents' feeling of being supported (Dickie, Schuurmans, & Schang, 1980).

The studies reviewed indicate that an analysis of the aspects of marriage that have an impact on parenting should include emotional support, cognitive support or agreement in childcare, and physical support or sharing childcare. These three aspects of support in the marriage appear conceptually distinguishable yet are related to one another. Pilot work with 38 parents suggested that spouses who share childcare (physical support) tended to be more emotionally supportive. This finding is based on observer ratings of husband–wife interaction (Dickie et al., 1981). Also, when these same parents were divided into those with high and low levels of agreement in childcare, the two groups differed significantly in ratings of emotional support. Nevertheless, emotional support, cognitive support, and physical support are conceptually distinct, and may relate differently to parenting competence and other dimensions of the marriage relationship for men and women.

Infant Characteristics.   Parents acknowledge that each of their children have their own unique characteristics that affect the parent–child interaction. Research is now catching up with this important subjective experience of parents (Lewis & Rosenblum, 1974). The possibility that infant characteristics may be related to the marriage relationship, as well as to parent–infant interactions, is suggested in an intriguing study by Cook (1979). It was found that fathers were more influenced by their infant's behavior than mothers were, especially if marriage satisfaction was low. Clearly, to understand the father–mother–infant triad, we need to understand more about the unique contribution of the infant.

Two characteristics of infants that may be particularly important are infant gender and infant social competence. Many parents have a preference for boys, a preference that is particularly strong among fathers (Hoffman, 1977). Lamb (1976) concluded that the emotional bond between fathers and their infant sons is stronger than the bond between fathers and their infant daughters. Furthermore, mothers and fathers treat their infant sons and daughters differently. Fathers expect to, and do show higher involvement with sons than daughters (Dickie, 1985; Parke, 1979). In other research, mothers talked to and touched infant daughters more than sons during feeding, but fathers in a play situation touched, visually stimulated, and looked at their sons more often than their daughters (Thoman, Barnett, & Leiderman, 1971; Thoman, Leiderman, & Olson, 1972).

Interactions between infant gender and parent gender have not been found in all studies. In studies that have relied more on self-report measures, fathers of sons and fathers of daughters have not differed in the extent to which they reported feeding, diapering, bathing, holding, or comforting their infants, or in number of play activities with their infants. Nor did infants' sex significantly influence fathers' enjoyment of parenting or how they felt during interactions with their infants (Entwistle & Doering, 1981; Grossman et al., 1980). The contrast between our results and these again illustrates that self-report and observational measures of father involvement yield different results.

Infant's social competence is a second infant variable related to mother–father–infant functioning. In a previous study (Dickie et al., 1980), fathers were more affected than mothers by variations in infants' social responsiveness. Fathers with more responsive and predictable infants (i.e., more socially competant infants) were more likely to be sensitive to their infants. Thus, infant social competence is a promising variable for further exploration.

AN EMPIRICAL STUDY OF
THE CONTEXT FOR PARENTING

This section presents results of an empirical study that was designed to examine the relationship between couples' and infants' functioning and parental competence, focusing on elements of what we have labeled *the conceptual context.* This included (a) cultural expectations as interpreted by the parents, (b) qualities of the marriage relationship, and (c) the individual characteristics of the infant.

Our premise was that fathers and mothers are very similar in their needs and in the variables that influence their parenting behavior. However, because cultural influences and levels of support are different for prospective fathers and mothers, we expected that a greater variety of variables might influence fathers' parenting skills compared with mothers'. The study focused on three classes of variables that could affect parental competence and marital relationships. It was designed to learn more about how the fathers' role behaviors influence the infant directly and indirectly. The ultimate objective was to clarify interrelationships within the mother-father–infant triad so that this knowledge could be used in future intervention programs.

METHODS

Trained observers rated husband–wife and parent–infant interactions of 46 white middle-class couples and their 4- to 8-month-old infants during a 2-hour observation. Most of the families were professional, and parents were in their early thirties. Thirty-two of the infants were firstborns, ten were secondborns, and four were thirdborns. Seventy percent of the mothers were full-time homemakers, and some of the mothers worked part-time, while others worked full-time.

Rating scales were adapted from Baumrind's (1971) observation schedule. Raters, who were unaware of the hypotheses, were trained until they reached 90% agreement on 7-point anchored scales for the variables under investigation. The observational ratings were complemented by questionnaire measures that focused on the marital relationship, expectations for child-care responsibilities, and identity in the parent role. Both self-report and observational measures were used. Validity should have been increased because parents are more likely to answer questionnaire items accurately when they have been observed (Lytton, 1971).

Parental competence was assessed by observers' ratings of the following specific aspects of parent–infant interaction: (a) verbal and non-verbal contingent responding, (b) emotional consistency, (c) appropriate stimulation,

(d) anticipation of infant needs, (e) reasonableness of expectations and routines, and (f) expression of warmth and pleasure. These variables have been identified as important determinants of successful parent–infant interaction (Belsky, Goode, & Most, 1980; Dickie & Gerber, 1980; Yarrow, Rubenstein, & Pedersen, 1975). Fathers and mothers were each given a summary score that combined parenting competence in all six areas. Principal Component Factor Analysis revealed these to be a single factor.

Expectations were assessed in two ways: (a) a comparison between parents' actual participation in child-care activities and their beliefs about ideal participation, and (b) a measure of the parents' identity in the parent role. To measure parental identity we used the "identity pie" measure designed by Cowan, Cowan, Coie, and Coie (1978): Parents divided a circle into parts representing their feelings of identity in various roles. The percent of the total given to parent role was considered to be a measure of parental identity.

The marriage relationship was assessed in two ways, observers' ratings and self-reports. Observers rated three aspects of spousal support. For each of these aspects there was one score per couple. These scores were: (a) emotional support (verbal and non-verbal indices of affection, balance of dominance, mutual respect, compatibility, communication, and satisfaction), (b) cognitive support (parental agreement in childcare), and (c) physical support (sharing of childcare and play with the baby).

Parents' perceptions of three aspects of their marriages were assessed by self-reports: (a) perceived support (feelings that their spouses had been supportive of them in the parent role), (b) communication (how frequently partners felt understood by their spouses and how freely they expressed their own needs and disagreements), and (c) satisfaction (with the spouses handling of 12 aspects of family life, including money, chores, time allocation, trust, sex, ·affection, relations with friends, relations with in-laws, jobs, personal relationships, childcare, and social interaction).

Infant variables included (a) gender and (b) observer ratings of social responsiveness. Ratings were based on infants' overall responsiveness to both parents, the degree of pleasure the infant showed in social interactions and the predictability and latency of responses.

RESULTS

Parental Expectations

In 31 of the 46 couples, both the husband and wife completed the questionnaire. Data from these questionnaires are shown in Table 6.1. The results show that mothers and fathers both recognized that mothers take major responsibility for all aspects of parenting (see Table 6.1, columns 1 & 2). However, the division of parental responsibilities depended on the particular aspects of parenting. Responsibility for physical care fell most heavily on mothers. In contrast, fathers took proportionately more responsibility for playing with their infants and for decision making.

It appeared from fathers' and mothers' reports of what they actually did that more than 100% of the job was getting done! For example, mothers and fathers each gave self-reports of their own contributions to the total parent responsibility taken for children's sleep schedules. The total for mothers and fathers was 114%. The extent to which reporting was self-serving depended on the task. Parents tended to overestimate their own work but to underestimate play. Mothers' and fathers' reports of play with their infants added to only 93%.

When parents' reports of their actual responsibility for childcare are compared with what they believed to be ideal, it can be seen that both parents wished to move toward more father participation in all aspects of childcare. Mothers believed it would be ideal to do less, and fathers believed it would be ideal to do more, than they actually did. This was true, although the ideal was not equal sharing between husband and wife in any area, including physical care, play, and decision making (see Table 6.1, columns 3 & 4).

Finally, columns 5 and 6 of Table 6.1 show the discrepancy between what parents said they actually did and their ideals. The discrepancy scores in the table represent scores for actual participation minus scores for what parents believed to be ideal. Negative scores indicate that actual participation is less than what parents call ideal; positive scores indicate that actual participation is more than the ideal. The discrepancy scores show that fathers believed they participate too little, and mothers believed that they participate too much. Fathers seemed most satisfied with the degree of responsibility they have assumed for decision making about childcare, and less satisfied with their responsibility for physical care. Mothers seemed most satisfied with the degree of responsibility they have assumed for play with infants and for decisions concerning medical care and the baby's immediate safety. Mothers and fathers both wanted greater father participation. However, ideally fathers envisioned increasing their child-care responsibilities less than the mothers envisioned decreasing their own responsibilities. Mothers' and fathers' discrepancy scores differed most for feeding, diapering, bathing, tending the infant at night and deciding about sleep schedules, clothing, toys, and furniture. Fathers thought they were close to the ideal in decision-making responsibilities, but their wives disagreed.

Although Table 6.1 addresses parental investment in childcare, another measure of emotional investment was included in the procedures. This was the "identity pie." Mothers reported a greater sense of identity in the

TABLE 6.1

Mothers and Fathers Reports of Their Actual and Ideal Responsibility
for Physical ChildCare, Playing, and Decision Making About Their Children.
(Scores express percent of total responsibility.)

	Actual Responsibility		Ideal Responsibility		Discrepancy Between Actual and Ideal[a]	
	Father N = 31	Mother N = 31	Father N = 31	Mother N = 31	Father N = 31	Mother N = 31
Physical Care						
Feed	18%	88%	26%	72%	− 8%	16%
Diaper and Bathe	19	84	29	68	− 10	16
Night Care	19	83	27	64	− 8	19
Taking Infant to Doctor	15	86	29	71	− 13	15
Playing	32	61	42	55	− 10	7
Decisions						
For Medical Care	38	60	42	55	− 4	5
For Immediate Safety Needs	44	55	45	52	− 1	3
For Sleep Schedules	34	80	33	60	− 1	20
For clothing, toys, furniture	26	89	32	63	− 6	26

[a]Negative number indicates parent is actually responsible for less childcare than his/her ideal. Positive number indicates parent actually responsible for more than his/her ideal.

parental role than fathers did (37% and 25% respectively). However, parents' feelings of identity were not proportional to their actual responsibility for childcare. Although parents reported that mothers took more than twice as much responsibility for child-care tasks as fathers did, mothers' and fathers' identity in the parental role was much more similar.

Table 6.2 reports the results of an extension of the analysis of the measures of actual responsibility and the discrepancy between actual and ideal. Correlations are presented between these measures and observers' ratings of parental competence as well as mothers' and fathers' self-reports of two aspects of the marriage relationship. A third aspect, marital satisfaction, showed no significant relationships and is omitted from the table. In addition, correlations with identity in the parent role (measured with the "identity pie") and extent of observed parental childcare and play are presented. The discrepancy between actual and ideal was significantly and negatively correlated with observed competence for fathers, but not for mothers. Fathers with the greatest discrepancy between actual and ideal responsibility for feeding, diapering, and bathing, were least competent in parenting. (See Table 6.2, columns 1 & 2.)

Fathers' competence appeared to depend less on their reported actual childcare time than on the degree to which fathers lived up to their expectations for responsibility in feeding, diapering, and bathing. Fathers' identity in the parent role was positively related to observers' ratings of competence. The more identity fathers reported feeling in the parental role, the greater the parenting competence.

Columns 1 and 2 of Table 6.2 also includes observer's assessments of the degree of responsibility fathers and mothers took for childcare and playing. There was a significant relationship between fathers' competence and the observers' assessment of their responsibility for childcare, and especially for playtime. Mothers' responsibility for childcare and mothers' parental identity did not show a significant relationship with observers' ratings of mothers' parental competence. Maternal identity and the amount of time spent in the mothering role did not affect maternal competence. However, observed maternal responsibility for play was negatively related to observers' ratings of mothers' competence. The greater the responsibility for play, the less competently mothers interacted with their infants.

What are we to make of the fact that parents' self-reports of responsibility for childcare and play were unrelated to observers' ratings of parental competence, but that observers' reports of actual childcare were related to parental competence? Perhaps the self-report measures were inaccurate. This seems unlikely, at least for physical care, because mothers' and fathers' independent judgments of responsibility were so similar. It seems more likely that both the observer reports and the self-reports were correct estimates of responsibility for childcare. The self-reports were estimates of

TABLE 6.2

Relationship of Observers' Ratings of Parental Competence and Self-Reports
of the Marriage Relationship with other Parenting Variables

| | Observer Ratings Of Overall Parental Competence | | Self-Reports of Marriage Relationship | | | |
| | | | Perceived Parental Support | | Spouse Communication | |
	Fathers	Mothers	Fathers	Mothers	Fathers	Mothers
SELF-REPORT						
Actual Responsibility						
Physical Care						
Feeding						
Diaper and Bathe		.27*		−.29**	−.34**	
Night Care				−.32**		
Taking Infant to Doctor						
Playing						−.27*
Decisions:						
For medical care	.30*	−.33*				
For Safety						
For Sleep						
For clothing, etc.						

Discrepancy Between Actual and Ideal

Physical Care:						
Feeding	-.40**					
Diaper and Bathe	-.34**					
Night Care			.51***	-.32**		-.22*
Taking Infant to Doctor				-.38***		-.22*
Playing				-.32**		
Decisions:						
For Medical Care				-.29**		-.22*
For Safety Needs						
For Sleep Schedules						
For clothing, etc.						
Identity in Parent Role	.40**					

OBSERVERS' REPORTS

Child Care	.31**				-.61***	
Play	.58***	-.28**		-.30**		

*p < .10
**p < .05
***p < .01

129

degree of responsibility for all childcare. However, observers measured the responsibility of each parent only when both parents were present. This may be the key to understanding how a father's perceptions of the father role relates to his competence in the role. More competent fathers seem more likely to live up to their ideals about responsibility for feeding, diapering, and bathing. Within current work structures, this means more involvement when fathers are home. The more competent fathers also felt more identity in the father role. They felt competent with their infants. Conversely, fathers who were less competent interacted less with infants in play and childcare, felt less identity as fathers, and more discrepancy between what they were doing and what they should be doing for their infants' physical care.

Mothers' competence was unrelated to the amount of time they spent with their infants or the discrepancy between their actual and ideal responsibilities, with the exception that observed play was negatively related to competence. It is interesting that mothers who played more than others with their infants when both parents were home interacted less competently with their infants. Perhaps these mothers felt a lack of support when their husbands were not involved in play with the infants. This might lower their competence scores.

Parents' reports of actual responsibility, and the discrepancy between actual and ideal were related to some aspects of the marriage relationship and not to others. These factors are associated with how much support from spouses husbands and wives felt in the parenting role. Once again, it was the discrepancy between actual and ideal childcare sharing that was most important (see Table 6.2, columns 3 through 6). Column 3 shows that fathers felt supported by their wives when there was a large discrepancy between how often they tended to the infant at night, and how often they thought they should be tending the infant.

Notice that it was not the actual amount of responsibility that wives took for tending the infant that was important to fathers, but the discrepancy between fathers' ideals and the actual situation: When fathers thought that they should be getting up at night, but were actually sleeping, they felt supported! Mothers felt supported by their husbands when they took less of the responsibility for infant diapering, bathing, and for taking the infant to the doctor, and presumably their husbands took more of this responsibility. Mothers also felt supported when there was little discrepancy between actual and ideal responsibility for taking the infant to the doctor, playing with the baby, and making medical decisions about the infant. The more supported mothers felt, the less responsibility for play they assumed and presumably the more their husbands assumed. Perhaps this perceived support also helped the mothers to be more competent with the infant.

Responsibility for childcare and discrepancy between actual and ideal had little relationship with spousal communication, but there were two interesting exceptions; fathers who were observed to take little responsibility for childcare and reported that they did little diapering and bathing, also reported the most open communication with their wives. There is no evidence that their wives shared this perception. Perhaps a husband who participates a great deal in childcare communicates less of his own needs to his spouse. His participation in childcare certainly supports his wife, but it may be at the cost of time for husband–wife communication, at least from the husband's point of view.

Summary and Discussion of Expectations. There are strong expectations that fathers will participate in parenting, and that fathers will be playmates for their infants. Both mothers and fathers wish ideally that fathers could participate more in all aspects of parenting. However, mothers seem to want even more father participation than fathers do. Therefore, these expectations may be an important source of mothers' and fathers' conflict.

Fathers' sense of identity in the parent role was related to their competence in that role. Fathers who were judged more competent were more likely to live up to their ideals for childcare responsibility. Considering current work structures, this means fathers were more involved at times when both parents were at home. Mothers' parental role perceptions were less related to their competence. However, the closer a father's participation was to his wife's ideal, the more the wife felt supported in parenting. The degree to which the father's participation approached the level that the couple expected seemed to be particularly important, not only for the infant's sake, but for the mother's feelings as well. The absolute amount of father involvement appeared to be less important than how the parents functioned and what they ideally wanted in their roles.

The Marriage Relationship

The second important aspect of the parenting context is the marriage relationship. Aspects of marital support were assessed in terms of their impact on parenting competence and the marriage relationship. We expected that spouses who supported each other's parenting emotionally, cognitively (by agreement on childcare), and physically (by actually sharing childcare), would score high on measures of parental competence. We also expected that support would have a greater impact on fathers than on mothers.

Table 6.3 shows the correlations between the three types of support in which we were interested, and observers' ratings of parental competence. All three types of support show the expected relationships. For fathers, especially, being in a supportive relationship and providing more caregiving support to the spouse was associated with greater parenting competence.

Table 6.4 shows how levels of spousal emotional and cognitive support were related to fathers' and mothers' observed parental competence. Distributions of each of the spousal support scores were divided at the median and analyses were computed. Notice that greater support was associated with greater competence for both parents. However, it was the fathers who gained the most from an emotionally supportive spousal relationship. Under conditions of high support, mothers and fathers did not differ in parenting competence. However, under conditions of low support, the fathers were significantly less competent than the mothers. For both fathers and mothers, emotional support in husband–wife interactions was most strongly associated with sensitive, contingent, and emotionally pertinent interaction with the infant. Although it is impossible to ascertain direction of effect we suspect that parents who are socially competent in the husband–wife dyad are most likely to be able to respond sensitively in the parent–infant dyad. The pattern of outcomes for spousal cognitive support is similar to that for emotional support. That is, cognitive support seemed less important for mothers' than for fathers' parenting skills. However, the interaction between parent gender and level of cognitive support was significant at only the .10 level. Spousal support by giving physical care to the infant had the least effect on parenting competence.

How does support in the parent role relate to other aspects of the marriage? Table 6.5 suggests that in this study the type of support that enhanced parent–infant interaction may not have enhanced all aspects of the marriage, especially from the husband's point of view. When fathers gave their wives emotional support in childcare and were competent with their infants, husband–wife communication suffered. These fathers were less likely to communicate their own needs or to express disagreement with their wives. They also expressed somewhat lower marriage satisfaction. Mothers, on the other hand, showed no such conflicts between aspects of the marriage and aspects of parental support. In fact, they felt most supported by their husbands, and believed there was the greatest husband–wife communication, when husbands gave cognitive support for parenting. That is, mothers felt that they were supported when their husbands agreed with them about child rearing. Emotional support and cooperation in childcare were not significantly related to mothers' perceptions of support, spouse communication, and marriage satisfaction.

Summary and Discussion of Marriage Relationship.   The marriage relationship provides a major aspect of the context for parenting. The earlier view that the father's primary parenting job is emotional support for his wife and, hence, to indirectly affect his infant, has been enlarged to

TABLE 6.3

Correlation between Parental Competence and Observed Parenting Supportiveness

	Observed Couple Supportiveness:			Observed Physical Support:	
	Emotional Support	Cognitive Support	Cooperation	For ChildCare	For Play
Father's Competence (N = 46)	.76***	.70***	.52***	.31*	.58***
Mother's Competence (N = 46)	.54***	.30*	.22	-.07	-.28*

*p < .05
**p < .01
***p < .001

133

TABLE 6.4
Association Between Observed Parenting Competence and
Two Measures of Spousal Support:
Emotional Support and Agreement in ChildCare

	Low of Emotional Support*	
	Low	High
Parent Competence Scores:		
Fathers	72.63	94.64
Mothers	87.00	97.32
	Agreement in ChildCare**	
	Low Agreement	High Agreement
Fathers	76.97	93.71
Mothers	90.00	95.24

*Main effect of Parent Gender: $F(1,88) = 8.49$, $p < .005$; main effect of Emotional Support: $F(1,88) = 28.71$, $p < .001$; Parent Gender x Support Interaction: $F(1,88) = 3.76$, $p < .05$.
**Main effect of Parent Gender: $F(1,88) = 7.14$, $p < .01$; Main effect of Agreement: $F(1,88) = 10.41$, $p < .001$; Parent Gender X Support Interaction: $F(1,88) = 2.85$, $p < .10$.

recognize that wives also support their husbands. Indeed, in this study it was fathers who seemed to benefit most from emotional support. For both mothers and fathers, emotional and cognitive support were strongly associated with sensitive, contingent, and emotionally pertinent interaction with their infants. Actual participation in childcare was also important for fathers' parenting skills.

Although supportive marriages seemed to enhance competent parenting, these results call for a closer examination of the relationship between marriage and parenting. Pedersen (1981) pointed out that research on marriage and parenting should examine in what ways parenting and marriage roles support, and in what ways they compete with one another. The concept that greater marriage satisfaction should support greater parenting satisfaction is only one view of the relationship. Another view is that the two might compete, especially for fathers, whose time with their wives is in direct conflict with time spent with their child. Those mothers whose limited employment allows them most individual time with their infants may encourage fathers to play with their infants when the fathers return home from work. Mothers, in turn, feel affirmed and supported when their husbands care for, and play with their infants. However, fathers may feel that time for spousal communication is reduced.

TABLE 6.5

Correlations of Observed Couple Supportiveness and Observed Parental Competence
with Self-Reported Aspects of the Marital Relationship

	Observed Couple Supportiveness:			Observed Parental Competence
	Emotional Support	Cognitive Support	Cooperation in ChildCare	
Self-Reports of Marriage:				
Fathers' Reports				
Support	-.31*			
Spouse Communication		-.23*	-.28*	-.25*
Marriage Satisfaction				-.26*
Mothers' Reports				
Support		.41***		
Communication		.36***		
Marriage Satisfaction				

*p < .10
**p < .05
***p < .01

135

The suggestion that the relationship between parenting and marriage roles differs for fathers and mothers is supported by Feldman, Nash, and Aschenbrenner's (1983) finding of only a moderate correlation between husbands' and wives' descriptions of the quality of their marriage. Perhaps the men based their marital assessment on direct interaction with their wives, whereas the wives based their marital assessment on how supportive of parenting their husbands were.

Our results indicate that not all systems of the family are enhanced by spousal parenting support. For the mother, support in childcare is associated with her perception that she and her husband communicate well. For the father, support in childcare is associated with his perception that he and his wife do not communicate well. Perhaps communications about childcare have different values for husbands and wives, and these values foster discrepant perceptions. Belsky (1979) discriminated between husband–wife communications about the infant and husband–wife communications about other matters. Only communication about the infant enhanced the father–infant relationship. Our data suggest that mothers feel supported by cognitive agreement with their husbands about childcare. Communication about the infant may help the mother because it is what she most wants to discuss with her husband. Although communication about the infant also fosters good father–infant interaction, it may not be what the father wants most to discuss with his wife. Involved fathers may be setting aside their own needs in order to support their wives and care for their infants. This is the essence of nurturant childcare. Although these fathers do well at childcare and supporting their wives, it may be at some cost to spousal communication about matters other than the infant. Feldman and Grossman (this volume) have suggested that good mothering involves maintaining a less egocentric orientation by focusing on the needs of others. Gilligan (1982) believed that a focus on serving others is more typical of women than men. Perhaps the competent fathers in our study are assuming a posture in parenting that has long been associated with competent mothering, other-oriented service that supports both mother and infant, but at least for this early infancy period, subordinates the fathers' own needs.

Infant Characteristics

The infant's characteristics were the final aspect of the context for parenting examined in this study. The question raised was: How does infant gender relate to spouses' observed participation in parenting and to competence in parenting. Infants' gender had a differential effect on fathers' and mothers' parenting, in two areas, parents' observed responsibility for childcare and sense of identity in the parent role. Table 6.6 shows these relationships for fathers and for mothers. Fathers with sons were more apt to participate in childcare than were fathers with daughters, whereas mothers showed the reverse. Fathers with sons also tended to report stronger feelings of parent identity than fathers with daughters, whereas mothers with daughters reported feeling stronger parent identity than those with sons, but the interaction between parent's and child's sex was significant only at the .10 level.

Although fathers were more involved with the physical care of sons than daughters, they played equally with sons and daughters and there was no difference in their competence with sons and daughters. Infants' gender had no direct relationship with observers' ratings of parental competence for mothers or fathers, nor did the babies' gender influence any aspect of parental support for each other. Mothers and fathers were equally support- ive of one another with sons and daughters. Aspects of the marriage relationship (perceived support, spousal communication, and marriage satisfaction) were also not affected by infant gender.

The second infant variable examined was infants' social competence based on the home observer's ratings of the infants' overall responsiveness, pleasure, and predictability in interactions. There was a positive relation- ship between infants' social competence and observed parental competence, support for each other and qualities of their marriage. Infant social competence, as judged by an observer, was related to both the mothers' ($r = .36, p < .05$) and fathers' ($r = .35, p < .05$) parenting competence. The infant's social competence was also related to spouses emotional support for one another ($r = .44, p < .05$), cognitive support for each other's parenting ($r = .27, p < .05$), and to the husband's support for his wife by giving physical care to the baby ($r = .35, p < .05$). In other words, parents who had more socially competent infants were more likely to interact competently with their infants and to support one another emotionally and cognitively. Again, because these data are correlational, the causal relation- ship cannot be determined. It is possible that infants' responsiveness and pleasure during interactions may serve to entice fathers into greater

TABLE 6.6
Infant Gender and Two Aspects of Parenting:
Observed Participation in ChildCare
and Self-Reported Identity in the Parent Role

	Participation in ChildCare*		Parent Role Identity**	
	Father	Mother	Father	Mother
Son	30%	70%	30%	35%
Daughter	15%	85%	20%	39%

*Main effect of Parent Gender: $F(1,78) = 297.57, p < .001$; Interaction with Infant Gender; $F = (1,78) = 17.33, p < .001$
**Main effect of Parent Gender: $F(1,55) = 11.58, p < .001$; Interaction with Infant Gender; $F = (1,55) = 2.78, p < .10$

interaction, or the fathers' greater participation may heighten the social competence of their infants. Finally, mothers of socially competent infants reported the most open communication with their spouses ($r = .28, p < .05$). No other aspect of the marriage relationship was related to infant's social competence.

Summary of Infant Characteristics.   Infant gender may influence parenting skill only indirectly in that it may influence the degree of responsibility fathers assume for childcare. Such qualities as infant gender and infant social competence may also serve to stimulate greater father participation and, in turn, foster greater father competence. It is also likely that families that are able to express emotional support for one another also take particular pleasure in one another. This shows up in husband–wife relationships and in infant–parent relationships. It is unclear whether it is the infant's social competence that elicits the parent's competence, or the parent's competence that elicits the infant's competence. But it seems likely that parents and infants affect one another in interactions that each enchance the pleasure and responsiveness of the other.

IMPLICATIONS OF FINDINGS
FOR POTENTIAL INTERVENTION

Intervention programs that seek to improve the functioning of the mother–father–infant triad should be viewed with caution. With the changing roles of men and women in our culture, new ways are needed to support families. Although an ideal program has yet to be devised, this review of research and the empirical findings underscore the importance of the context of parenting for intervention programs. Before interventions are designed we should consider first the impact of role expectations, second, the interaction of parents' support for each other and husband–wife communication and, third, the characteristics of the infant.

Expectations

Mothers and fathers both want more father participation in childcare, although mothers seem to want even more father participation than their husbands do. Both parents expect much father participation in play and in decision making concerning the infant. This differs from the conception that mothers want to monopolize childcare and feel competition with their husbands. Because husbands and wives may differ in their role expectations, interventions should help parents address this issue and should reduce potential conflict.

As couples integrate parenting into their lives, they need to consider not one ideal division of roles, but a variety of divisions. Discrepancies between actual and ideal role arrangements are as important as parents' actual division of responsibilities. Interventions that increase expectations without providing mechanisms for participation may serve to increase frustration and potentially decrease fathers' competence and mothers' sense of support.

Programs should foster fathers' feelings of identity in parenting. This may mean some decrease in fathers' identity with work roles but, as Shirley Feldman (personal communication, May 31, 1984) and Jay Belsky (personal communication, May 31, 1984) pointed out, this may be important for improving the fathers' parenting competence.

The Marriage Relationship

In intact families, the marriage relationship is a major determinant of the context for parenting. Intervention programs should be fashioned with the understanding that the marriage relationship may be the most important source of support for parenting. However, the traditional concept of the father as provider and source of support for his wife, must be modified to recognize the father's need for support as well. Mothering may be a more "buffered" system in the sense that it is less vulnerable to the whims of social circumstance. Mothers also may have more social support than fathers outside of marriage for the parental role. It may be especially fruitful to include the father in intervention efforts because fathers who have emotional and cognitive support can be as competent at parenting as their wives are.

Intervention programs should incorporate both cognitive components as well as husband–wife support components. Cognitive components are focused on questions concerning how to parent. In our studies, emotional and cognitive support for both mothers and fathers was strongly associated with sensitive, contingent, and emotionally pertinent parent–infant interaction. However, those intervening in the mother–father–infant traid need to recognize that enhancement of the couple's role as parental partners may encroach on the couple's role as marital partners. Moreover, emphasis on parenting may be experienced differently by mothers and fathers. Mothers' encouragment of fathers' interest and communication about the infant may increase fathers' involvement and mothers' sense of support. Increased involvement in parenting may increase fathers' parenting competence, but may compete with the time they spend with wives.

Intervention should facilitate communication, not only about parenting issues, but about marital issues as well. Wente and Crockenberg (1976) reported that men who were in discussion groups for new parents talked freely about the difficulties of missing sleep since the baby's arrival, but rarely talked about the husband–wife relationship. What parents focus on most in discussion groups may not, in fact, be the most important issues. Should fathers be encouraged to express their needs to their wives? In our study, the most competent fathers and most supportive fathers were men who were more likely to subordinate their needs in service to the family. We do not know whether this is a temporary phenomenon, one that is adaptive for the infant's first year, or whether resentment may grow that will eventually lead to less marital satisfaction and less successful parenting.

The interaction between different aspects of the marriage relationship, and the finding that men and women may perceive it differently, underscores the complexity of the context for parenting. The belief that we can have more of everything (more father involvement, more communication about parenting issues, and more communication about non-parenting issues) may be based on a failure to recognize that more of one may lead to less of another.

Infant Characteristics

Infants themselves contribute to the functioning of the mother–father–infant triad. Fathers, particularly, may be influenced toward greater or lesser involvement by the infant's gender or social responsiveness. Intervention programs should help parents recognize that infant characteristics can influence them. If fathers' greater involvement contributes to infants' social responsiveness, then support for fathers' interactions with their infants may be especially important.

Researchers advocating interventions need to recognize that parenting does not occur in isolation, but in a context, and that intervention in one relationship, such as that of the mother and infant, will have ramifications for others, such as the husband–wife and father–infant relationships. There are important questions about how role expectations, the marriage, and the qualities of the infant interact. Research on the mother–father–infant triad should help unravel these intricate interactions. Our studies also suggest that a unifying focus for observation and intervention might be social competence. Social competence would be fostered by both parents' decentering, that is putting themselves in each others' place by understanding each others' expectations, by encouraging sensitivity to each others' cues, by providing support, by knowing their own feelings, and how their behavior affects the other. Will this improve overall family functioning? Future studies will tell.

REFERENCES

Barry, W. A. (1970). Marriage research and conflict: An integrative review. *Psychological Bulletin, 73,* 41-55.

Baumrind, D. (1971). Current patterns of parental authority. *Developmental Psychology Monographs, 4,* 1-101.

Belsky, J. (1979). Mother–father–infant interaction: A naturalistic observational study. *Developmental Psychology, 15,* 601-607.

Belsky, J., Goode, M., & Most, R. (1980). Maternal stimulation and infant exploratory competence: Cross-sectional, correlational and experimental analyses. *Child Development, 51,* 1163-1178.

Bernard, J. (1974). *The future of motherhood.* New York: Penguin.

Biller, H. B. (1981). The father and sex role development. In M. E. Lamb (Ed.), *The role of the father in child development* (2nd ed., pp. 489-552). New York: Wiley.

Block, J., & Morrison, A. (1981). Parental agreement–disagreement on child-rearing orientations and gender-related personality correlates in children. *Child Development, 52,* 965-974.

Bloom-Feshbach, J. (1981). Historical perspectives on the father's role. In M. E. Lamb (Ed.), *The role of the father in child development* (2nd ed., pp. 71-112). New York: Wiley.

Brazelton, T. B. (1973). Neonatal behavior assessment scale. *Clinics in Developmental Medicine, 50.* London: Spastics International Medical Publications.

Bronfenbrenner, U. (1977). Toward an experimental ecology of human development. *American Psychologist, 32,* 513-531.

Chadwick, B., Albrecht, S., & Kunz, P. (1976). Marital and family role satisfaction. *Journal of Marriage and the Family. 38,* 431-440.

Clarke-Stewart, K. A. (1978). And daddy makes three: The father's impact on mother and young child. *Child Development, 49,* 466-479.

Cook, N. I. (1979, March). *An analysis of marital and infant factors in evolving family relationships.* Paper presented at the meeting of the Society for Research in Child Development, San Francisco.

Cowan, C. P., & Cowan, P. A. (1983, September). *Mens involvement in the family: Implications for family well being.* Paper presented at the meetings of the American Psychological Association, Anaheim, CA.

Cowan, C. P., Cowan, P., Coie, L., & Coie, J. D. (1978). Becoming a family: The impact of a first child's birth on the couple's relationship. In W. B. Miller & L. F. Newan (Eds.), *The first child and family formation* (pp. 296-324). Chapel Hill, NC: Carolina Population Center.

Cowan, P. A., Curtis-Boles, H., Garrett, E. T., Coysh, W. S., Ball, F. L. J., Boles, A. J., Heming, G., & Cowan, C. P. (1983, August). *Individual and couple satisfaction during family formation: A longitudinal study.* Symposium presented at the meetings of the American Psychological Association, Anaheim, CA.

Dickie, J. R. (1985, April). *Infant effects in context: The mother–father–infant triad.* Paper presented at the Society for Research in Child Development, Toronto.

Dickie, J. R., & Gerber, S. C. (1980). Training in social competence: The effect on mothers, fathers and infants. *Child Development, 51,* 1248-1251.

Dickie, J. R., Schuurmans, S. M., & Schang, B. (1980, September). *Mothers, fathers, infants— What makes the triad work?* Paper presented at the American Psychological Association meeting, Montreal.

Dickie, J. R., Van Gent, E., Hoogerwerf, K., Martinez, I., & Dieterman, B. (1981, April). *Mother, father, infant triad: Who affects whose satisfaction?* Paper presented at The Society for Research in Child Development, Boston.

Entwisle, D. R., & Doering, S. G. (1981). *The first birth: A family turning point.* Baltimore: The John Hopkins Press.

Feldman, S. S., & Nash, S. C. (1984). The transition from expectancy to parenthood: Impact of the first born child on men and women. *Sex Roles, 11,* 61–78.

Feldman, S. S., Nash, S. C., Aschenbrenner, B. G. (1983). Antecedents of fathering. *Child Development, 54,* 1628–1636.

Frank, E., Anderson, C., & Rubenstein, D. (1980). Marital role ideals and perception of marital role behavior in distressed and non-distressed couples. *Journal of Marital and Family Therapy, 6,* 55–63.

Gilligan, C. (1982). *In a different voice.* Cambridge, MA: Harvard University Press.

Grossman, F., Eichler, L., & Winickoff, S. (1980). *Pregnancy, birth, and parenthood.* San Francisco: Jossey-Bass.

Gutmann, D. (1975). Parenthood: Key to the comparative psychology of the life-cycle? In N. Daton & L. Ginsberg (Eds.), *Life-span developmental psychology* (pp. 167–184). New York: Academic Press.

Hobbs, D. (1968). Transition to parenthood: A replication and an extension. *Journal of Marriage and Family, 30,* 413–417.

Hobbs, D., & Cole, S. (1976). Transition to parenthood: A decade replication. *Journal of Marriage and Family, 38,* 723–31.

Hoffman, L. W. (1977). Changes in family roles, socialization and sex differences. *American Psychologist, 32,* 644–658.

Hoffman, L. W. (1978). Effects of the first child on woman's role. In W. Miller & L. Newman (Eds.), *The first child and family formation* (pp. 340–367). Chapel Hill, NC: Carolina Population Center.

Hoffman, M. L. (1981). The role of the father in moral internalization. In M. E. Lamb (Ed.), *The role of the father in child development* (2nd ed., pp. 359–378). New York: Wiley.

Lamb, M. E. (1976). *The role of the father in child development.* New York: Wiley.

Lamb, M. E. (1981). Fathers and child development: An integrative overview. In M. E. Lamb (Ed.), *The role of the father in child development* (2nd ed., pp. 1–70). New York: Wiley.

Levine, J. A., Pleck, J. H., & Lamb, M. E. (1983). The fatherhood project. In M. E. Lamb & A. Sagi (Eds.), *Fatherhood and family policy* (pp. 101–111). Hillsdale, NJ: Lawrence Erlbaum Associates.

Lewis, M., & Rosenblum, L. A. (1974). *The effect of the infant on its caregiver.* New York: Wiley.

Lewis, M., & Weinraub, M. (1976). The father's role in the child's social network. In M. E. Lamb (Ed.), *The role of the father in child development* (pp. 157–184). New York: Wiley.

Lytton, H. (1971). Observation studies of parent-child interaction: A methodological review. *Child Development, 42,* 651–684.

Myers, B. J. (1980, April). *Fathers and mothers of newborns: An intervention to improve parenting.* Paper presented at the Southeastern conference on human development, Alexandria, VA.

Parke, R. D. (1979). Perspectives on father-infant interaction. In J. Osofsky (Ed.), *The handbook of infant development* (pp. 549–590). New York: Wiley.

Parke, R. D., Hymel, S., Power, T. G., & Tinsley, B. R. (1980). Fathers and Risk: A hospital based model of intervention. In D. B. Sawin, R. C. Haskins, L. O. Walker, & J. A. Penticuff (Eds.), *Psychosocial risks in infant-environment transactions* (pp. 174–189). New York: Bruner/Mazel.

Pedersen, F. A. (1981). Father influences in a family context. In M. E. Lamb (Ed.), *The role of the father in child development* (2nd ed., pp. 295–317). New York: Wiley.

Pedersen, F. A., Zaslow, M. J., Cain, R. L., & Anderson, B. J. (1980, April). *Caesarean childbirth: The importance of a family perspective.* Paper presented at the International Conference on Infant Studies, New Haven, CT.

Radin, N. (1981). The role of the father in cognitive, academic and intellectual development. In M. E. Lamb (Ed.), *The role of the father in child development* (2nd ed., pp. 379–427). New York: Wiley.

Russell, C. (1974). Transition to parenthood: Problems and gratifications. *Journal of Marriage and the Family, 36,* 294–302.

Sagi, A., & Sharon, N. (1983). Costs and benefits of increased paternal involvement in child rearing: The societal perspective. In M. E. Lamb & A. Sagi (Eds.), *Fatherhood and family policy* (pp. 219–233). Hillsdale, NJ: Laurence Erlbaum Associates.

Shereshefsky, P., & Yarrow, L. (1973). *Psychological aspects of a first pregnancy and early postnatal adaptation.* New York: Raven Press.

Spanier, G., & Lewis, R. (1980). Marital quality: A review of the seventies. *Journal of Marriage and the family, 42,* 825–839.

Thoman, E. B., Barnett, C., & Leiderman, P. H. (1971). Feeding behaviors of newborn infants as a function of parity of the mother. *Child Development, 42,* 1471–1483.

Thoman, E. B., Leiderman, P. H., & Olson, J. P. (1972). Neonate-mother interaction during breast feeding. *Developmental Psychology, 6,* 110–118.

Wandersman, L. P. (1980). The adjustment of fathers to their first baby: The role of parenting groups and marital relationship. *Birth and Family Journal, 7,* 155–161.

Weinberg, S. L., & Richardson, M. S. (1981). Dimensions of stress in early parenting. *Journal of Consulting and Clinical Psychology, 49,* 686–693.

Wente, A., & Crockenberg, S. (1976). Transition to parenthood: Lamaze preparation, adjustment difficulty and the husband-wife relationship. *Family Coordinator, 24,* 351–357.

Yarrow, L. J., MacTurk, R. H., Vietze, P. M., McCarthy, M. E., Klein, R. P., & McQuiston, S. (1984). Developmental course of parental stimulation and its relationship to mastery motivation during infancy. *Developmental Psychology, 20,* 492–503.

Yarrow, L., Rubenstein, J., & Pedersen, F. (1975). *Infant and environment.* New York: Wiley.

Zaslow, M. J., Pedersen, F. A., Kramer, E., & Cain, R. L. (1981, April). *"Postpartum depression" in new fathers.* Paper presented at the meeting of the Society for Research in Child Development, Boston.

Zelazo, P. R., Kotelchuck, M., Barber, L., & David, J. (1977, March). *Fathers and sons: An experimental facilitation of attachment behaviors.* Paper presented at the biennial meeting of the Society for Research in Child Development, New Orleans.

Men's Involvement in Parenthood:
Identifying the Antecedents and Understanding the Barriers

Carolyn Pape Cowan
Philip A. Cowan
University of California, Berkeley

In his review of research on the role of the father, Nash (1965) pointed out that Carmichael's (1954) comprehensive *Manual of Child Psychology* failed to list "father" in the index. As recently as 1975, Lamb described fathers as "the forgotten contributors to child development" (p. 245). It has taken several decades of research to establish empirically that men can be competent caretakers of newborns (Lamb, 1975; Parke, 1979; Parke & Sawin, 1975), that at least some are centrally involved in the rearing of their children (Pruett, 1983, 1984; Radin & Russell, 1982), and that fathers have distinct positive effects on their children's development (Clarke-Stewart, 1977; Lamb, 1981; Yogman, 1982, 1983).

Although both men and women increasingly support the idea of more equal participation in the day-to-day business of family making (Araji, 1977), and there is some evidence of slightly increased participation by fathers in the care of their children (Pleck, 1981), an impressive array of studies documents the fact that behavioral change has not kept pace with the shift in ideology. Regardless of whether couples are living together or married, or whether one or both partners work full time, women still retain the primary responsibility for household tasks and childcare (Pleck & Rustad, 1980; Robinson, 1977; Stafford, Backman, & Dibona, 1977; Szinovacz, 1977).

Within these larger trends, however, men differ in the extent of their participation in family life. Several researchers have begun to explore what it is that leads some men to become happily involved in the care of their children, some to become active but less satisfied fathers, and others to participate only infrequently in looking after their children's needs (e.g.,

Barnett & Baruch, 1983; Feldman, Nash, & Aschenbrenner, 1983; Palkovitz, 1984). We address this complex question using both quantitative and qualitative data from our longitudinal study of couples becoming families in the 1980s. We show how contemporary fathers fight an uphill battle against their socialization history, societal constraints, and complex dynamics within the couple relationship that both encourage and discourage their participation in childrearing. The unifying theme of the chapter is that although the father's role has usually been narrowly defined as a relationship between men and their children, how involved men become in that relationship and how stressed or satisfied they feel in the early years of parenthood depends on what is happening in many aspects of life within and outside the family.

A FIVE-DOMAIN MODEL OF FAMILY STRUCTURE

Until recently, there has been little theoretical rationale for the choice of variables in studies of the transition to parenthood. A few researchers have been attempting to construct a limited number of categories to define the universe from which they select their measures (Belsky, 1981, 1984; Feldman, this volume; Fisher, Kokes, Ransom, Phillips, & Rudd, 1985; Grossman, Eichler, & Winickoff, 1980; Heinicke, 1984; Parke & Tinsley, 1982). We have argued that regardless of how the variables are ultimately grouped, they focus on five domains of the family system (Cowan et al., 1985).

1. the characteristics of each individual in the family;
2. the husband–wife relationship;
3. the parent–child relationships;
4. the relation between the nuclear family and the family of origin (the intergenerational view); and
5. the balance between external sources of stress and support, including social networks and jobs/careers.

As shown in Fig. 7.1, each domain focuses on a different level of analysis of variables within the family system or between the family and other social systems. In prior research, domains that we see as central have been included within other categories and not given the emphasis that is their due. Variables describing the couple relationship, for example, have been hidden in the general category of "mothers' social support." Important family of origin influences have been lost within the category of "social networks." Although our diagram has some similarity with those of Belsky (1984) and Parke and Tinsley (1982; Tinsley & Parke, 1984), it differs in its representation of parents as separate individuals who have separate relationships with the child and with important people and institutions outside the nuclear family.

FIG. 7.1   A model of family structure during the transition to parenthood.

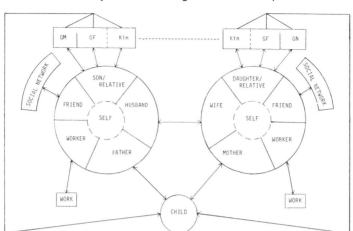

Figure 7.1 reflects our assumption that the couple relationship functions as a mediator, shaping the impact of changes in all domains on every individual and relationship in the family. A father who experiences a dip in his self-esteem, for example, may find that his relationship with his wife feels more tense, which, in turn, can affect his relationships at work, with his parents, or with his new baby. Tensions in his relationship with the child can reverberate in the marriage and lead to increased stress at work. We argue that the impact of negative events in any domain can disrupt the marital relationship, and affect men's feelings about themselves, their relationships with other family members, and those outside the family. Because each domain refers to a different level of the family system and because our data demonstrate the interconnections among domains (C. P. Cowan & P. A. Cowan, in press; P. A. Cowan & C. P. Cowan, in press; Cowan et al., 1985), we have come to think of Fig. 7.1 as a structural model for looking at the family in transition. Because men and women change in different ways as they become parents (see the following), the husband–wife relationship almost inevitably enters a period of disequilibrium. As partners' attempt to cope with change in the family structure, then, they often experience alterations in the dynamics of their relationship as a couple. We argue that both structural and process models are necessary for us to understand individual and couple adaptation during this major adult shift from partners to parents.

Application of the Model to Father Involvement

An examination of previous research indicates that antecedents of father involvement can be found in each of the domains outlined in our model.

Individual Characteristics.   Gamble and Belsky (cited in Yogman, 1983) suggest that fathers with higher self-esteem tend to be more involved in childcare in the early infant period. Russell (1978) found that fathers who described themselves as more instrumental were more likely to share childrearing tasks, whereas Palkovitz (1984) found that men who were more instrumental and expressive (i.e., more androgynous) were more involved with their young infants. Barnett and Baruch (1983) used the same instrument as Palkovitz in investigating fathers' involvement in the care of their kindergarteners and fourth graders: They reported that androgyny was unrelated to fathers' participation. Clearly, the data are not entirely consistent but they demonstrate that self-reported personality characteristics of fathers are often associated with men's participation in the rearing of their young children. The correlations, of course, do not establish whether men's personality characteristics are antecedents of their involvement in the care of their children.

Marital Quality.   Feldman, Nash, and Aschenbrenner (1983) followed 30 middle- and upper middle-class couples from late pregnancy through the first 6–8 months postpartum and found that fathers with higher marital satisfaction were more involved with their children. Yogman (1983) also found that men with more positive marital relationships were more involved with their infants. A dissenting note has been sounded by Crouter and Huston (1985) in a study of rural dual-earner families. They reported that the more husbands loved their wives, the less they tended to be involved with their young children. These authors speculated that children might be perceived as an intrusion on more cohesive marital relationships. Although Crouter and Huston's data come from a longitudinal study, the results reported in their paper focused on concurrent postpartum correlations. Feldman and her colleagues examined fathers' involvement and satisfaction by following families through the transition to parenthood and obtaining marital data predating the arrival of the baby. It is interesting that Feldman et al.'s (1983) conclusion about the link between the quality of couple relationships and fathers' involvement is the strongest of all. "The quality of the marital dyad, whether reported by husband or wife, is the one most consistently powerful predictor of paternal involvement and satisfaction" (p. 1634). This is a specific example of Grossman et al.'s (1980) general finding that marital satisfaction is linked to many indices of individual satisfaction and adaptation for men and women, and to their adaptation in the relationship with their young children.

One direct way in which the husband-wife relationship can influence father participation is through the wife's support of her husband as an active parent. Barnett and Baruch (1983) found that the more wives endorsed a nontraditional role for men, the more their husbands were involved in childcare. Similarly, Strassberg (1978) found that fathers with higher levels of participation in childrearing perceived their wives to be more supportive of that involvement.

Parent-Child Relationships. Palkovitz (1984) focused on men's parenting ideology and found that men who believed that a father's involvement was important to his child's development tended to become more involved with their own children. Although several recent investigators have predicted that previous experience with children would be related to increased involvement, no such connections have been found. The hypothesis that fathers might be more involved with sons than with daughters has been supported in some studies (Lamb, 1978; Parke, 1979) but not in all (Russell, 1983).

The Three-Generational View. Do men's own childhood experiences shape their disposition to become involved in childcare? Social learning and role theories (Bandura & Walters, 1963; Sarbin & Allen, 1968) imply that fathers will tend to imitate the patterns they observed in their family of origin. Psychodynamic theories rely on the construct of identification to explain the same phenomenon; in addition, they suggest a compensatory pattern in which fathers attempt to make up for a perceived lack of nurturance in their growing up years by trying to create a more positive family experience for their children (e.g., Herzog, 1979). Barnett and Baruch's (1983) findings support the compensatory view. The lower the emotional quality of a father's relationship with his own father, the higher his level of participation with his preadolescent child. Radin and Goldsmith's findings (1983) showed similar trends for father-son but not father-daughter relationships.

Outside the Family. We are not aware of studies of the impact of social support on father involvement, but there have been a number of studies examining the relationship between men's and women's work and their child-care arrangements. The findings generally indicate that men's participation in childcare increases slightly when their wives work outside the home (e.g., Barnett & Baruch, 1983; Pleck, 1981) and that this effect is more visible when the children are under 3 years old (Russell, 1982). When men themselves spend more hours at work (Russell, 1983) or are more psychologically involved in their jobs (Feldman et al., 1983), they tend to spend less time with their children.

Because investigators use different methods and measures, we should expect to find contradictory findings in this area of research. Nevertheless, the data from existing studies suggest that events in each domain of family life are correlated with how much men participate in the rearing of their children. Longitudinal data collected before the birth of the child can help us determine which of the correlates function as antecedents and which are consequents of father involvement. Our model suggests that combining information from the domains may lead to a more complete picture of how father involvement emerges. Our expectation is that the extent to which fathers participate in the care of their children is not solely a function of men's personality characteristics or even an outgrowth of their actual relationships with their children. Rather, father involvement evolves from a matrix of influences that begin to exert their effects in the family of origin and continue to affect men throughout pregnancy and the early years of childrearing.

BECOMING A FAMILY PROJECT

Our longitudinal research and intervention study has three primary goals: (a) to assess the impact of the transition to first-time parenthood on men, women, and marriage; (b) to assess the effectiveness of a preventive intervention on couples' adjustment to parenthood; and (c) to examine the impact of couple relationship quality on the development of young children. When the study began, 72 couples were expecting their first child and 24 couples had not yet decided whether to have children. They were recruited with the help of a number of obstetrician/gynecologists in private practice and one Health Maintenance Organization, and with announcements in several community newsletters in the greater San Francisco Bay Area. All were invited to participate in a study of how contemporary couples think about, arrange, and experience their lives during the period of family formation. We told spouses that we wanted to understand more about how contemporary couples go about becoming families. We wanted to know more about how they handled the stresses of this major adult transition and how couples who felt they were doing well and not so well managed their lives.

At the beginning of the study, the participants ranged in age from 21 to 49, with a mean age of 30.5 years for the men and 29 years for the women. Partners had been living together from 8 months to 12 years, with an average of 4.8 years; the majority were married. They live in 28 Bay Area communities and represent a wide range of socioeconomic status (SES) and income from working class to upper middle class. Approximately 15% of the participants are black, Asian-American, and Hispanic, and 85% are Caucasian. In the first 2 years of their child's life 54% of the mothers were employed outside the home. Of the employed mothers 67% were working half time when the child was 6 months old, and 50% were working half time when the child was 18 months old. Prior to an initial 2-hour interview with one of three staff couples, the expectant couples were randomly assigned to one of three conditions; couples who had not yet decided about having children comprised a fourth condition.

I. Intervention Group. After the initial interview and the completion of a battery of questionnaires focused on the five domains of family life represented in Fig. 7.1, the 24 couples in the Intervention condition began meeting weekly in small couples groups from late pregnancy until the babies reached about 3 months of age—6 months of meetings in all. The groups were co-led by couples trained to help partners focus on their experiences as individuals and as partners while they moved from couple to family life. We mention the intervention and its effects on the participants only briefly; this aspect of the study has been described in detail elsewhere (C. P. Cowan, in press; C. P. Cowan & P. A. Cowan, 1987).

II. Nonintervention Group. Another set of 24 couples was interviewed and completed the questionnaires about their individual and marital lives at the same times as those in the Intervention Group, but they did not participate in a couples group. These couples are referred to as the Nonintervention parents.

III. Postnatal Control Group. A third set of 24 couples completed the questionnaires only after birth. They served as a control for the assessments in late pregnancy, which participants in our pilot study (Cowan, Cowan, Coie, & Coie, 1978) described as an intervention in itself. Because we are most concerned in this chapter with predictability from pregnancy to 18 months postpartum, data from these couples are not included in this report.

IV. Nonparent Control Group. Finally, 24 couples who had not yet decided whether to become parents were recruited from the same sources as the expectant parents. None of these couples was experiencing fertility problems or had chosen medical procedures to make parenthood impossible (vasectomies or tubal ligations). Followed over the same length of time, the Nonparent couples served as a comparison group to evaluate changes in couples making the transition to parenthood.

The findings we report here are from 62 couples—47 of the initial 48 in conditions I and II followed from pregnancy until the children were 18 months old, and 15 of the original 24 nonparent couples who remained childless over the same period of time.

Change and Consistency
in Men, Women, and Marriage

Change.   Our longitudinal findings support previous cross-sectional research on women's transition to parenthood and document the fact that this period is equally disequilibrating for men. From pregnancy to 6 months after birth, marital satisfaction scores (Locke & Wallace, 1959) in new parents declined significantly, with another drop from 6 to 18 months postpartum. Assessments of the nonparent couples over a comparable period revealed essentially stable marital satisfaction scores. Clearly, then, declining satisfaction with marriage is associated with the arrival of a first child—for both men and women. What is it about becoming a parent that leads to this widely reported finding?

We have shown (C. P. Cowan & P. A. Cowan, 1987; P. A. Cowan & C. P. Cowan, in press; Cowan et al., 1985) that between pregnancy and 18 months postpartum there are major changes in men, women, and marriage. Many of these changes are unexpected or negative in all five domains of family life: parents' sense of self, marital roles and communication patterns, parent–child relationships, three-generation relationships, and life stress and social support. Among our findings are:

- On an instrument called "The Pie," men and women divided a circle to represent how large each aspect of themselves felt, not how much time they spent in each role. Men's and women's sense of self as "parent" increased from pregnancy to 18 months after birth while "partner" or "lover" aspects of self decreased.
- New parents adopted more traditional divisions of family labor than they described in pregnancy—more gender-linked than either spouse expected. Partners reported being less satisfied with their mutual role arrangements once they became parents.
- Marital conflict increased for 92% of the couples. Both men and women felt more distance in the marriage and described negative changes in their sexual relationship.
- Although there were no systematic changes in their permissive-protective and child-centered parenting attitudes, men who were not in our Intervention groups adopted more authoritarian and control-ling attitudes toward their children during the pregnancy-to-parenthood transition.
- Spouses' relationships with their parents became more salient and often more stressful; some were dramatically renegotiated.
- Both mothers and fathers reported initial increases, then declines in support from friends and family.
- Although men tended to increase their work involvement, women

reduced their employment drastically. Eighteen months after childbirth, 48% of the women, compared with 92% of the men, were working between half and full time outside the home.

These changes in the lives of new parents were a contrast to the stability or positive change reported by childless couples over the same period of time.

Consistency.   Although both individuals and couples showed substantial shifts over the transition to parenthood, we found, as Belsky (1984) did, a great deal of consistency in individual differences over time. It was possible to predict adaptation and distress at the 18-month follow-up from data obtained almost 2 years earlier during pregnancy. Test–retest correlations for self-esteem, role satisfaction, amount of conflict and disagreement, and marital satisfaction ranged from .31 to .83. Parents' self-reported symptoms of depression on the Center for the Epidemiological Study of Depression Scale (CES-D; Radloff, 1977) 18 months after giving birth were predictable from multiple regression equations using pregnancy data (R = .61 to .75). We also see that fathers' involvement, satisfaction, and parenting stress at 18 months postpartum are related to their satisfaction with themselves and their marriage before the baby's birth.

These findings suggest that it is possible to identify individuals and couples who are at risk for distress in the early period of family formation: Those who reported more difficulty after the birth of their first child tended to be those reporting more distress or dissatisfaction before the baby arrived. In other words, although babies trigger changes in their parents, they do not appear to create dysfunction where it was not present before. The findings reinforce our conviction that preventive interventions focusing on couple relationships might profitably be directed to the period before children become a focus of family life.

His and Her Transitions

Like "his and her marriages" described by Bernard (1974), our data suggest "his and her transitions to parenthood" (Cowan, et al., 1985). There were significant male–female differences in the timing of marital satisfaction changes. Overall, new mothers showed their largest decline from pregnancy to 6 months postpartum, whereas men's views of the marriage revealed no significant change over that time. Fathers' precipitous drop in marital satisfaction occurred between 6 and 18 months after the birth of their first child. Because all but one of the recent longitudinal studies of becoming a family end during the first year after birth, the negative impact of becoming a father on men's perceptions of marriage has probably been underestimated.

During the period of becoming a family, new fathers and mothers became increasingly dissimilar in self-descriptions, roles, and perceptions of their mutual lives, usually in the direction of increased gender stereotyping. Because this trend was not evident for the childless couples, we can be reasonably confident in attributing the gender differentiation over this period of time to the circumstances associated with the birth of a first child. Furthermore, for couples making the transition to parenthood, it was gender differentiation, rather than change per se, that was associated with difficulties in the marriage. The more different husbands and wives became from one another between pregnancy and 6 months after birth, and the greater their increase in conflict, the greater their decline in marital satisfaction from pregnancy to 18 months postpartum.

In summary, as men are becoming fathers, they and their wives are changing in different ways, and the "passing of ships in the night" feeling that many partners describe tends to put a strain on their marriage. These findings provide a context for understanding what leads men to become involved in the care of their young children, what supports their role as active parents, and what limits their participation in childrearing.

FATHER INVOLVEMENT, SATISFACTION, AND STRESS

Measures

In our study, the main measures of father involvement and satisfaction come from a self-report instrument called "Who Does What?" created for the study. (Cowan et al., 1978), and a questionnaire developed by William Coysh (1983) about men's early models of fathering, prior experiences with young children, and involvement in the care of their 18-month-olds. The data reported in this section come from the subsample of fathers in Coysh's dissertation study and from all the fathers in the larger study.

At each assessment period, both parents filled out the 36-item *Who Does What?* scale: three subscales of 12 items each ask partners to describe the couple's division of household tasks, family decisions, and child-related tasks. Each item is described on a scale from 1 ("she does it all"), through 5 ("we share this about equally"), to 9 ("he does it all"). Each partner indicates "how it is now" and "how I'd like it to be" for each item at each time period. Father involvement is the average of scores from the 12 items describing typical activities of caring for children like feeding, changing diapers, playing, and taking the baby to the doctor. During pregnancy, ratings of child-related tasks were "how I expect it will be" and "how I'd like it to be."

We should emphasize that we are reporting on a relative measure of father involvement—how much he does of the total amount of being with, playing with, and looking after the baby. From Coysh's (1983) study of our sample, we know that in absolute terms, the average amount of time fathers spent in child-related tasks was 26 hours a week, compared to mothers' average of 121 hours. Thus, even when we refer to some fathers as more involved relative to other men in the study, it is clear that fathers were substantially less involved in childcare than mothers in almost every case.

A check on the potential bias of self-reported role arrangements is the correspondence between husbands' and wives' ratings. Although each partner gave him or herself somewhat higher ratings of involvement than the spouse did, correlations between spouses' ratings of their expectations or actual arrangements were quite high: $r = .75$ in pregnancy; $r = .79$ at 6 months postpartum; and $r = .80$ at 18 months postpartum.

We created two indices of satisfaction with the division of childrearing tasks. The first was derived from a sum of the absolute discrepancies between ratings of "how it is" and "how I'd like it to be." The second, which we will focus on in this report, was a simple rating made after filling out the child-care items in response to the question "In general, how satisfied are you with the way you and your partner divide the family tasks related to children?" Responses ranged on a 5-step scale from very satisfied, through neutral, to very dissatisfied. The correlation between the two indices at 18 months postpartum was .38 ($df = 45$; $p < .008$); although significantly associated, they reflect different aspects of men's satisfaction with their level of participation in the day to day tasks of rearing their children. The discrepancy measure may reflect how close fathers come to meeting their ideals, whereas the overall rating may provide a more direct measure of how men feel about the current arrangements.

The Parenting Stress Index (PSI; Abidin, 1980, 1981) served as our main measure of stress in the parent role. A 150-item scale assessing aspects of difficulty associated with the parent role, the child's temperament, and the parent's response to typical child behavior, the PSI differentiates known groups of stressed and non-stressed parents and is sensitive to interventions designed to help parents cope with children experiencing physical or psychological problems (Lafiosca, 1981; Zimmerman, 1979).

The Effects of Time
and the Intervention on Fathers

We have noted that at 6 months postpartum men did not become as involved in child-care tasks as they had predicted they would during pregnancy. By 18 months postpartum, however, husbands and wives reported greater participation by fathers than they had at the 6-month follow-up. There was a tendency ($p = .11$) for the men who had been in the couples group intervention to show greater increases in their involvement in child care than the men in the control group.

Six months after the birth, men who had participated in the intervention tended to be less satisfied with their involvement in child-care tasks than they had expected to be in late pregnancy. By the time their babies were 18 months old, however, their satisfaction with the division of childcare was significantly higher than it was earlier and greater than that of the Nonintervention fathers. By contrast, Nonintervention fathers showed no change in satisfaction with their involvement over time. The group discussions seemed to sensitize men to the day-to-day needs of an infant and to the gap between what they had intended to do and what they were actually doing. This dissatisfaction may have motivated their somewhat greater increases in participation from 6 to 18 months after birth.

Although total Parenting Stress scores did not show significant changes from 6 to 18 months after birth, both men and women described greater stress over time on the Child Domain subscales of the PSI. That is, as their children grew from infants to toddlers, parents described the children as more demanding and difficult and their interactions with the children as more negative. The intervention did not appear to affect parents' overall level of parenting stress.

We have described the overall impact of the intervention elsewhere (C. P. Cowan, in press; C. P. Cowan & P. A. Cowan, 1987). Here it is sufficient to note that its primary effect was not on father involvement or stress, but rather on men's and women's evaluation of their marriage—the central focus of the intervention. Parents in both Intervention and Nonintervention samples showed a decline in marital satisfaction from pregnancy to 6 months postpartum, although Intervention couples showed a more subtle decline at this 3-months post-Intervention follow-up. One year later, at 18 months postpartum, the effects of the intervention were even clearer. For men and women who had been in a couples group, satisfaction with marriage had remained stable for the year from 6 to 18 months postpartum, whereas the satisfaction of couples without the intervention had declined even more sharply than it had earlier.

When the babies were 18 months old, 16% of the original Nonparent sample and 12.5% of the parents who had not participated in the intervention had separated or divorced. All of the intervention participants remained in intact marriages. It should be clear from the findings of negative change in both of the new parent subsamples that the intervention did not prevent partners from experiencing the typical changes and strains of new parenthood. Nevertheless, participation in an ongoing couples group with trained leaders appeared to prevent those strains from having a serious negative impact on satisfaction with the overall marriage and on the intactness of the family.

"Ingredients" of Father Involvement, Satisfaction, and Parenting Stress

Our general hypothesis was that individual differences in father involvement and satisfaction can best be accounted for by a combination of variables from the family domains we have just outlined. To test this model, we constructed multiple regression equations of (a) father involvement, (b) satisfaction with involvement, and (c) parenting stress on a set of independent variables chosen from each of the domains. For each of the three target variables, we constructed a concurrent equation describing the relationship between the family domain variables and the target variables at 18 months postpartum, and a predictive equation assessing the connection between the variables assessed in late pregnancy and the target variables 21 months later.

To narrow down the choice of variables from each domain, we began with an exploratory set of simple correlations based on a partial sample of the data. Guided by these results, we entered eight variables in the concurrent regressions:

(i) perceived positive relationships in fathers' family of origin as assessed at 18 months postpartum (high cohesiveness and expressiveness and low conflict on the Family Environment Scale (Moos & Moos, 1975);

(ii) fathers' self-esteem;

(iii) fathers' participation in household (non-child-care) tasks;

(iv) fathers' satisfaction with their contributions to marital decision making (e.g., making purchases, spending leisure time, initiating lovemaking);

(v) fathers' marital satisfaction;

(vi) fathers' child-centered parenting attitudes (men's tendency to report that they would choose to meet their child's needs rather than their own when the two are in conflict);

(vii) fathers' employment (none, part-time, full-time);

(viii) mothers' employment (none, part-time, full-time).

We should note that life stress and social support did not appear to be related to father involvement and satisfaction variables, but life stress was highly correlated with parenting stress.

In the equations predicting father involvement, satisfaction, and parenting stress from pregnancy data, we eliminated men's and women's work from the regressions because there was very little variance in late pregnancy in fathers' hours and women's work patterns were in flux. In these predictive equations, we increased the focus on men's anticipated involvement in the father role by including their late pregnancy predictions of how much they would be involved in each of the 12 child-care tasks.

We chose the "backward elimination" technique to construct the multiple regression equations because it facilitated a test of our model. First, it enters into the equation all the measures that we expected would contribute to variance in the target. Then, it removes one measure at a time to assess whether the removal would significantly reduce the size of the multiple correlation. If the reduced correlation is statistically significant, the variable is retained; if not, it is eliminated (Pedhazur, 1982). The results of these analyses are summarized in Table 7.1. Beta weights describing the relative amount of variance explained are listed only when the variable was retained in the final step of the analysis. In a few cases the variable was not retained but the simple correlation was statistically significant; these are included in a separate column in the table. In our discussion of each equation we generally describe variables in the order of the domains as they are listed: family of origin (i); self (ii); couple (iii, iv, v); parent–child (vi); work (vii, viii). We comment on those that contribute most to the criterion variance as indexed by their beta weights.

Father Involvement.   Six of the eight variables entered into the multiple regression were retained by the backward elimination technique. Fathers who participated more in caring for their 18-month-olds had a slight tendency to remember the relationships in their families of origin as having been more cohesive and expressive and less conflictful. Not surprisingly, the variable with the highest beta weight was household task involvement: The more men took responsibility for household tasks the more they were involved in childcare. Men's satisfaction with the couple's decision making was the second most important contributor to variation in their involvement in caring for their children. From the parent–child domain we see that child-centered attitudes about parenting were associated with greater participation in childcare. Work patterns of both parents were also a significant part of the fatherhood picture: More involved fathers were employed fewer hours than other men, and their wives worked more hours outside the home than other women at this stage of becoming a family. The multiple R of .68 indicates that these concurrent factors account for almost half (46%) of the variance in father involvement. Neither self-esteem nor marital satisfaction were included in the final regression equation, but the simple correlation between men's satisfaction with marriage and their involvement in child care was statistically significant ($r = .21$).

It could be argued that participation in household tasks, childrearing attitudes, and parental work patterns might be consequences of decisions about father involvement, but data obtained before the babies were born suggest that this is not the case. The pattern of correlations from pregnancy to 18 months postpartum is quite similar to the concurrent correlations, suggesting that the variables listed in the table function as antecedents of

TABLE 7.1

Correlates of father involvement, satisfaction, and parenting stress:
Multiple regressions concurrent at 18 months and predictive
from the prenatal period to 18 months

	Involvement		Satisfaction		Parenting Stress	
	beta[a]	simple r	beta[a]	simple r	beta[a]	simple r
Concurrent						
i positive relationships in family of origin	.09	—	—	(.36)	—	—
ii self-esteem	—	—	—	—	-.23	—
iii participation in household tasks	.48	—	.07	—	—	—
iv satisfaction with couple decision making	.33	—	.68	—	—	—
v marital satisfaction	—	(.21)	—	(.48)	-.41	—
vi child-centered parenting attitudes	.18	—	.17	—	-.18	—
vii father's employment	-.14	—	.06	—	—	—
viii mother's employment	.29	—	.14	—	—	—
R	.68***		.72***		.68***	
R^2	.46		.51		.47	

Predictive

i	positive relationships in family of origin	.09	—	-.40
ii	self-esteem	—	.33	-.19
iii	participation in household tasks	.42	.34	—
iv	satisfaction with couple decision making	.27	.15	-.20
v	marital satisfaction	.08	.27	-.27
via	child-centered parenting attitudes	.19	.36	—
vib	predicted involvement in child care	.30	.13	-.30
R		.56**	64**	.59**
R^2		.32	.40	.35

[a]Listed beta coefficients are those that were retained in the analysis. The simple correlation coefficients listed were significant although the variables were not retained in the analysis.

*p < .01
**p < .001
***p < .0001

men's participation in childcare. Fathers who shared more of the child-care tasks at 18 months postpartum had a tendency in pregnancy to remember relationships in their family of origin as more cohesive and expressive, and lower in conflict. At that time they were already more involved in household tasks and more satisfied with couple decision making than men who later took less part in the direct care of their children. Marital satisfaction contributed a small amount to the predictive regression with a tendency for more satisfied men to be more responsible for the tasks of caring for the child. The more involved fathers-to-be were already psychologically invested in that role; they held more child-centered parenting attitudes, and they showed by their predictions on the *Who Does What?* scale that they expected to be more involved in childcare. In total, the multiple correlation of .56 accounted for 32% of the variance in father involvement at 18 months postpartum. Again, men's pre-birth self-esteem did not enter the regression as a direct predictor of father involvement.

Satisfaction With Involvement.   Our discrepancy measure of satisfaction with childrearing ("how it is" compared with "how I'd like it to be") yielded only marginally significant concurrent and predictive equations. It may be that because this measure of satisfaction is affected by variations in both actual and ideal division of labor, the task of accounting for individual differences is much more complex. The separate global rating of satisfaction with the arrangements for caring for the child, however, provides further support for our hypothesis that men's overall evaluation of their role in childcare is associated with a combination of variables from the family domains.

Note that the ingredients of men's satisfaction with their involvement with their 18-month-olds differed markedly from the ingredients of their level of involvement. By far the greatest proportion of variance in men's satisfaction with the couple's division of child-care tasks was accounted for by their satisfaction with couple decision making. In addition, there were small amounts of variance attributable to men's participation in household tasks, their child-centered parenting attitudes, and both their own and their wives' employment ($R = .72$; R = squared = .51). Neither self-esteem nor marital satisfaction remained in the multiple regression equation but both showed substantial simple correlations with men's satisfaction with childcare ($r = .36$ and .48 respectively).

Fathers' satisfaction with involvement at 18 months was predictable from a cluster of measures obtained in pregnancy. Men who were later satisfied with their role in the care of their children had higher self-esteem before the birth, had participated more in household tasks, and tended to have greater satisfaction with couple decision making and the overall marital relationship, held more child-centered parenting attitudes, and predicted greater involvement in childrearing. The predictive equation accounted for 40% of the variance in later satisfaction ratings. Although correlations do not establish the direction of influence between self- or marital variables and men's evaluation of involvement with their children, we can argue from a comparison of the predictive and concurrent regression equations that men's feelings about themselves, their marriage, and their role as fathers preceeded their feelings about their role in caring for their children.

Parenting Stress.   Fathers who described themselves as experiencing more difficulty in the parent role at 18 months postpartum described their families of origin as less cohesive, less warm, and more conflictful, had lower self-esteem, and were more dissatisfied with their marriages. These variables all contributed substantially to the equation. In addition, they tended to report less child-centered attitudes about parenting. This combination of variables produced a multiple R of .68, accounting for 47% of the variance in fathers' parenting stress.

Here again, the predictive regressions help us to determine the antecedents of fathers' parenting stress: less positive relationships in the family of origin, lower self-esteem, lower satisfaction with couple decision making and the overall marriage, and less predicted involvement in caring for their children. Pregnancy variables combined to predict 35% of the variance in parenting stress in fathers of 18-month-old children.

Connections Among Outcome Variables.   Although the concurrent correlations at 18 months postpartum indicate that fathers who were more involved in caring for their children were more satisfied with that role, ($r = .38$; $p < .004$), amount of involvement and level of satisfaction were not directly related to the amount of stress men reported in their role as parents. Yet, the data obtained 1 year earlier at the 6-month postpartum follow-up reveal that in the early months of new parenthood, more involved fathers were not only more satisfied with their participation ($r = .47$; $p < .001$), but they tended to have lower parenting stress ($r = .26$; $p < .05$). It may be that once the first few months of parenthood have passed, men's experience of stress in the parent role becomes less connected with how involved they are in caring for their children and linked more with their stress or satisfaction with other family domains.

Implications of the Multiple Regressions

The most notable fact in Table 7.1 is that the multiple regression equations for involvement, satisfaction, and parenting stress differ considerably. The "ingredients" of father involvement appear to be located in a cluster of variables defining psychological investment in home and family tasks, satisfaction with couple decision making, and couple work patterns. Men who are less involved in the care of their young children are less involved in household tasks and less satisfied with the couple's pattern of making decisions. These fathers are employed more hours and their wives are involved in paid work fewer hours than more involved fathers.

Men's satisfaction with the division of child-care tasks is most strongly related to their satisfaction with couple decision making. Men's marital satisfaction and self-esteem are correlates of their child-care satisfaction, but appear to be eliminated from the regression equation because they are redundant with the couple decision-making variable. The men who were later happier with their participation in the care of their children, had tended before the birth to have higher self-esteem, more child-centered attitudes about parenting, and expectations of greater involvement in their children's care.

As is the case in men's satisfaction with their role as a parent, their parenting stress appears to be associated more with evaluations of themselves and their marriage (at 18 months postpartum) than with their own work patterns or child-centered attitudes. Less cohesion in the family of origin, especially as perceived in pregnancy, appears to be an ingredient of the strain fathers experience in their relationships with their young children. Unlike some of the studies cited previously, we find that earlier relationships in the family of origin appear to have a direct rather than compensatory connection to the fatherhood experience. Perhaps if we assessed the quality of mother–child and father–child relationships in the family of origin separately, we might have found more evidence for our observation that many men wanted to establish better relationships with their children than they had with their father when they were growing up.

Although the domains we have assessed do not always enter significantly into every regression equation, our model (Fig. 7.1) receives a substantial amount of support when we look at the three outcome variables in this study. Concurrent multiple correlations range between .68 and .72, accounting for almost half of the variance in the criterion measures. Although predictive multiple correlations were lower, ranging from .56 to .63, it is impressive to account for 30% to 40% of the variance in outcome measures using data obtained 2 years earlier. A combination of variables from several domains always accounts for more of the variance in outcome than any domain taken singly, and all five domains contribute significantly and meaningfully to variation in one or more aspects of the father's role with his 18-month-old.

What is not fully revealed in these quantitative data is the central role that we feel the couple relationship plays in shaping the nature of a man's relationship with his child. Although marital satisfaction was not included in the concurrent regression for father involvement and only marginally contributory to the predictive regression, it was an important predictor and concurrent correlate of men's child-care satisfaction and the best correlate of men's stress in the parent role. These findings can be interpreted in several ways:

1. It is possible that the state of the marriage is not a central determinant of the extent to which fathers participate in child-care tasks, although given other data, this conclusion seems unlikely. A simple correlation indicated that marital satisfaction showed a low but statistically significant association with father involvement. Thus, the multiple regression analysis may be creating a misleading impression. In the process of identifying combinations of measures that account for variance in the criterion, the regression strategy casts out those that are "redundant." In this case, marital satisfaction may have been excluded because it did not explain more variance in the criterion than the other variables already included in the regression.

2. Other marital variables (sharing of household tasks and satisfaction with couple decision making) were ingredients of father involvement. Thus, even if marital satisfaction is not a major ingredient of father involvement, the quality of the marital relationship as it plays out in the division of labor and decisions is a central correlate of fathers' participation in child-care tasks.

3. It is possible that marital satisfaction is an indirect ingredient of father involvement through its statistically significant correlations with other measures of the marital relationship (e.g., sharing of household tasks) and with variables in the other domains (e.g., self-esteem). This speculation will be examined in future quantitative analyses as we develop and test path models of the correlations in our data set. For now, we focus on the qualitative data from our interviews and meetings with groups of couples in the Intervention that lend support to our hypothesis that the couple relationship functions as a mediator of father involvement through its effect on events in each domain of the family system.

4. We have not yet completed analysis of partners' patterns as a couple as they affect the father's role. One hint comes from the finding that men are more involved when they work less and their wives work more. A similar finding from *The Pie* suggests that men are more involved in childcare when their "parent" piece is larger ($r = .32$) and their wives' "parent" piece is smaller ($r = .41$).

A FAMILY SYSTEM VIEW OF SUPPORTS
AND BARRIERS TO FATHER INVOLVEMENT

Our quantitative and qualitative data point in the same direction—to the study of fathering as a family affair. Although we are not yet at the point where we can apply complex path analyses to the data, our interviews and group discussions with men and women convince us that the determinants of fathers' child-care involvement, satisfaction, and stress are not rooted solely in their inner dynamics. The role a father plays with his child emerges from a complex, circular interaction pattern in which each family domain affects and is affected by all of the others. Static pictures created with data gathered at arbitrary points in time fail to do justice to the balancing act set in motion during the transition to parenthood. First, each partner engages in an intrapersonal struggle as he or she attempts to juggle new, competing demands from various aspects of self (see Fig. 7.1). Second, husbands and wives become involved in an interpersonal balancing act as they attempt to resolve their separate intrapersonal struggles and keep their relationship as a couple alive. The process of creating these balances influences a father's involvement in the family, and his involvement, in turn, influences how each family member feels and the quality of the relationships among them (cf. Parke, 1979; Pedersen, 1980; Pedersen, Anderson & Cain, 1977).

There is an unfortunate tendency, we believe, to assume that fathers are not involved with their children because they lack motivation or because they consider their work to be more important than being with their children. This is not our impression. At each assessment period in our study, many fathers talked about their desire to be more involved with their children and their wives than they were. Some might argue that these fathers were saying what they thought we wanted to hear rather than what they wanted to be doing. We observed these men developing intense relationships with their babies. Although they were not spending nearly as much time with their sons or daughters as their wives were, most fathers were actively involved in some daily care and soothing of their babies. Like their wives, men described a sense of wonder as their infants began to discover and explore the world around them. Why were they not as active in sharing the care of their babies as they had expected to be? Our view, consistent with Russell's (1983), is that despite some support for the idea of a new definition of fatherhood, there are powerful barriers to men actually becoming equal participants in family making. Men bump up against these barriers in relationships between the generations, in the workplace, with their wives, and within themselves.

The Three-Generation Perspective.   In his study of father involvement, Coysh (1983) failed to find any correlations between men's prior experience with children or with adult models and their involvement with their own children. Nevertheless, it was clear that the quality of men's relationships with their own fathers was a powerful reference point for their own parenting plans. A few men wanted to recreate the warm childhood relationships they had experienced with their dads, but the majority were determined to be more involved with their children than their fathers had been with them. Throughout the interviews in our study, we have been moved by stories of men who experienced little warmth from their fathers in their growing up years; many are finding it difficult to be the kind of nurturant fathers that they had wanted. Recall that cohesion, expressiveness, and low conflict in the family of origin accounted for a small but significant amount of variance in fathers' involvement and a larger amount of the variance in parenting stress. Men who want to be highly involved with their children but do not have good models of the kind of family they hope to create must struggle to overcome their own early family patterns. Clearly, knowing only what one does not want to be provides little foundation for creating one's "ideal" parent. Despite the wish for compensation in the new generation, carry-over seems to account for much of what actually happens. Here is an area where the patterns of both husbands' and wives' early experiences may help us understand when generational relationship patterns begin to shift (cf. Radin, in press).

A man's parents continue to have a powerful impact on his ideology and behavior. The more men attempted to take an active role in the care of their children, the more mixed or negative feedback they reported from their own parents. Men described both amusing and painful examples of being questioned by their mothers or fathers about their role with the baby and about getting ahead in their work. To compound matters, the grandparents often directed all conversation about the baby to the child's mother. It seemed clear to us that many of the grandparents found their children's attempts to establish more egalitarian family roles a threat or implied criticism of the "old way" of family making. Because the parents in our study care very much about their parents' reactions, this intergenerational tension becomes one of the subtle barriers to fathers becoming as involved in the family as they had hoped to be.

When there was conflict between the generations, the impact of the grandparents on the development of the father's role was often determined by the state of the couple relationship. When men's or women's parents were critical of the new family unit, couples already in difficulty tended to become even more tense, which could easily trigger increased friction between the new parents and the grandparents. By contrast, when the new parents felt fairly secure in their relationship with one another, partners could usually support each other and maintain cordial relations with their parents, even if the two generations were following different patterns.

Sense of Self.   Multiple regressions and simple correlations showed that self-esteem was an ingredient of men's satisfaction and stress as parents. Especially in our couple Intervention groups, we could see how men's self-esteem and feelings of competence played a central role in the early trial-and-error arrangements they made to tend their infants. They clearly expected their wives to be competent with the babies right from the start. We were surprised at how little time fathers allowed themselves for uncertainty, and how quickly mothers tended to step in the moment their partner or the baby looked uneasy. Given men's discomfort with feeling incompetent, it took a minimum of implicit criticism or "help" for them to hand the baby back to "the expert," as many men dubbed their wives.

It became clear that men's individual feelings of competence and self-esteem were intertwined with parent–child and couple relationship issues. Coysh (1983) found that a father's involvement and satisfaction with his role as parent were highly correlated with both his rating of how competent his wife thinks he is and with her actual ratings of his competence in caring for their child. Thus, just as studies of new mothers find that the ones who feel their husbands are supportive of their new role make the best adjustment (Grossman et al., 1980), our data and observations suggest that the more men feel supported in the parent role by their wives the more they tend to stay involved in the care of their young children.

Work.   The multiple regression equations only begin to hint at the importance of parents' employment patterns for father involvement. When men work fewer hours and women work more, men tend to become more involved with their young children. But the job market in this country is structured to keep fathers at work and mothers at home while children are young. Paternity leaves, if they are offered at all, are usually short, often teasing both father and mother with a taste of what it could be like to share parenting. New fathers gave countless examples of continuing demands at work and direct disapproval if they suggested wanting to spend more time with their children. Women who returned to work part time when their children were young reported being relegated to less important projects or losing their former positions. When both partners worked outside the home, the difficulty of finding excellent and affordable childcare often drained parents' natural excitement about parenthood and increased their anxiety about leaving their children in someone else's care.

Some new data from a 1984 survey of leading industrial, financial, and service companies (Catalyst, in press) corroborate parents' impression of employers' reluctance to get involved with these serious family–work dilemmas. The Catalyst survey reports that companies rarely name leave policies in a way that men will recognize them as referring to paternity or parental leave. Of the companies surveyed, 90% had a policy of allowing men "personal leave," with the result that male employees were often unaware that they were eligible for time off to be with their children. When asked how much leave time was considered reasonable for men, 62% of the staff members surveyed replied "none" and 17% suggested a maximum of 2½ weeks. Management especially thought time off for men to parent was unreasonable.

In our study, even when fathers overcame the social pressures to work full time and cut back their hours in order to stay home more, the marked differences between men's and women's wages often placed an additional financial burden on the new family. These practical realities can be the last straw, pushing partners to assume more traditional parenting arrangements than they had originally intended (cf. Coysh, 1983).

Although we have been describing parents' work arrangements as part of an outside-the-family domain, it was evident that some central aspects of the couple relationship mediated the impact of work on family life and vice versa. First, the decisions about whether and when women would return to work, and the process by which these decisions were made, usually reflected previously established couple problem-solving patterns. As they attempted the highly stressful juggling of family and work, some couples appeared to be handling the stress without its taking a toll on their relationship; others blamed work tensions and childrearing pressures for the fact that their marriage felt like it was "on hold." To understand this complex inside- and outside-the-family dilemma requires a closer look at what goes on between partners as they tackle these family decisions.

The Dynamics of the Couple Relationship.   The tenor of contemporary scientific and popular writing on male and female roles suggests that women generally want more participation from fathers in childcare than men are willing to give. Our observations reveal a more complicated state of affairs. As they cope with the challenges of becoming a family, dynamic tensions within each parent and in the marriage tend to discourage men's active involvement in the care of their children.

New mothers are often ambivalent about their husbands becoming very involved with the baby. At a 6-month postpartum interview, one woman not yet back at work described her mixed feelings clearly: "I love seeing the closeness between him and the baby, especially since I didn't have that with my father, but if he does well at his work *and* his relationship with the baby, what's my special contribution?" Just as men are uncertain about their competence in the parent role, women find it difficult to give up their historically significant role as the main expert on childrearing.

A "marital gavotte" keeps new parents coming together and backing away from shared parenting. What we saw and talked about in our couples groups was that women who left space for their husbands to become involved with the baby—through active encouragement or through their own involvement in work outside the family—found that men took more responsibility for the care of the children. This observation is supported by the finding that men are more involved when their own "parent" aspect of self is larger, but their wives' "parent" is smaller. Men who "hung in there" despite feelings of incompetence and inadequate role models, began to feel connected to their infants, a feeling that soon had its own rewards and resulted in even more involvement with the babies. Similarly, husbands who felt support by their wives as they developed their own ways of handling the baby tended to be more involved in the care of their 18-month-olds.

The gavotte is often apparent around feeding the infant. In our part of the country, nurses and doctors seem to be emphasizing breastfeeding to the exclusion of all else; supplemental bottles are not mentioned or are frowned upon in the early postpartum period. Aware of the health benefits of breastfeeding but unaware of other important avenues for having an effect on their infants, fathers get the idea that there is little of importance they can do during the newborn period. Because holding a squalling infant before feeding, or changing a diaper after do not feel like significant contributions to childrearing to most men, many fathers feel unnecessary or pushed out of a central role with their newborns in the first weeks of parenthood. They back away and turn to their work where they know they can make a real contribution to the family's welfare. Although we are not questioning the merits of breastfeeding, we wish to illustrate how experts' advice about a practice that involves the mother's relationship with the baby may have unintended consequences for the father's relationship with the baby and with his wife.

Even when there is no unambiguous or unambivalent solution to a problem, men and women must work out a way to resolve these internal and interpersonal dilemmas. How successfully they do so can affect both partners' feelings about their relationship. Ball (1984) interviewed a subset of the couples in our study after both partners had watched a videotape of themselves discussing a current "who does what?" problem. She found that marital satisfaction was related not to whether spouses found a solution but to how they approached the problem and whether they felt understood and "on the same side of the net."

Moving from adversaries to partners is not always easy. Research by Levenson and Gottman (1983; Gottman & Levenson, 1985) indicates that there are marked gender differences in coping with conflict, especially in maritally dissatisfied couples. In these less happy couples, men tend to have more difficulty managing their arousal and tend to withdraw or "stonewall"; women are more easily able to express conflict and move on. Applying this formulation to couples making the transition to parenthood, we find an ironic twist: Spousal differences inherent in the transition generate increased marital conflict, which may be exacerbated further by men's and women's typical styles of managing their emotions as they try to resolve their disagreements. Instead of moving to the same side of the court, new fathers and mothers may find themselves facing each other across a higher and tighter net.

CONCLUSIONS

Each domain of family life that we have examined contains potential support and barriers for fathers who want to be actively involved in the care of their children. The domains are interrelated in circular fashion so that what happens to a man's self-esteem, for example, both reflects and influences the quality of his experience as a parent. Although our qualitative data provide support for our central hypothesis—that the couple relationship is the most influential domain—this must be tested more directly in our future analyses and in studies of other families.

Our study supports the view that although men and women in the 1980s are far from adopting egalitarian family roles, both fathers and mothers are predicting more sharing of childrearing than they are able to enact. In our study, couples who were able to move in the direction of shared parenting were more likely to be satisfied with themselves and their marriage. This does not imply that the more traditional arrangements in which fathers are primarily wage earners and mothers homemakers are somehow less adaptive. Fathers tend to be less involved in childcare in more traditional families, but there are not inevitable links between those arrangements and men's or women's dissatisfaction or dysfunction. The magnitude of the correlations we have found, although statistically significant, leave room for alternative paths to self-esteem and satisfaction with marriage. It is clear that there is still a range of family arrangement styles desired by contemporary couples.

Neither traditional nor egalitarian arrangements guarantee nirvana. Our observations lead us to the belief that the processes by which partners work out their division of family labor (Cowan & Cowan, 1981) are even more critical to satisfaction with family life than are the actual arrangements. In our study, a number of couples have made active collaborative decisions to have more traditional family arrangements; both partners support and feel comfortable with this way of rearing their young children. Other spouses are trying to share childcare and continue careers; they report both gratification and fairly high levels of individual and marital stress. In our view, the task of researchers has only begun. What remains is to find an approach that allows us to establish family typologies that can reveal the multiple pathways to both adaptation and dysfunction in contemporary families.

The new thinking about the importance of father's role certainly has not penetrated to the general public. Most writing in the research literature and popular press continues to promote the fiction that what is primary in early child and family development occurs between mother and child. Parents take these "experts" seriously. What we focus on or omit as researchers contributes to the barriers men bump against as they try to become involved in their families. As researchers and clinicians, we cannot simply petition government and business leaders to change policies that affect families. We too have an obligation to help remove the barriers and provide more supports to make it easier for men to become as involved in their family's development as they wish to be. We do not mean to imply that men should become more involved in the lives of their children. Our data support the notion that contemporary fathers want a more central role in the rearing of their children and are more satisfied with themselves and their marriages when they find ways to be involved in rearing their children. It seems clear that research, interventions, and policies must support men and women so that they can create whatever kinds of family arrangements satisfy both partners' images of life as a family.

ACKNOWLEDGMENTS

This research was supported by NIMH grant R01 MH-31109. The authors gratefully acknowledge major contributions to the longitudinal study by Gertrude Heming, data manager, Ellen Garrett and William Coysh, Harriet Curtis-Boles and Abner J. Boles III, the other intervention group leaders, and Dena Cowan, data processing.

REFERENCES

Abidin, R. (1980). *Parent education and intervention handbook.* Springfield: Thomas.

Abidin, R. (1981). *The parenting stress index: A concurrent validity study using medical utilization data.* Unpublished manuscript, Institute of Clinical Psychology, University of Virginia.

Araji, S. K. (1977). Husbands' and wives' attitude-behavior congruence in family roles. *Journal of Marriage and the Family, 39,* 309–320.

Ball, F. L. J. (1984). *Understanding and satisfaction in marital problem solving: A hermeneutic inquiry.* Unpublished dissertation, University of California, Berkeley.

Bandura, A., & Walters, R. H. (1963). *Social learning and personality development.* New York: Holt, Rinehart & Winston.

Barnett, R. C., & Baruch, G. K. (1983, August). *Determinants of fathers' participation in family work.* Paper presented at the meeting of the American Psychological Association, Anaheim, CA.

Belsky, J. (1981). Early human experience: A family perspective. *Developmental Psychology, 17,* 3–23.

Belsky, J. (1984). The determinants of parenting: A process model. *Child Development, 55,* 83–96.

Bernard, J. (1974). *The future of marriage.* New York: World.

Carmichael, L. (Ed.). (1954). *Manual of child psychology* (2nd ed.). New York: Wiley.

Catalyst (in press). Workplace policies: New options for fathers. In P. Bronstein & C. P. Cowan (Eds.), *Fatherhood today: Men's changing role in the family.* New York: Wiley.

Clarke-Stewart, A. (1977). *Child care in the family.* New York: Academic Press.

Cowan, C. P. (in press). Working with men becoming fathers: The impact of a couples group intervention. In P. Bronstein & C. P. Cowan (Eds.), *Fatherhood today: Men's changing role in the family.* NY: Wiley.

Cowan, C. P., & Cowan, P. A. (1981, August). *Conflicts for partners becoming parents.* Paper presented at the meeting of the American Psychological Association, Los Angeles, CA.

Cowan, C. P., & Cowan, P. A. (1987). A preventive intervention for couples becoming parents. In C. F. Z. Boukydis (Ed.), *Research on support for parents and infants in the postnatal period.* Hillsdale, NJ: Ablex.

Cowan, C. P., Cowan, P. A., Coie, L., & Coie, J. D. (1978). Becoming a family: The impact of a first child's birth on the couple's relationship. In W. B. Miller & L. F. Newman (Eds.), *The first child and family formation* (pp. 296–324). Chapel Hill, NC: Carolina Population Center.

Cowan, C. P., Cowan, P. A., Heming, G., Garrett, E., Coysh, W. S., Curtis-Boles, H., & Boles, A. J. (1985, December). Transitions to parenthood: His, hers, and theirs. *Journal of Family Issues, 4,* 451–482.

Cowan, P. A., & Cowan, C. P. (in press). Changes in marriage during the transition to parenthood: Must we blame the baby? In G. Y. Michaels & W. A. Goldberg (Eds.), *Transition to parenthood: Current theory and research.* Cambridge: Cambridge University Press.

Coysh, W. S. (1983). *Factors influencing men's roles in caring for their children and the effects of father involvement.* Doctoral dissertation, University of California, Berkeley.

Crouter, A. C., & Huston, T. L. (1985, April). *Social-psychological and contextual antecedents of fathering in dual-earner families.* Paper presented at the meeting of the Society for Research in Child Development, Toronto.

Feldman, S. S., Nash, S. C., & Aschenbrenner, B. G. (1983). Antecedents of fathering. *Child Development, 54,* 1628–1636.

Fisher, L., Kokes, R., Ransom, D. C., Phillips, S. L., & Rudd, P. (1985). Alternative strategies for creating "relational" data. *Family Process, 24,* 213–224.

Gottman, J. M., & Levenson, R. W. (1985). A valid procedure for obtaining self-report of affect in marital interaction. *Journal of consulting and clinical psychology, 53,* 151–160.

Grossman, F., Eichler, L., & Winickoff, S. (1980). *Pregnancy, birth, and parenthood.* San Francisco: Jossey-Bass.

Heinicke, C. M. (1984). Impact of prebirth personality and marital functioning on family development: A framework and suggestions for further study. *Developmental psychology, 20,* 1044–1053.

Herzog, J. (1979). Patterns of expectant fatherhood. *Dialogue, 3,* 55–65.

Lafiosca, T. (1981). *The relationship of parent stress to anxiety, approval motivation, and children's behavioral problems.* Unpublished doctoral dissertation, University of Virginia, Institute of Clinical Psychology.

Lamb, M. E. (1975). Fathers: Forgotten contributors to child development. *Human Development, 18,* 245–266.

Lamb, M. E. (1978). Influence of the child on marital quality and family interaction during the prenatal, perinatal, and infancy periods. In R. M. Lerner, & G. B. Spanier (Eds.), *Child influences on marital and family interaction: A lifespan perspective.* New York: Academic Press.

Lamb, M. E. (Ed.). (1981). *The role of the father in child development* (2nd ed.). New York: Wiley.

Levenson, R. W., & Gottman, J. M. (1983). Marital interaction: Physiological linkage and affective exchange. *Journal of Personality and Social Psychology, 45,* 587-597.

Locke, H., & Wallace, K. (1959). Short marital adjustment and prediction tests: Their reliability and validity. *Marriage and Family Living, 21,* 251-255.

Moos, R. H., & Moos, B. S. (1975). Families. In R. H. Moos (Ed.), *Evaluating correctional and community settings* (pp. 179-198). New York: Wiley.

Nash, J. (1965). The father in contemporary culture and current psychological literature. *Child Development, 36,* 261-298.

Palkovitz, R. (1984). Parental attitudes and fathers' interactions with their 5-month-old infants. *Developmental Psychology, 20,* 1054-1060.

Parke, R. D. (1979). Perspectives on father-infant interaction. In J. Osofsky (Ed.), *Handbook of infant development* (pp. 549-590). New York: Wiley.

Parke, R. D., & Sawin, D. (1975, March). *Infant characteristics and behavior as elicitors of maternal and paternal responsibility in the newborn period: Some findings, some observations, and some unresolved issues.* Paper presented at the meeting of the Society for Research in Child Development, Denver, CO.

Parke, R. D., & Tinsley, B. R. (1982). The early environment of the at-risk infant: Expanding the social context. In D. Bricker (Ed.), *Intervention with at-risk and handicapped infants: From research to application* (pp. 153-177). Baltimore: University Park.

Pedersen, F. A. (1980). *The father-infant relationship: Observational studies in the family setting.* New York: Praeger.

Pedersen, F. A., Anderson, B. J., & Cain, R. L. (1977, March). *An approach to understanding linkages between the parent-infant and spouse relationships.* Paper presented at the Society for Research in Child Development, New Orleans, LA.

Pedhazur, E. J. (1982). *Multiple regression in behavioral research: Explanation and prediction* (2nd ed.). New York: Holt, Rinehart & Winston.

Pleck, J. H. (1981, August). *Changing patterns of work and family roles.* Paper presented at the meeting of the American Psychological Association, Los Angeles.

Pleck, J. H., & Rustad, M. (1980). *Husbands' and wives' time in family work and paid work in the 1975-1976 study of time use.* Unpublished manuscript, Wellesley College Center for Research on Women, Wellesley, MA.

Pruett, K. D. (1983). Infants of primary nurturing fathers. *The Psychoanalytic Study of the Child, 38,* 257-281.

Pruett, K. D. (1984). Children of the father-mothers: Infants of primary nurturing fathers. In J. Call, F. Galenson, & K. Tyson (Eds.), *Frontiers of infant psychiatry* (Vol. 2, pp. 375-380). New York: Basic Books.

Radin, N. (in press). Primary caregiving fathers of long duration. In P. Bronstein & C. P. Cowan (Eds.), Fatherhood today: changing role in the family. N.Y.: Wiley.

Radin, N., & Goldsmith, R. (1983, April). *Predictors of father involvement in childcare.* Paper presented at the meeting of the Society for Research in Child Development, Detroit.

Radin, N., & Russell, G. (1982). The effect of fathers on child development: A consideration of traditional families and those with highly involved fathers. In M. E. Lamb & A. Sagi (Eds.), *Fatherhood and social policy* (pp. 191-218). Hillsdale, NJ: Lawrence Erlbaum Associates.

Radloff, L. (1977). Sex differences in depression: The effects of occupation and marital status. *Sex Roles, 1,* 249-265.

Robinson, J. (1977). *Changes in American's use of time: 1975-1976—a progress report.* Cleveland, OH: Communications Research Center, Cleveland State University.

Russell, G. (1978). The father role and its relation to masculinity, femininity, and androgyny. *Child Development, 49,* 1174-1181.

Russell, G. (1982). Effects of maternal employment status on fathers' involvement in child care and play. *Australian and New Zealand Journal of Sociology, 18,* 172-179.

Russell, G. (1983). *The changing role of fathers?* St. Lucian, Queensland: University of Queensland Press.

Sarbin, T. R., & Allen, V. L. (1968). Role theory. In G. Linzey & E. Aronson (Eds.), *The handbook of social psychology* (Vol. I, 2nd ed., pp. 488-567). Reading, MA: Addison Wesley.

Stafford, R., Backman, E., & Dibona, P. (1977). The division of labor among cohabiting and married couples. *Journal of Marriage and the Family, 39,* 43-57.

Strassberg, S. (1978). Paternal involvement with firstborns during infancy. *Dissertation Abstracts International, 39,* 2528B-2529B. (University Microfilms No. 7819833).

Szinovacz, M. E. (1977). Role allocation, family structure and female employment. *Journal of Marriage and the Family, 39,* 781-791.

Tinsley, B. R., & Parke, R. D. (1984). Grandparents as support and socialization agents. In M. Lewis (Ed.), *Beyond the dyad* (pp. 161-194). New York: Plenum.

Yogman, M. W. (1982). Development of the father-infant relationship. In H. Fitzgerald, B. Lester, & M. W. Yogman (Eds.), *Theory and research in behavioural pediatrics* (Vol. I, pp. 221-279). New York: Plenum.

Yogman, M. W. (1983). Competence and performance of fathers and infants. In A. Macfarlance (Ed.), *Progress in child health* (pp. 130-156). London: Churchill Livingston.

Zimmerman, J. L. (1979). *The relationship between support systems and stress in families with a handicapped child.* Unpublished doctoral dissertation, University of Virginia.

Father-Infant Caregiving and Play with Preterm and Full-Term Infants[1]

Michael W. Yogman, M.D.
*Department of Pediatrics, Harvard Medical School
and The Children's Hospital*

A father's involvement with his infant can be influenced by forces within the family, most notably, mother's wishes and the harmony of the couple's relationship, and by forces outside the family. These may be economic and employment policies or the practices of social institutions such as hospitals and schools. Stress of any kind, whether due to personal loss and the accompanying grief, job loss, or illness in the family, can have a major impact on the father. The effects may be either positive, as a catalyst for growth, or negative. The birth of a high-risk premature infant confronts the father, as well as the mother, with a major stress. This stress may have a direct facilitating or interfering effect on the father–infant relationship. It may also have an indirect effect on the infant mediated through its effect on the father's support of the mother. These effects are illustrated in Fig. 8.1.

Although the mother's support of the father's role also deserves study, this chapter restricts itself to families in which mothers are primary caregivers and the discussion focuses on fathers' support for mothers. A major coping mechanism for dealing with stress is the utilization of supports, and the father is the most readily available source of support for the mother within the family. The father's support may take four different forms: emotional support, help with caregiving tasks, financial support, and the mobilization and recruitment of additional supports and resources from the community at large.

Evidence for the stressful effect of a premature birth is suggested by data

---

[1]Portions of this chapter have appeared previously as *The Father's Role with Preterm and Fullterm Infants* by M. Yogman, 1984.

FIG. 8.1 Schematic diagram of direct and indirect effects of premature birth on father-infant relationship and infant outcome.

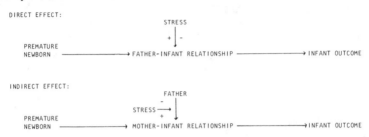

from a study in England (Jeffcoate, Humphrey, & Lloyd, 1979), in which mothers and fathers were interviewed during the first weeks after a premature birth. Both parents of premature infants reported more depression, anxiety, emotional turmoil, and difficulty caring for the baby than a matched group of parents of full-term infants. It needs to be emphasized that fathers, especially, need permission to express their feelings of fear and grief during this perinatal period because it violates the stereotype of masculinity. Zilboorg (1931) examined the interaction of psychodynamic and sociocultural influences on postpartum reactions in men and women many years ago and suggested that men are more likely than women to develop symptoms of extreme regression, psychosis, or paranoia because depression is a socially unacceptable symptom in males. According to Zilboorg, society instructs men to view passivity, impotence, and crying as a threat to their self-image. Although the social stigma of male depression may be less prevalent today, professionals working with fathers in a nursery for premature newborns may still need to view bizarre and regressive behavior as less pathological than in other situations, and as analogous to maternal depression.

Initially after a premature birth, the father often develops a primary role in decision making either because the infant has been transferred to a different hospital or because of the physical incapacity of the mother. When they visit, parents are often terrified about basic questions of survival, and fathers may focus on physiological data and laboratory values, perhaps as a way of fending off an emotional attachment to their babies before knowing anything certain about survival. Fathers may suffer a double burden in that extended family members may expect them to remain strong and even to recruit the help that will "fix" things and insure the baby's survival. However, once fathers of premature infants begin to interact with their newborns in an intensive care nursery, they do so with behaviors similar to those described for fathers of full-term infants; they respond more to newborn limb movements and talk less to the baby than mothers do (Marton, Minde, & Perrotta, 1981; Parke & Tinsley, 1982).

This chapter discusses father behavior and its effect in the context of a longitudinal study of 10 preterm and 10 full-term infants during the first 18 months of life. We were able to study father's indirect effects on the infant by helping his wife with caregiving tasks. We also studied the father's direct effects on the infant by engaging the infant in play. Help with caregiving tasks can be conceptualized as support for the mother, who typically is the primary caregiver. That is, the father's help supports the mother, thus indirectly influencing the mother's relationship with the infant. We chose to focus on this indirect effect of paternal caregiving rather than to focus on paternal caregiving and its direct impact on the infant. We also studied the direct influence of paternal play on the infant.

Father–Infant play

The role of fathers as play partners with full-term infants has been widely studied. Most research has shown that fathers spend one fourth to one third of time that mothers spend with their infants (Clarke-Stewart, 1980; Kotelchuck, 1976; Pedersen & Robson, 1969). Regardless of the amount of time spent, fathers' play with full-term infants tends to be more stimulating, vigorous, arousing, and state-disruptive (Lamb, 1977; Power & Parke, 1979; Yogman, 1981) than is the play of mothers.

In our studies of fathers' play with infants between age 2 and 5 months, father–infant dyads were filmed in our laboratory. During en-face play, fathers were instructed simply to play with their infants without using any toys and without picking the babies up (Yogman, 1982). We were specifically interested in categories of play called *games* because we felt they marked moments of shared affect and mutual delight. We operationally defined a *game* as an episode during which an adult uses a repeating set of behaviors to either engage or maintain the infant's attention in an affectively positive manner (Stern, 1974; Yogman, 1981). Using this definition, we reliably identified such episodes from en-face play, described them in a narrative form, and then categorized them, using seven categories with predetermined descriptions of the adult's activity. The seven categories included pure tactile contact, conventional and non-conventional visual behavior, conventional and non-conventional limb movement, verbal games, and combinations (Yogman, 1981).

When we compared mothers' and fathers' play with full-term infants, we found that fathers engaged their infants in tactile and limb movement games in which they attempted to arouse the infant. Mothers more commonly played visual games in which they displayed distal motor movements; these movements were observed by the infants and appeared to be attempts to maintain visual attention (Yogman, 1981). Typical paternal games were labelled by fathers as "pull to sit," "button your lip," or "three-point tapping" games.

Studies of the games parents play with 8-month-old infants show similar findings for mothers and fathers: Mothers played more distal games, whereas fathers engaged in more physical games (Power & Parke, 1979). Stern (1974) has suggested that the goal of such games is to facilitate an optimal level of arousal in the infant in order to foster the infant's attention to social signals. The more proximal games of fathers with infants may serve to modulate the infant's attention and arousal in a more accentuated fashion than occurs during the more distal games of mothers with infants. These findings are surprisingly robust in that similar findings have been replicated with different age infants in different situations.

The differences between fathers and mothers in play and the quality of vigorous stimulation persist, even in studies of primary caregiver fathers in the United States (Field, 1978; Yogman, 1982), and in studies of non-traditional fathers with paternity leave in Sweden (Frodi, Lamb, Hwang, & Frodi, 1982; Lamb, Frodi, Hwang, Frodi, & Steinberg, 1982). It is interesting to speculate that differences between maternal and paternal play may become less tied to parental gender as social institutions and sex stereotypes change along with the socialization of young children. In contrast, the performance of caregiving tasks may be relatively more modifiable and more closely related to role rather than to gender.

Influences on Later Development of Preterm Infants

Although the impact of paternal caregiving and play with preterm infants on later development has not been previously studied, the influence of maternal involvement and perinatal events has been well studied. Preterm infants are known to be at high risk for later mental and neurological disorders (Caputo, Goldstein, & Taub, 1979; Drillien, 1964; Parmelee & Haber, 1973) and families of preterms are also at risk for parenting disorders (Klaus & Kennell, 1976). However, it is also becoming increasingly apparent that most premature infants do appear to show social and cognitive competence comparable to full-term infants by the end of the first year of life (Brown & Bakeman, 1980), if caregivers can be helped to provide them with optimal care for recovery. A number of researchers have concluded that social factors have more predictive value for the child's development than do perinatal hazards (Beckwith & Cohen, 1980; Werner, Bierman, & French, 1971). An understanding of how these social variables affect future competence is critical.

Attempts to assess risk by focusing on single prenatal, perinatal, or neonatal stress factors have resulted in some significant correlations with later outcome measures, but they cannot accurately predict the outcome of individual infants (Niswander & Gordon, 1972; Parmelee & Haber, 1973;

Parmelee, Sigman, Kopp, & Haber, 1975; Sameroff & Chandler, 1975; Sigman & Parmelee, 1979). Although clustering single factors produced better correlations, individual babies' developmental course could still not be predicted (Parmelee et al., 1975; Sigman & Parmelee, 1979).

A transactional model of development seems most useful. The model takes into account the feedback system from the behavior of a particular infant to the caregiving environment, and the quality of that environment to individually care for that infant (Sameroff & Chandler, 1975). In a non-supportive environment, the behavioral repertoire of the poorly organized infant may suppress caregivers' potentially optimal behavioral patterns that are necessary to facilitate the recovery of the baby. These non-optimal caregiving patterns could then exacerbate the already disorganized and stressed baby. On the other hand, in a supportive environment that compensates for the infant's poor organization by appropriate stimulation and structuring, the at-risk infant is able to elicit caregiving behavior that, in turn, facilitates recovery and emerging organization (Als, Lester, & Brazelton, 1979). We know that as newborns, preterm infants have difficulty maintaining prolonged states of alertness and shutting out stressful stimuli (Als et al., 1979) and that, in the early months, mothers of preterm infants can be overly active and intrusive compared with mothers of full-term infants (Field, 1979a; Goldberg, 1978).

Supporting evidence for a transactional model comes from the UCLA longitudinal study (Beckworth & Cohen, 1980). In a longitudinal study following the development of preterm and full-term infants, Beckwith and Cohen measured outcome after 2 years using the Gesell and Bayley tests. The group of infants that had both severe perinatal hazards and high levels of reciprocal social interaction with their mothers scored higher than a group of infants that had suffered milder perinatal complications, but had less optimal social interaction. With some exceptions (J. L. Gaiter, personal communication, June 1, 1984; Parke, this volume) most studies that are guided by a transactional model of development have primarily investigated the mother's contributions to the caregiving environment of the premature infant. Instead, our study focuses on the father's contributions.

METHOD

Sample

Ten preterm and 10 full-term infants were seen longitudinally at 1, 3, 5, 9, and 18 months of age (corrected for gestational ages of the infants). The characteristics of the participating families, the majority of whom were white, can be seen in Table 8.1. The two groups differed on perinatal characteristics and on birth order but not on social class or other demographic characteristics. Five preterm and four full-term infants were female. Infants' age at the time of assessments were corrected for weeks of prematurity, with the date determined from the mother's expected date of delivery if the pregnancy had gone to fullterm. The behavioral measures discussed in this chapter were part of a larger project that included assessments of neonatal behavior, infant medical complications, developmental (Bayley) status, free play and home environment (Brazelton, 1982).

Measures of Caregiving Behavior.   We assessed paternal caregiving using parental questionnaires. Fathers' participation in caregiving at 1, 5, and 18 months, was assessed by means of a caregiving scale, derived from questionnaires that fathers filled out at the appropriate time postterm. The questionnaire asked fathers to record in checklist fashion their caregiving activities during the previous 2 weeks. Specifically, the father recorded how many days per week he (a) got the infant up, (b) dressed, (c) bathed, and (d) diapered the infant, (e) put the infant to bed, (f) took the infant to the doctor, (g) comforted the infant when he/she fretted, and (h) comforted the infant when he/she cried at night.

Measures of Social Play.   Our measures of father–infant play were based on laboratory observations at 5 months corrected age. Infants were videotaped in face-to-face interaction with each parent using a method developed by Brazelton, Tronick, Adamson, Als, & Wise, (1975), and Yogman (1982) for studying early social interaction. The procedure consisted of a 3-minute play episode with mother, a 3-minute still face episode, a 3-minute reunion episode with mother, followed by a 3-minute play episode with father, each separated by 30 seconds of infant alone. The infant, when alert and calm, was seated in an infant seat placed on a table surrounded by curtains. The parent entered from behind the curtain, sat in front of the infant, and was instructed to play without using toys and without removing the infant from the seat. The unstructured nature of this type of interaction is designed to place maximal demands on the social capabilities of the participants. During the interaction, one video camera focused on the infant, and the other on the parent. The two images appeared simultaneously on a split-screen monitor, which showed a single frontal view of adult and infant along with a digital time display. Sound was recorded simultaneously.

Within each interaction period we were interested in the categories of play we defined as *games* as in our earlier studies of full-term infants (Yogman, 1981). All videotapes were reviewed in order to describe the components of these games. Each episode that met the definition of a game was described in detailed narrative form. In a second step, descriptions of the games were then categorized as tactile, conventional and nonconventional limb movement, conventional and nonconventional visual, pure verbal,

TABLE 8.1
Father–Infant Games Sample Characteristics

Family Demographic Characteristics	Preterm		Full-Term		
	Mean	SD	Mean	SD	Signif.
Sex of Infant					
Male	5		4		
Female	5		6		
Birth Order					
First-Born	8		2		
Later-Born	2		8		
Hollingshead Four-Factor Index of Social Class					
I–II (Upper)	4		7		
III (Middle)	3		0		
IV–V (Lower)	3		3		
Mother's Age	27.0	4.03	29.8	3.52	
Father's Age	30.1	4.82	31.5	5.84	

Neonatal Medical and Pediatric Measures

Gestational Age (Weeks)	30.2	2.19	39.9	0.58	*
Birth Weight (Grams)	1389.5	407.65	3446.2	405.41	*
Apgar 1 Minute	5.3	3.31	8.4	0.52	*
Apgar 5 Minutes	7.5	1.51	9.2	0.42	*
Obstetric Comp. Scale (Parmelee)	67.8	12.56	123.3	11.61	*
Postnatal Comp. Scale (Parmelee)	74.2	31.07	160.0	0.00	*
Newborn Neuro. Exam (Parmelee)	15.8	6.10	17.2	2.62	
Days to Discharge	41.7	20.44	3.2	0.79	*
Pediatric Comp. Scale (Parmelee)					
At 5 Months	105.6	25.14	124.6	20.53	
At 9 Months	105.0	19.81	111.6	17.93	
At 18 Months	16.8	1.67	17.4	1.17	

*$p < 0.05$

182

and combination games according to a system devised by Crawley et al. (1978), which was modified and described in a previous study (Yogman, 1981). Behavioral interactions were then grouped into arousing and non-arousing games. *Arousing games* were defined as proximal, and included tactile and limb movement games. These were assumed to encourage a higher level of arousal in the infant than the nonarousing games. An example is moving the infant's limbs rhythmically in space. Distal games, including verbal and visual games, were assumed to maintain rather than arouse infant attention, and were labelled *nonarousing games* in contrast to the more energetic tactile or kinesthetic type. An example is the parent imitating the infant's coos. Because frequencies of specific types of games were relatively low, analysis focused on the more general categories of games: arousing and nonarousing. Combinations of types were not included in this analysis. Coding reliability was established on discrete behaviors coded as part of the original narrative descriptions and was maintained at 85% agreement for infant behaviors and 80% agreement for adult behaviors.

RESULTS

Caregiving.   Although fathers still did far less caregiving than mothers, fathers of the preterm infants reported doing more of the caregiving for each task, at each age, than the comparison group of fathers of full-term infants (Yogman, 1984). Although all fathers helped with diapering, the fathers of preterm infants were more likely to take infants to the physician, to bathe babies, and to get up at night to console them at age 18 months. The stress of premature birth appears to have encouraged fathers to provide more caregiving support to mothers. Because in this sample parity and term status overlap, future research is necessary to unravel these relationships. Not surprisingly, first-time fathers reported contributing more than other fathers did to taking care of their infants at 1 month.

Fathers' perceptions of their caregiving may not represent the actual help they provide. Therefore, we also asked mothers to rate their husbands' caretaking involvement using a similar scale, and we were able to look at the discrepancy scores between these reports for the families in which both parents completed the scales. For this comparison, the variables were made dichotomous: Fathers either helped or did not help on a regular basis during the week. Because of the small sample size for whom data are available from both parents, statistical comparisons were not performed and differences are reported descriptively.

Mothers, like fathers, also reported that fathers of preterm infants did more of the caregiving than the comparison group of fathers of full-term infants did. However, there was a larger discrepancy between mothers' and fathers' reports for the preterm group than the full-term group. Under the stress associated with premature birth, especially at 1 month, either fathers of preterms showed a tendency to overrate themselves, compared to their wives' reports, or their wives tended to underrate them. At 1 month this tendency was evident on seven of the eight items for the preterm fathers, in contrast to only two of the items for full-term fathers. However, at 5 and at 18 months there were few differences between fathers of preterm and full-term infants in discrepancies between maternal and paternal reports. There were no consistencies over time in the specific items on which parents disagreed.

In addition, we were interested in whether infants' risk status at birth influenced the father's participation in caretaking early in the infant's life. As already noted, we found that fathers of preterm infants generally rated their own caretaking higher than did fathers of full-term infants. However, we found that, within the preterm group, greater medical risk did not predict increased caretaking by fathers. The preterm group varied widely in neonatal medical risk. This was indicated by scales measuring (a) obstetrical complications, (b) postnatal complications, (c) neonatal neurological status, and (d) duration of hospitalization after birth, as well as by (e) an overall clinical rating of neonatal medical complications. These indices of perinatal risk were not related to father caretaking at 1 month.

Play.   The results presented in Table 8.2 shows that fathers of preterm infants played fewer and shorter games and fewer arousing games, than did fathers of full-term infants. Fathers and their preterm infants played an average of 0.8 games (of any type) and spent an average of 11.3 seconds in play during the 3 minutes of observation. Fathers and full-term infants played more games: An average of 1.9 games, averaging 27.7 seconds of play. Although this difference appears striking, it is not statistically significant, in part because of the small sample size, although the shorter duration of paternal play with preterm infants showed a nonsignificant trend $(= .10)$.[2]

Fathers played more arousing games with full-term than with preterm infants (an average of 1. 5 arousing games with full-terms as opposed to an average of 0.6 arousing games with preterms). This was, again, not a statistically significant difference. Fathers played very few nonarousing games in general, and the birth status of infants did not significantly affect the number of fathers' nonarousing games. Fathers showed a trend $(p < . 10)$ to play arousing games longer (with both summed duration and mean duration of each episode) with full-term infants than with preterms, and the

---

[2]Because of the small sample size and skewed distribution of the games variable, a conservative statistical test (the Kolmogarov-Smirnov test) was used. Striking differences would be required for the results to be statistically significant.

TABLE 8.2
Comparison of preterm and full-term groups on number and duration of games

| | Preterm | | | | Full-term | | | |
| | Number | | Total Duration (seconds) | | Number | | Total Duration (seconds) | |
	X̄	SD	X̄	SD	X̄	SD	X̄	SD
All games with father	0.8	1.0	11.3	14.1	1.9	2.7	27.7	40.1
Arousing games with father	0.6	1.0	6.0	11.2	1.5	1.9	20.9	27.5
Nonarousing games with father	0.2	0.42	5.3	12.0	0.3	.94	5.1	16.1
Tactile	0.4	.09	4.6	9.7	0.4	0.7	4.7	11.2
Nonconventional limb movement	0.2	.42	7.4	3.3	1.0	1.5	14.3	23.2
Conventional limb movement	0	0	0	0	0.1	0.3	1.9	6.0
Visual Non-motor	0.1	.31	1.7	5.3	0.3	0.9	5.1	16.1
Visual Conventional	0	0	0	0	0	0	0	0
Verbal	0.1	.3	3.6	11.3	0	0	0	0

length of each nonarousing game was longer with preterm infants. Fathers were less able to directly engage their preterm infants in play compared to the full-term infants. When they did, the games lasted for a shorter time, particularly if the games were arousing. The specific types of games played are listed at the bottom of Table 8.3. Tactile games were the most common games played by fathers of preterm infants although their mean frequency was only 0.4. With full-term infants, nonconventional limb movement games were most common with a mean frequency of 1.0.

Longitudinal Relationships

Father's early caregiving involvement with their infants was generally not predictive of later father–infant social interaction. In fact, there were basically zero-order correlations between fathers' early caregiving and father–infant games during the face-to-face play session at 5 months postterm. It appears that paternal involvement in engaging their infants in play is unrelated to their participation in caregiving tasks.

In our study, we also examined the relationship between infants' developmental course and fathers' involvement in play with their infants. It may be noted that the preterm infant group did have significantly lower mean Bayley scores than the full-term group at both 9 and 18 months (see Table 8.3). We first examined the simple correlations between the number of father–infant games during the lab session at 5 months and Bayley scores. In spite of the diversity of interactive play adaptations between fathers and premature infants, we found a significant association between the father's ability to engage his preterm infant in play in the 5-month sessions and the infant's developmental outcome at 9 and 18 months postterm on the Bayley Test. Table 8.4 shows the correlations. The total number of games played by fathers (as well as by both parents combined), was significantly corre-

TABLE 8.3
Bayley Scales of Infant Development

	Preterm		Fullterm		Signif.
	Mean	SD	Mean	SD	
9 Months					
MDI	103.1	9.01	120.1	8.61	*
PDI	89.9	12.06	108.0	16.79	*
18 Months					
MDI	102.0	13.83	117.0	15.22	*
PDI	90.9	22.05	109.5	13.05	*

$*p < 0.05$

lated with the Bayley Mental Development Index (MDI) at 18 months. These correlations were as high or higher than those for games with mother alone and were higher than correlations for measures of perinatal complications or a neonatal neurological assessment, which were not significant. If we consider the impact of arousing and nonarousing games separately, it becomes evident that it is the frequency of arousing games that better predicts Bayley MDI outcome at 18 months. Because correlation coefficients can be deceptive with small sample sizes, Fig. 8.2 shows a scatter plot for the number of father–infant games on the X-axis and Bayley MDI scores on the Y-axis so that one can see the relationship for the individual infants. The total duration of all games played with both parents was also significantly correlated with MDI scores at 9 and 18 months and with the Psychomotor Development Index (PDI) at 18 months, whereas the number and duration of arousing games with both parents was correlated with the MDI at 18 months.

TABLE 8.4

Correlations Between Father–Infant Games
and Bayley Mental Development Index (MDI)
and Psychomotor Development Index (PDI)†

	Bayley 9		Bayley 18	
	MDI	*PDI*	*MDI*	*PDI*
Number of Games with Both Parents	.61	.43	.77*	.58
With Father	.45	.16	.79*	.15
With Mother	.59	.45	.68	.63
Number of Arousing Games with Both Parents	.50	.15	.80*	.28
Number of Nonarousing Games with Both Parents	.55	.43	.44	.62
Duration of All Games With Both Parents	.70*	.61	.85*	.72*
Duration of Arousing Games With Both Parents	.45	.03	.77*	.15
Duration of Nonarousing Games With Both Parents	.67*	.62	.40	.80*

†From Yogman, 1984
*$p < 0.05$

FIG. 8.2   Scatter plot for preterm infants of total number of games with father at 5 months versus Bayley MDI scores at 18 months.

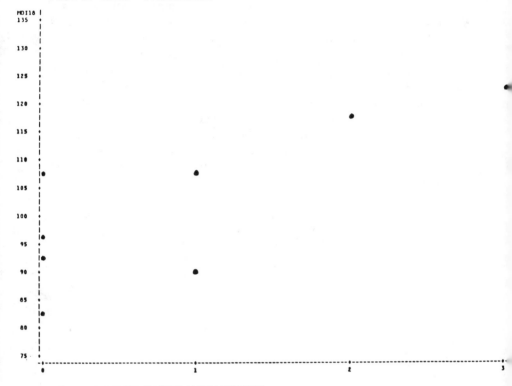

PLOT OF MDI8 = FNUMGAME

TOTAL NUMBER GAMES WITH FATHER

DISCUSSION

Paternal Caregiving

Although fathers still did far less caregiving than mothers, fathers of the preterm infants reported doing more of the caregiving for each task at each age than the comparison group of fathers of full-term infants (Yogman, 1984).

In considering the influences of the father's caregiving behavior on the mother and on the infant's development, the situation is unclear. To be effective, the father's indirect role of providing emotional and physical support for the mother must truly fit her emotional needs. Clearly, premature infants are harder to feed, console, and care for and they require more trips to the doctor for medical care. Fathers did provide more help with these tasks independently of their capacities as play partners. However, the indices of caregiving showed no association with the mother–infant relationship as assessed by our measure of mother–infant games, a measure of maternal responsivity from the Caldwell HOME scale (Bradley & Caldwell, 1976), nor any association with infant outcome on the Bayley. Without more in depth interviews with parents, we do not know which mothers truly felt emotionally supported. If the father's involvement was seen as competitive, it could have adversely influenced both the marital relationship and the infant.

Social Play. Studies of direct paternal interaction with preterm infants have produced conflicting findings, in part because of different measures, because the infants are often quite heterogeneous in medical complications and behavioral difficulty, and because parental reactions are also quite variable. In two studies of preterm infants at 3 months postterm, infants' face-to-face play with fathers and mothers was quite similar (Marton, Minde, & Perrotta, 1981; Parke & Tinsley, 1982) except for more maternal instrumental touching. A study at 4 months postterm found that fathers played more games than mothers did with their preterm infants, although fathers played with preterms less than with full-term infants (Field, 1979b). Our fathers also displayed less arousing play with preterm than full-term infants, and this may have been accentuated by the face-to-face methodology, which constrained fathers by restricting them from picking the infant up from the chair. Because of order effects, we did not compare infant play with mothers vs. fathers.

One suggested explanation of these findings is that the infant's behavior has a strong influence on the parent. For example, it is very difficult for a parent to interact with a stressed infant, an infant that has difficulty with motor activity and tone, with state regulation and hypersensitivity to stimulation. In such an instance, the tendency of many fathers to excite and vigorously stimulate their infants may stress an already vulnerable infant, interfere with social interaction, and may lead a father to feel failure and withdraw. Alternatively, a father may adapt to the baby's needs by limiting his arousing stimulation with the baby to specific periods when the baby can tolerate it.

Longitudinal Relationships
Between Social Play and the Bayley Assessments

The measure of social interaction that we used, games during en-face play, was significantly correlated with Bayley outcome assessments even though measures of obstetric and pediatric complications and a neonatal neurological exam showed no significant correlations with outcome. As noted earlier, Beckwith and Cohen (1980) have reported similar findings for social interaction between mothers and their preterm infants: Infants with higher scores for reciprocal social interactions, but severe medical complications, performed better at age 2 years than infants with lower scores for reciprocal social interaction and milder perinatal complications.

One can speculate about the path of influence reflected by the associations between father–infant play at 5 months and developmental outcome at 18 months. The games at 5 months may reflect both the degree of infant behavioral organization, such as maintenance of an alert socially responsive state for prolonged periods, and a father's sensitivity to his preterm infant's cues. The experience of social contingency and reciprocity may facilitate the infant's feelings of mastery and effectance (Tronick, Cohn, & Shea, 1986; White, 1959) and may enhance the infant's motivation and performance on the Bayley exam.

The diversity of father play with premature infants and effects on developmental outcomes may be illustrated with three case descriptions (Yogman, 1984):

Case I

Allan was the third infant born to a family with two older boys, one of whom was born prematurely. He was delivered after a 32-week uncomplicated pregnancy; and had a weight 1820 grams and had good Apgars of 7 and 7. He developed moderately severe hyaline membrane disease requiring intubation and ventilation for 5 days. He recovered rapidly, gained weight by day 10, and was discharged home after 23 days at 36 weeks post conceptional age. The father in this family was very involved, providing both emotional support for his wife and helping with caregiving. He was able to engage his baby in several arousing games at the 5-month session by waiting over a minute until the baby was ready, readjusting his infant's position in the seat, and engaging the infant in a mildly arousing arm waving game eliciting responsive smiles and vocalizations. The father seemed quite sensitive to his infant's fatigue and need for periods of time out. The infant's outcome at 9 and 18 months post term was good, as reflected in his Bayley scores. At 18 months the MDI was 117, and the PDI was 113. (p. 368)

The second case is a more severely ill infant and illustrates the difficulties faced by some fathers in making an adjustment.

Case II

Jeffrey was the first infant born to parents in their early 30s, born prematurely after a 29-week pregnancy. He weighed 1080 grams at birth. His Apgars were 1 and 7 and he was felt to be small-for-gestational age. After a prolonged neonatal hospitalization complicated by mild hyaline membrane disease and more severe apnea, this infant was discharged home at 36 weeks of age post term, weighing 1500 grams after a 52-day hospitalization. As a newborn, the baby was irritable and difficult to console. He had considerable problems with sleep, feeding, and crying in the first few weeks at home. Both parents worked at a local TV/radio station, had quite variable and unpredictable schedules, returned to work quite rapidly and were isolated from their extended families. In early interviews, the father described feeling "left out and unnecessary" and noted the presence of marital conflict. Even when the baby was a month postterm, the father still felt the baby was "a guest rather than his." In spite of these feelings, the father reported that he helped with a substantial portion of the caregiving. When the family was seen for a 5 month face-to-face session, the father interacted with the baby with continual tapping and shaking the infant's limbs in spite of the fact that the infant spent much of the interaction looking away from his father, squirming, and finally fussing and crying. At this time, the father could not adjust to the infant's need for time out, continually shifted his behavior, never allowing this labile infant to organize around a specific pattern of play, and often interacted with intrusive and overwhelming stimulation. By the time the infant was 9 months postterm, both parents were much calmer, more organized and less in conflict. They were able for the first time to discuss their previous fears about brain damage. The mother was now pregnant again, and the infant was doing better than expected on the Bayley exam. At 9 months, the MDI and PDI were each 99. This family then moved to California and no further follow-up was possible. (pp. 368–369)

The third case was one of the most severely ill infants in the study.

Case III

Alva was the first baby born to 27-year-old dual career parents. The mother had had one previous miscarriage. She delivered at 27 weeks weighing 950 grams, with Apgars of 5 and 7. She developed severe hyaline membrane disease, required ventilatory support for a week, was intubated and in high oxygen concentrations for over 6 weeks, and developed apnea as well as broncopulmonary dyspasia. She was thought to have a periventricular hemorrhage and had focal hypertonicity and hyperreflexia in her right leg. She was hospitalized over 80 days and was finally discharged home at 39 weeks post term. She also had a congenital esotropia of her left eye with strabismus that eventually required thick glasses and several operations. Needless to say, both parents were initially quite terrified. Once home, Alva had frequent periods of inconsolable crying, requiring swaddling and frequent feeding. The parents were unable to take her out and mother decided not to go back to work. Father adjusted his schedule by leaving work a bit early each day and was very involved both in providing emotional and physical support to the mother and in direct interaction with Alva. Slowly she began to gain weight. When she was seen at 5 months post term, in spite of her difficulties with vision and maintenance of truncal motor tone, father, by providing postural support, was able to engage his 8-month-old daughter by wiggling his fingers in front of her face saying, "Fingers; remember, *fingers,*" at which she would quiet and still and eventually brighten. When she began to avert her gaze, he would sensitively back off, as he had learned to respect her need for time out.

Project staff were so concerned about her motor tone after this visit that they advised the parents to work with an early intervention program. After considering this, the parents followed through and began weekly visits.

Four months later, when seen in the lab, Alva had improved dramatically and on a measure of social play she demonstrated a sense of persistence and mastery after pulling up to stand. When she turned her attention to a prohibited toy, a tape recorder, father anticipated her behavior and was able to distract her with an alternative wind-up toy. Her Bayley scores at 18 months reflect the continued sensitive environmental structuring by her father as well as her mother (MDI = 107, PDI = 113). Although her motor tone was still slightly increased, her vision was now more adequate, she now talked in phrases, her play was more creative, her sleep behavior was more organized, and she had even begun to have occasional tantrums. (pp. 369–370)

In discussing the effects of stress on fathers and premature infants, it is first important to emphasize the medical, behavioral, and interactional variability of these infants. Our small sample size makes it impossible to draw firm conclusions but rather to generate more informed hypotheses.

When father's direct role as a play partner for his premature infant is timed to the recovery and physiological stability of the baby, the outcome seems best. His ability to engage the baby affectively requires a much greater sensitivity to the individuality of the baby than is usually required with a full-term infant. When this occurs, it may illustrate the process of stress catalyzing growth; the fathers' vigorous interactive play with his infant may encourage the baby to maintain a moderately high level of arousal that may, in turn, facilitate the differentiation of sensorimotor skills, the development of mastery motivation, task persistence, and modulated assertiveness all reflected on the Bayley assessment.

Because we did not see any evidence for parents perceiving their preterm infants as vulnerable, fragile, and needing overprotection, that others have reported (Minde et al., 1978) it is tempting to speculate that father's ability to engage their babies in games allowed them to counter a family perception of the baby as fragile and vulnerable when that perception no longer fit.

Finally, our clinical impression in working with these families was that the ability of fathers and infants to engage in game playing at 5 months also reflected the mother's sanction and encouragement of the father's direct involvement with his infant. It seemed that a coherent paternal role that fit the needs of mother, father, and infant was more adaptive than simply high or low involvement. Stress of any kind may accentuate the need for a couple to cooperate in rearing their child. Premature birth is one example of this. Further studies need to look more carefully at the effects of stress on this family process and on the mechanisms of influence on paternal involvement and infant outcomes.

ACKNOWLEDGMENTS

Research support from the National Foundation March of Dimes, NICHD Grant No. 10889 and the Maternal and Child Health Grant No. MGR-250400 is gratefully acknowledged. I would like to thank colleagues in much of this research including Suzanne Dixon, M.D.; Ed Tronick, Ph.D.; T. B. Brazelton, M.D.; Heidelise Als, Ph.D.; Barry Lester, Ph.D.; Joel Hoffman, Ph.D.; Carey Halsey, M.A.; Nancy Jordan, M.A.; Diana Dill, M.A.; Emmy Burrows, and Joan Gilman.

REFERENCES

Als, H., Lester, B. M., & Brazelton, T. B. (1979). Dynamics of the behavioral organization of a premature infant. In T. Field (Ed.), *Infants born at risk* (pp. 173–193). New York: Spectrum Medical & Scientific Books.

Beckwith, L., & Cohen, S. E. (1980). Interactions of preterm infants with their caregivers and test performance at age 2. In T. Field (Ed.), *High risk infants and children* (pp. 155–178). New York: Academic Press.

Bradley, R., & Caldwell, B. (1976). Early home environment and changes in mental test performance in children from 6 to 36 months. *Developmental Psychology, 12,* 93–97.

Brazelton, T. B. (1982). Early intervention: What does it mean? In H. Fitzgerald, B. Lester, & M. W. Yogman (Eds.), *Theory and research in behavioral pediatrics* (Vol. I, pp. 1–31). New York: Plenum Press.

Brazelton, T. B., Tronick, E., Adamson, L., Als, H., & Wise, S. (1975). Early mother–infant reciprocity. In R. Hinde (Ed.), *Parent–infant interaction* (pp. 137–154). Ciba Foundation Symposium No. 33, Amsterdam: Elsevier.

Brown, J. V., & Bakeman, R. (1980). Relationship of human mothers with their infants during the first year of life: Effects of prematurity. In R. W. Bell & W. P. Smotherman (Eds.), *Maternal influences and early behavior* (pp. 227–239). Holliswood, NY: Spectrum.

Caputo, D. V., Goldstein, K. M., & Taub, H. B. (1979). Development of prematurely born children through middle childhood. In T. Field (Ed.), *Infants born at risk* (pp. 119–249). New York: Spectrum Medical & Scientific Books.

Clarke-Stewart, K. A. (1980). The father's contribution to children's cognitive and social development in early childhood. In F. A. Pedersen (Ed.), *The father-infant relationship: Observational studies in a family setting* (pp. 111–146). New York: Holt, Rinehart & Winston.

Crawley, S., Rogers, P., Friedman, S., Iacobbo, M., Criticos, A., Richardson, L., & Thompson, M. (1978). Developmental changes in the structure of mother-infant play. *Developmental Psychology, 14,* 30–36.

Drillien, C. M. (1964). *The growth and development of the prematurely born infant.* Baltimore: Williams & Wilkins.

Field, T. M. (1978). Interaction behaviors of primary versus secondary caretaker fathers. *Developmental Psychology, 14,* 183–184.

Field, T. M. (1979a). Interaction patterns of preterm and full-term infants. In T. M. Field (Ed.), *Infants born at risk: Behavior and development* (pp. 333–356). New York: Spectrum Medical & Scientific Books.

Field, T. M. (1979b). Games parents play with normal and high-risk infants. *Child Psychiatry and Human Development, 10,* 41–48.

Frodi, A., Lamb, M., Hwang, C., & Frodi, M. (1982, March). *Increased paternal involvement and family relationships.* Paper presented to International Conference on Infant Studies, Austin, TX.

Goldberg, S. (1978). Prematurity: Effects on parent-infant interaction. *Journal of Pediatric Psychology, 3,* 137–144.

Jeffcoate, J. A., Humphrey, M. E., & Lloyd, J. K. (1979). Role perception and response to stress in fathers and mothers following pre-term delivery. *Social Science and Medicine, 1304,* 139–145.

Klaus, M., & Kennell, J. (1976). *Maternal infant bonding.* St. Louis: C. V. Mosby.

Kotelchuck, M. (1976). The infant's relationship to the father: Experimental evidence. In M. Lamb (Ed.), *The role of the father in child development* (pp. 329–344). New York: Wiley.

Lamb, M. E. (1977). Father-infant and mother-infant interaction in the first year of life. *Child Development, 48,* 167–181.

Lamb, M. Frodi, A., Hwang, C., Frodi, M., & Steinberg, J. (1982). Mother and father-infant interaction involving play and holding in traditional and non-traditional Swedish families. *Developmental Psychology, 18,* 215–221.

Marton, P., Minde, K., & Perrotta, M. (1981). The role of the father for the infant at risk. *American Journal of Orthopsychiatry, 51,* 672–679.

Minde, K., Trehub, S., Carter, C., Boukydis, C., Celhoffer, L., & Marton, P. (1978). Mother-child relationships in the premature nursery—an observational study. *Pediatrics, 61,* 373–379.

Niswander, K. R., & Gordon, M. (Eds.). (1972). *The collaborative perinatal study of the National Institute of Neurological Diseases and Stroke: The women and their pregnancies.* Philadelphia: W. B. Saunders.

Parmelee, A. H., & Haber, A. (1973). Who is the "at-risk infant?" *Clinical Obstetrics and Gynecology, 16,* 376–387.

Parmelee, A. H., Sigman, M., Kopp, C. B., & Haber, A. (1975). The concept of a cumulative risk score for infants. In N. R. Willis (Ed.), *Aberrant development in infancy, Human and animal studies* (pp. 113–121). Hillsdale, NJ: Lawrence Erlbaum Associates.

Parke, R., & Tinsley, B. (1982). The early environment of the at-risk infant. In D. D. Bricker (Ed.), *Intervention with at risk and handicapped infants* (pp. 153–177). Baltimore: University Park Press.

Pedersen, F. A., & Robson, K. S. (1969). Father participation in infancy. *American Journal of Orthopsychiatry, 39,* 466–472.

Power, T. G., & Parke, R. D. (1979, March). *Toward a taxonomy of father-infant and mother-infant play patterns.* Paper presented to the Society for Research in Child Development, San Francisco.

Sameroff, A. J., & Chandler, M. J. (1975). Reproductive risk and the continuum of caretaking casualty. In F. D. Horowitz (Ed.), *Review of child development research* (Vol. 4, pp. 187-244). Chicago: The University of Chicago Press.

Sigman, M., & Parmelee, A. H. (1979). Longitudinal evaluation of the preterm infant. In T. M. Field (Ed.), *Infants born at risk* (pp. 193-219). New York: Spectrum Medical & Scientific Books.

Stern, D. (1974). The goal and structure of mother-infant play. *Journal of American Academy of Child Psychiatry, 13,* 402.

Tronick, E., Cohn, J., & Shea, E. (1986). Transfer of affect between mothers and infants. In T. B. Brazelton & M. W. Yogman (Eds.), *Affective development in infancy* (pp. 11-25). Norwood, NJ: Ablex.

Werner, E. E., Bierman, J. J., & French, F. E. (1971). *The children of Kauai.* Honolulu: University of Hawaii Press.

White, R. (1959). Motivation reconsidered: The concept of competence. *Psychological Review, 66,* 297-333.

Yogman, M. W. (1981). Games fathers and mothers play with their infants. *Infant Mental Health Journal, 2,* 241-248.

Yogman, M. W. (1982). Development of the father-infant relationship. In H. Fitzgerald, B. Lester, & M. Yogman (Eds.), *Theory and research in behavioral Pediatrics* (Vol. I, pp. 221-279). New York: Plenum Press.

Yogman, M. W. (1984). The father's role with preterm and fullterm infants. In J. Call, E. Galenson, & R. Tyson (Eds.), *Frontiers of infant psychiatry* (Vol. 2, pp. 363-374). New York: Basic Books.

Zilboorg, G. (1931). Depressive reactions to parenthood. *American Journal of Psychiatry, 10,* 927.

Fathers and Their At-Risk Infants
Conceptual and Empirical Analyses

Ross D. Parke
University of Illinois at Champaign-Urbana

Edward R. Anderson
University of Virginia

The aim of this chapter is to explore the role of the father in the development of the at-risk infant. To a large extent, the study of fathering has been restricted to term infants. The expansion of our analysis of fathering to include other types of infants is an important step in assessing the limitations of our generalizations about fathering in infancy. The study of fathers has changed and matured over the past decade. These indices of growth can be summarized by a set of assumptions concerning the appropriate conceptual framework for understanding the father's role in infancy.

THEORETICAL ASSUMPTIONS

First, to fully understand the changing nature of the father's role in the family, it is necessary to recognize the interdependence among the roles and functions of all family members (Parke & Tinsley, 1982). It is being increasingly recognized that families are best viewed as social systems. Consequently, to understand the behavior of one member of a family, the complementary behaviors of other members also need to be recognized and assessed. For example, as men's roles in families shift, changes in women's roles in families must also be monitored.

Second, fathers indirectly influence other family members, in addition to their direct influence through interaction. Examples of fathers' indirect impact include various ways in which fathers modify and mediate mother--child relationships. In turn, women affect their children indirectly through their husbands by modifying both the quantity and quality of father–child interaction (Lewis & Feiring, 1981; Parke, 1979, 1981; Parke, Power, & Gottman, 1979). In addition, recognition is being given to the embeddedness of families within a variety of other social systems, including both formal and informal support systems as well as the cultures in which they exist (Bronfenbrenner, 1979; Cochran & Brassard, 1979; Parke & Tinsley, 1982).

A further assumption that guides our essay is the importance of distinguishing among individual time, family time, and historical time. *Individual time* is each family member's life course. *Family time* is defined as the timing of transitional life events for the family as a unit (e.g., marriage, parenthood, children leaving the family). *Historical time* provides the social conditions for individual and family transitions; an example is the 1960s—Vietnam War era. These distinctions are important because individual, family, and historical time do not always harmonize (Elder & Rockwell, 1979; Hareven, 1977). For example, a family event, such as the birth of a child—the transition to parenthood—may have very profound effects on a man who has just begun a career in contrast to one who has advanced to a stable occupational position. Moreover, individual and family time are both embedded within the social conditions and values of the historical time in which they exist (Hareven, 1977). The role of father, as is the case with any social role, is responsive to such fluctuations. To illustrate these assumptions, the impact of the birth of a premature infant on family functioning is discussed.

The Impact of Preterm and Handicapped Infants on the Mother–Child Relationship

The birth of a premature infant is often a stressful event, as evidenced by descriptions portraying parents with infants in at-risk nurseries as shocked, angry, and otherwise emotionally distraught (Kennedy, 1973; Slade, Redl, & Manguten, 1977). Similarly, parents of handicapped infants express a similar emotional sequence of disappointment, denial, anger, and guilt (Holt, 1957; Legeay & Keogh, 1966; Klause & Kennell, 1982; Marion, 1981). Reactions to the birth of a premature infant are unlikely to be similar across families. The degree of stress associated with this event is determined, in part, by the parents' subjective perceptions of the event. In turn, it is assumed that their perceptions will influence their interactions with their infants. This cognitive–mediational approach suggests that parental knowledge, expectations, and labeling must be considered in order to understand the degree of stress as well as the parents' treatment of their infant (Leiderman, 1982; Parke, 1978; Sameroff, 1982).

The survival rate of the low birth weight infant has increased greatly in recent years due to advances in medical care and technology (Klause & Fanaroff, 1979). Many of these "new" survivors often have serious medical difficulties as well as a higher rate of short- and long-term developmental problems than normal infants. Caputo and Mandell (1970) point out a number of outcomes that may make the low birth weight "at risk" for possible parental maltreatment. Some of the outcomes may alter the parent–child relationship in the early postpartum months, whereas others may not affect the parent–child dyad until the child is beyond infancy.

It is generally accepted that some disequilibrium is initiated by the birth of any infant, caused by the additional tasks associated with caregiving, modifications of schedules and activities, and readjustment in the marital relationship (Cowan & Cowan, 1984; Entwisle & Doering, 1981). In addition, the birth of a premature infant has consequences that further increase familial stress in a number of ways. First, the immature development of the infant may require special medical support procedures, which in turn may lead to separation of the mother and her infant. Although early separation may cause short-term stress on the family, follow-up studies indicate no long-term impact (i.e., 2 years) of this type of separation on the development of these infants (Leiderman, 1981, 1982).

Second, the low birth weight premature infant violates many parental expectations. In addition to arriving early, often before parental preparations for birth are completed, these infants differ from full-terms in their appearance, cries, feeding needs, interactional demands, and developmental progress, which, in turn, can contribute further to the stress associated with their arrival (Brooks & Hochberg, 1960; Frodi et al., 1978). For example, in their study, Frodi et al. documented that in addition to their appearance, the high-pitched cry patterns of the premature infant are rated by parents as more disturbing, irritating, and annoying. In addition, the parents who reported found premature infants less pleasant and they were less eager to interact with a preterm than a full-term infant. More recently, Stern and Hildebrandt (1984) found that mothers rated infants who were labeled *premature* as less physically developed, less attentive, slower, less smart, quieter, more sleepy, and more passive than the same infants were when labeled *full-term.* These studies provide support for the existence of a prematurity stereotype among adults. In turn, these perceptions may lead to a self-fulfilling prophecy whereby the premature infant comes to exhibit the expected negative behavior. These findings underscore the value of a cognitive mediational approach (Parke, 1978). Violations of expectations are not restricted to preterm infants; other studies indicate that handicapped infants also violate parental expectations of rearing a normal well-functioning child (Canning & Pueschel, 1978).

Preterm infants place greater demands on their caregivers than term infants. For example, feeding disturbances are more common among low birth weight infants (Klaus & Fanaroff, 1979). Moreover, premature infants are behaviorally different than their term peers; as Goldberg (1979) reported, premature infants spend less time alert, are more difficult to keep in alert states, and are less responsive to sights and sounds than term infants, and provide less distinctive cues to guide parental treatment. In view of these behavioral characteristics, it is not surprising that parents have to work "harder" when interacting with a premature infant. Brown and Bakeman (1980) have documented that preterm infants are more difficult and less satisfying to feed than term infants; during feeding interactions, preterms contributed less to maintenance of the interactive flow than term infants and the burden of maintaining the interaction fell disproportionately on the mothers of these preterms. Other observational studies of Down's Syndrome children (Stoneman, Brody, & Abbott, 1983), developmentally delayed infants (Vietze, Abernathy, Ashe, & Faulstich, 1978), or severely handicapped infants (Walker, 1982) report a similar pattern of reduced responsivity during social interchanges. Together, these studies confirm that children with a variety of limiting conditions are less responsive during parent–child interaction.

Not only does the preterm infant modify caregiver behavior, expectations concerning developmental timetables may be altered as well. Recently, Smith, Leiderman, Selz, MacPherson, and Bingham (1981) found that mothers of preterm infants rated developmental milestones for their own child and a typical full-term child differently. In rating their own children, they predicted substantial lags for their own child until approximately 2 years of age. Beyond 2 years, they expected more rapid development in social psychomotor, and cognitive development than the rate of progress expected by the mothers of full-term infants. To expect preterms to surpass full-term babies in their rates of development after 2 years may be unrealistic and may, in turn, be a contributing factor in later dysfunctional parent–child relationships, such as child abuse (Egeland & Brunnquell, 1979).

In the remainder of this chapter, it is argued that an expanded characterization of the social context of the premature infant as well as the handicapped and retarded infant is necessary to better understand the nature of the environment in which these infants and children develop.

FATHERS AND TRIADS: EXPANDING THE CONTEXT OF DEVELOPMENT

The Father–Infant Relationship

In recent years, the father's role in infancy has been increasingly recognized (Lamb, 1981; Parke, 1981; Parke & Tinsley, 1984). Fathers are active and interested contributors in early infancy and competent in their execution of early caregiving tasks, such as feeding and diapering (Parke &

Sawin, 1976, 1980). Until recently, the focus was nearly exclusively on fathers of term infants, but researchers have begun to explore the special role of fathers in families with preterm infants as well as handicapped and retarded infants. Fathers' roles in caregiving and play with normal full-term infants as well as with special infants, such as premature and handicapped infants, are examined.

The birth of a premature infant elicits greater father involvement in caregiving; this heightened involvement may, in part, be due to the additional time, energy, and skill required to care for preterm infants. A recent investigation by Yogman (1982) illustrates this. Twenty preterm and 20 full-term infants were followed longitudinally from birth to 18 months. On the basis of father reports of routine caregiving at 1, 5, and 18 months, Yogman found that fathers of the preterm infants reported engaging in more of the caregiving tasks at each age than the comparison group of fathers of full-term infants. The differences were especially marked and statistically significant by 18 months, when fathers were more likely to take the infant to a physician, to bathe the infant, and to get up at night to console their infant.

Although the birth of an infant prematurely appears to often elicit greater father participation in caregiving, not all investigators find such a relationship. In our recent short-term longitudinal study of the development of preterm infants (Parke, 1984), we followed 44 families—24 full-term and 20 preterm infants from birth to 12 months of age. Families were observed at the hospital and in the home at 3 weeks, 3 months, 8 months, and 12 months. Two types of observations were made: (a) mother–father–infant triad during a 10-minute feeding period and a 10-minute unstructured observation period, (b) separate mother–infant and father–infant dyads in unstructured 10-minute observation sessions. The preterm infants were less than 2500 grams (x = 2000 grams) and less than 37 weeks gestation (x = 32 weeks gestation). Although the preterm infants were at higher risk than full-terms according to the Obstetrical Risk Index (preterm $\overline{X}$ = 4.8; term $\overline{X}$ = 1.2; $p < .001$), as a sample they were a relatively healthy set of preterm infants. In contrast to the Yogman sample, the infants in our sample were less at risk. As part of our assessment battery, parents were asked to record the amount of caretaking they provided their infants during the course of 1 week following each of the home visits. A specially prepared diary was provided by the project staff. Parents recorded the amount of time mother and father each spent in feeding, diapering, and bathing. Other methodological work (Anderson, 1984), in which independent observers' ratings of these caregiving activities were compared with parental diary records, indicated that parents are moderately reliable recorders of these types of caregiving activities. Analyses of the families across 12 months indicated only one main effect for all contexts (feeding, diapering, and bathing); namely, sex of parent (average $F = 141.00$; $p < .001$). Mothers were consistently more involved than fathers in all facets of caregiving, across all time points, for both full-term and preterm infants.

How do we reconcile these discrepancies? Both the Yogman data on fathers of preterms and the extensive data on fathers of infants delivered by Caesarean Section (Grossman, Eichler, & Winickoff, 1980; Vietze, MacTurk, McCarthy, Klein, & Yarrow, 1980) suggest that fathers modify their levels of involvement to assist when mothers are unable to cope due either to their own condition or to the increased demands imposed by the infant. In our study, the relatively healthy status of our preterm infants may have obviated the necessity for increased father involvement.

However, before we assume that father involvement always increases under conditions of impaired health of the infant, consider the case of infants who are born with a handicapping condition. Does father participation increase in the case of handicapped infants? Although the data are neither abundant nor entirely consistent, research suggests that fathers of retarded infants and children tend not to show increased involvement in childcare. In fact, the level of participation in caregiving of fathers of retarded children is relatively low (Andrew, 1968; Holt, 1957). Lamb (1984) suggested that:

> This reflects the fact that fathers obtain less satisfaction from retarded than normal children (Cummings, 1976) and the fact that paternal involvement— unlike maternal involvement is discretionary. The paternal role is defined in such a way that fathers can increase or decrease their involvement depending on their preferences and satisfactions whereas traditionally mothers are expected to show equivalent commitment to all their children—regardless of personal preferences or the individual characteristics of their children. (p. 16–17)

It is clear that the conditions that will overcome the role differentiation of mothers and fathers have yet to be well specified. Although severity of infant medical condition is clearly implicated, no simple linear relationship between this factor and father involvement is evident. A curvilinear hypothesis could integrate much of the existing literature. This hypothesis suggests that father involvement will be highest in the case of moderately difficult circumstances that limit the mother's ability to adequately manage caregiving routines, but that it will be less under either normal circumstances or under extreme circumstances, such as with handicapped infants. In the case of handicapped infants, a variety of factors will determine the nature of the father's reactions including the severity of the condition, as well as the short-term versus long-term nature of the condition. However, the difficulty of adequately evaluating a hypothesis of this form severely limits its utility. Moreover, in the case of handicapped infants, the critical factor of the longevity of the limiting condition may be an important determinant of father involvement. Our point is simply to call for further exploration of this issue and prevent any premature closure on this issue.

Mother–Father Differences in Style of Interaction

Do mothers and fathers differ in their interactions with their infants? Do mother and fathers treat preterm infants differently than full-terms? Our own longitudinal study, as well as other recent investigations, can help answer these questions.

In our study, mother–infant and father–infant dyads were observed for a 10-minute period interacting with their infant in a non-feeding situation. Based on analyses of variance, mothers vocalized, kissed, and touched more than fathers (all $p < .05$) and engaged in more caregiving in the form of checking and adjusting the infant than fathers ($p < .05$). These differences were evident for preterm and term infants suggesting that the traditional stylistic distinctions between mothers and fathers holds for parents of preterms as well. Although the analyses of variance failed to reveal any differences between mothers and fathers in physical play (bounce, toss, and lifting behaviors), a discriminant function analysis revealed that fathers of full-terms were more physical in their interactions than fathers of preterms. Mothers, on the other hand, were more verbal with their preterm than their full-term infants, but were more affectionate with full-terms than with preterms. Finally, both parents provided more caregiving to their preterm infants than to their full-term infants (Anderson, 1984).

Other investigators have confirmed some of these patterns, especially the differences in play patterns of fathers of preterm and full-term infants. Yogman (this volume) studied fathers of preterm and full-term infants during a 3-minute episode of face-to-face play in the laboratory between ages 2 and 5 months. The games were then categorized as arousing if they involved proximal activities such as tactile and limb movement games or as nonarousing if they were assumed to maintain, rather than arouse the infant's attention, as was the case with verbal and visual games. Fathers of preterm infants played fewer and shorter games, and fewer arousing games, than did fathers of full-term infants. Fathers of preterm infants also were less able to directly engage their babies in play, compared with fathers of full-term infants. Possibly, fathers assume that the premature infant is fragile and unable to withstand robust physical stimulation that, in turn, leads to an inhibition of fathers' usual play style. Vigorous stimulation may stress and disorganize an already vulnerable infant because preterm infants have more difficulty with motor activity, poorer tone and state regulation, and hypersensitivity. In view of this feedback, fathers may, in turn, not only shift their play style to a less stressful mode, but may also interact less.

It would be worthwhile to study how fathers of infants with varying types of handicapping conditions modify their play patterns. Observational studies by Walker (1982), of the social interactions between mothers and handicapped infants, suggest that the handicapped infant is less reinforcing, less interesting, and a more difficult social partner. In Walker's studies, mothers accounted for a large share of the playful stimulation, while the infant's contribution was severely limited. Parallel work with fathers using an observational strategy would help illuminate further the father's role in the early development of handicapped infants. In view of the important role of physical play in the development of social competence, intervention strategies might be developed to increase the degree of physical interaction between preterm infants and their fathers (MacDonald & Parke, 1984, Power & Parke, 1982).

The Family Triad: Mother–Father–Infant

Models that limit examination of the effects of interaction patterns to only the father–infant and mother–infant dyads, and to the direct effects of one individual on another, are inadequate for understanding the impact of social interaction patterns in families, and especially in families with preterm infants or handicapped infants (Lewis & Feiring, 1981; Parke, Power, & Gottman, 1979; Parke & Tinsley, 1982).

Triadic contexts in which mother, father, and infant interact together, merit further examination. Similarly, indirect, as well as direct paths of mutual influence within families are important. A parent may influence a child through the mediation of another family member's impact (e.g., a mother may contribute to the father's positive affect toward his child by praising his caregiving skill). Another way one parent may indirectly influence the child's treatment by other agents is to modify the infant's behavior. Child behavior patterns that develop as a result of parent–child interaction may, in turn, affect the child's treatment by other social agents. For example, irritable infant patterns induced by an insensitive and impatient mother may, in turn, make the infant more difficult for the father to handle and pacify. Thus, patterns developed in interaction with one parent may alter interaction patterns with another caregiver. In larger families siblings can play a similar mediating role.

The triadic setting can modify the nature of parent–infant interaction patterns. Parents have been shown to behave differently when alone with their infants than when interacting with the infant in the presence of the other parent. In our earlier studies (Parke, Grossman, & Tinsley, 1981; Parke & O'Leary, 1976), the presence of the other parent significantly altered the behavior of the partner. Although there was an overall reduction in the level of interaction in the presence of a spouse, not all behaviors decreased. Specifically, each parent expressed more positive affect (smiling) toward their infant and showed a higher level of exploration when the other parent was present.

In our study of preterm infants we find similar patterns. First, the overall level of activity was reduced in the triadic context in comparison with the dyadic setting. This is consistent with earlier second-order effect findings (Lamb, 1979; Parke, 1979). Parental vocalization, touching, kissing, caregiving, and playing were all significantly lower in the triadic, compared with the dyadic contexts ($p < .05$ for each measure). Finally, parents of full-term infants interacted more with each other in the family triad, than did parents of preterms. Specifically, parents of full-term infants looked at and vocalized to their spouses and smiled at their spouses more often than parents of preterm infants did ($p < .05$ for all measures). Possibly the heightened demand of managing and interacting with a preterm, in contrast with a full-term infant may compete with, and reduce spousal interaction. Moreover, this finding is consistent with other data that are discussed later, suggesting that the premature birth of an infant may have a negative impact on the spousal relationship.

Recent research with Down Syndrome infants and their parents also underscores the importance of examining the family triad (Stoneman et al., 1983). These investigators found, as with normal infants, that the behavior of both mothers and fathers decreased when the other parent was present. However, fathers were more affected than mothers. Although mothers remained involved with their children in both the dyadic and triadic contexts, fathers tended to play a less active role when the mother was present. "This is consistent with research suggesting that mothers continue to assume a managing, parenting role across family groupings; whereas in mother–father–child triads, fathers tend to defer to mothers decreasing their interaction time with children" (Stoneman et al., 1983, p. 599). However, this effect was not different for families of retarded and non-retarded children.

As a number of recent studies have demonstrated, spousal support is an important factor in mediating both parental competence and infant outcome (Belsky & Volling, this volume; Dickie, this volume; Pederson, Anderson, & Cain, 1980). Although much research has been devoted to families of healthy infants, the marital relationship may be particularly important in the case of preterm or handicapped infants. A supportive spousal relationship can serve to buffer or diminish the negative impact of giving birth to a handicapped or retarded infant. Support for this hypothesis comes from a study of maternal adjustment to having a handicapped child (Friedrich, 1979). Marital satisfaction was found to be the best predictor of maternal coping behavior.

Unfortunately, stressful events, such as the birth of a premature or retarded infant, may often have a disruptive impact on the marital relationship. In turn, this disruption may reduce the level of mutual support that spouses provide each other in stressful circumstances. Of relevance to this issue is the work of Leiderman (1981) and Leiderman and Seashore (1975). These investigators examined the relationship of prematurity to marital stability. In the 2-year period following hospital discharge, marital discord, often leading to separation or divorce, was higher for the families of preterm infants who were initially separated from their mothers. As Leiderman and Seashore (1975) suggest, "separation in the newborn period does have an effect, albeit non-specific, by acting through the family as a stress that creates disequilibrium in the nuclear family structure" (pp. 229–230). The Leiderman work provides further support for considering the family unit, but it is not specifically clear how the birth of a preterm infant affects relationships among family members.

Just as in the case of preterm infants, the birth of a retarded child often has a negative impact on the marital relationship. Specifically, a number of investigators have found extensive marital and family disruption as a result of the birth of a retarded or handicapped child (Farber, 1959, 1960; Holt, 1957; Lonsdale, 1978; Tew, Lawrence, Payne, & Rawnsley, 1977). Moreover, non-retarded siblings tend to be negatively affected (Farber, 1960; Holt, 1957) and further childbearing tends to diminish (Carver & Carver, 1972).

The importance of these findings is clear: In order to understand either the mother–infant or father–infant relationship, the total set of relationships among the members of the family needs to be assessed. Although interviews are helpful, they are not sufficient; rather, direct observations of both mother and father alone with their infants, as well as the mother, father, and infant together, are necessary to understand the effects of the birth of either a premature of handicapped infant.

BEYOND THE TRIAD: EXTRA-FAMILIAL SUPPORT SYSTEMS AND THE AT-RISK INFANT

A further extension of our theoretical framework—from the dyad to the traid, to the family in its ecological context—is needed to understand the environment and the development of either the at-risk or retarded infant. Families do not exist as units independent of other social organizations within society. Thus, families need to be viewed within their social context, and recognition of the role of the community as a modifier of family modes of interaction is necessary for an adequate theory of early development.

To understand the specific functions that extra familial support systems play in modulating interaction patterns in families of premature and handicapped or retarded infants, an appreciation of the problems associated with the care of these types of infants is necessary. Infants who are born prematurely or with a handicapping condition may be at risk as a result of parents' limited knowledge of development, their inappropriate skills for infant care, and the stress associated with the care and rearing of a preterm infant. Extrafamilial support systems can function to alleviate these problems by providing accurate timetables for the development of infants with special problems, monitoring parents' infant care practices with provision of corrective feedback, and providing parents with relief from stress associated with the birth and care of preterm or handicapped infant.

There are a variety of support systems of special relevance to at-risk infants and their families. Two kinds of support systems operate: formal (e.g., health-care facilities, social service agencies, recreational facilities) and informal (e.g., extended families, neighbors, and co-workers). These programs serve the educational function of providing child-care information, as well as alleviating stress associated with premature or ill infants. Support systems that serve an educational function include: hospital-based courses in childcare and childbearing, visiting nurse programs, well-baby clinics, follow-up programs, and parent-discussion groups. Some other supportive programs that offer stress relief are: family and group day-care facilities, babysitting services, mother's helpers, homemaker and housekeeping services, drop-off centers, crisis nurseries, and hot lines.

Evidence is limited in support of the role of formal and informal support systems that attempt to regulate family ability to cope with at-risk infants. Therefore, we review some illustrative studies of the role of support systems in modifying family management of infant care and development. Although some recent studies involve informal social support systems, many of the studies have primarily involved modification of the formal support systems available to families. Finally, in some cases, formal and informal support are provided together, which underlines the interconnectedness of these two levels of social support for families.

The Impact of Informal Support Systems

A number of studies have suggested that there is a positive relationship between informal social networks and a family's adaptation to stressful events, such as divorce (Hetherington, Cox, & Cox, 1982) and job loss (Bronfenbrenner & Crouter, 1982). Of particular relevance are recent investigations concerning the relationship between social networks and mother–child interaction.

A number of investigators have examined the impact of social networks on mother–infant interaction, and have found a positive relationship between the level of maternal social support and subscales from the HOME scale

(Pascoe, Loda, Jeffries & Earp, 1981; Unger, 1979). More recently, Crinic, Greenberg, Ragozin, Robinson, and Basham (1983), using samples of both preterm and full-term infants, reported positive relationships between infor-mal social support and the quality of mother–infant interaction. These investigations suggest that social support may affect infant developmental outcomes indirectly through modifying the nature of parent–child interac-tion patterns.

Moreover, Crockenberg (1981) found that the extent to which a mother utilized social support networks was related to the infant's pattern of attachment to her. Especially in the case of irritable infants (a characteris-tic common in many premature infants), utilization of social support was associated with secure attachment. This study provides an excellent illustra-tion of the interplay of individual characteristics (temperament) and the role of the social environment (social support networks) on later patterns of infant–mother attachment. In view of the evidence that the quality of early attachment is associated with later peer social competence (Pastor, 1981), this finding is of particular importance.

Unfortunately, little evidence is available concerning the utilization and impact of social support systems on families of preterm infants. It is assumed that social networks will be particularly important to the families of preterm infants who are under greater initial stress than families of term infants. Although many of the children in the Pascoe et al. study were either born prematurely or were ill as infants, no assessments were made of the social networks of these families when their children were infants.

In our recent longitudinal project (Parke, 1984), we found a number of differences in the patterns of social support utilization among families of preterm and full-term infants. At each time point, parents completed a social support questionnaire that tapped the extent to which families used either informal or formal support agents. Second, the purpose of this use was separately evaluated (i.e., social, emotional, informational, or physical). A number of findings are noteworthy.

First, there were clear sex differences in the patterns of social support utilization. As is commonly found, (Gottlieb, 1981) mothers have more overall contact with individuals outside the family than fathers do ($p < .01$). When the purpose of the contact was examined, mothers again were higher than fathers, in contact with informal networks for information purposes ($p < .01$), for assistance with home baby care ($p < .10$), for alleviating worry or upset about their baby ($p < .01$) and for relaxation and enjoyment ($p < .10$). Although mothers utilized informal networks more than fathers, this sex difference was evident in the first 3 months postpartum. Current analyses are being run to evaluate the pattern at later time points in the first year.

Second, during the hospital period, fathers of preterms sought information more often from formal support agencies, such as professional or social service agencies, than did fathers of full-terms ($p < .02$). Over time, and presumably as the crisis passed, fathers decreased their reliance on formal agencies, and by 3 months there were no differences between fathers of preterm, and fathers of full-term infants. In contrast, mothers of preterms did not differ from mothers of full-terms in their use of formal agencies for information in the early postpartum period. Fathers and mothers, in short, appear to have distinctive styles of support seeking. Possibly, males see information seeking from formal sources as role-consistent; whereas females are more comfortable utilizing informal social networks. Overall, the results underscore the importance of distinguishing formal from informal support systems and suggest the necessity of providing formal support systems, especially for fathers. Further analysis will indicate the impact of these patterns of support utilization for family functioning and infant development.

The Impact of Formal Support Systems

Formal support systems, according to our findings, may be of particular importance for fathers. In recent years, a number of investigators have used the early postpartum period to provide supportive intervention for fathers. This is demonstrated by our hospital-based study with full-term infants (Parke, Hymel, Power, & Tinsley, 1980). During the mother's postpartum hospitalization, one group of fathers was shown a short videotape that modeled positive father–infant interaction and caretaking involvement with young infants. In comparison to a control group of fathers who saw no videotape, fathers who viewed the film in the hospital increased their knowledge about infant perceptual abilities, believed more strongly that infants need stimulation, and were more responsive to their infants during feeding and play. Based on parental diary reports of caretaking activities in the home at 3 months, fathers of boys who saw the film were more likely to diaper and feed their infants than fathers in the no-film control group. However, the film intervention had no efect on fathers of girls. In summary, the film intervention significantly modified selected aspects of father behavior and attitudes both in the hospital and through the first 3 months of their infants' lives.

Further evidence of the effectiveness of this type of film intervention during the postpartum period comes from a recent study by Arbuckle (1983). In this project, Arbuckle used a film intervention developed by Parke (1980). Entitled, "Becoming a Family," the film demonstrated the same behaviors, such as feeding and diapering, playing, and infant capabilities, as were included in the Parke et al. (1980) film intervention. In contrast to the earlier film, this film depicted both mothers and fathers actively engaged in caregiving and game playing. Assessment of the impact of the film 4 to 6 weeks later indicated that first-time fathers who saw the film, in comparison to a no-film control group of fathers, had greater knowledge of infant sensory and cogntive capabilities and were higher in their perception of the importance of providing the infant affection and stimulation. Moreover, the experimental fathers reported higher levels of involvement in the daily caregiving of their babies 4 to 6 weeks after the intervention. No sex of infant differences were found. In spite of the limitation of this study by the reliance on self-report measures, the similarity of the findings across these two film intervention studies underscores the potential value of this approach for modifying paternal behavior. Further work is clearly justified; particularly important would be studies that isolate the effective components of these film intervention programs.

Programs for modifying father behavior with at-risk infants would appear to be worthwhile extensions of this work.

THE ROLE OF HISTORICAL TIME

A final caution is in order. It is important to recognize the historical boundedness of our data about fathers' role in early infancy (Parke & Tinsley, 1984). A number of changes in a variety of areas have taken place over the past 25 years that together may have significantly altered the ways in which men define the fathering role. Shifts in sex-role ideology, work patterns for men and women, age of timing of parenthood, as well as significant changes in medical practices have altered the climate in which men are immersed as they make the transition to fatherhood. Consider the shifts in the medical sphere. Current evidence suggests that caesarean-section deliveries and possibly preterm births in some cases are associated with increased father involvement with their infants. It is not possible from the available data to assess whether the shifts in delivery practices, such as the increase in cesarean sections, affect fathers of different cohorts in similar ways. Examination of samples to assess this issue would be worthwhile because it is not clear whether these changes would have produced similar shifts in father involvement in another time period. For example, in a more traditional era, characterized by more rigid gender roles for mothers and fathers, a caesarean-section delivery may not necessarily have led to increased paternal involvement. Female members of the family's social network such as friends or relatives (parents or in-laws) may have been called upon to assist the new mother. However, because there has been a cultural shift toward decreased geographical proximity between many families and extended kin, family support systems would then be less available which, in turn, might increase the likelihood of father involvement. Given that the use of social networks for childcare-related activity is negatively correlated with the father's involvement in childcare (Bloom-Feshbach, 1979), it is suggested that if the grandparents and other members of the social network are helping with childcare in a situation such as a caesarean-section birth, there is less impetus and opportunity for the father to be involved in this type of support. Thus, several societal trends may have converged to create a situation in which fathers are naturally encouraged to increase their participation in caregiving.

In summary, it is argued that more attention needs to be given to the role of historical change in accounting for current profiles of fathering. Critical to this pursuit is to determine which aspects of family processes are most likely to be altered by historical events and which processes are less amenable to historical change.

CONCLUSIONS

In this chapter, it has been argued that the understanding of fathers' role in the development of the at-risk infant will be most profitably achieved by expanding our conceptual approach. To complement our explorations of the father-infant dyad, studies of the family triad of mother–father and infant are necessary. In addition, the family is embedded in a set of informal and formal social support systems that can significantly modify the interaction patterns of family members and thereby affect the developing infant. Our review suggests that more attention needs to be devoted to describing the impact of infants who are at different degrees of risk for later developmental problems. Preterm infants represent only a single class of risk-infants and even within this class there is considerable variability. Consideration of how such parameters of risk such as severity of the problems, the longevity of the condition, the prognosis for successful treatment individually and in combination affect the nature of early interaction patterns with parents and alter the marital relationship is necessary. To adequately investigate these issues multiple research strategies including observational as well as self-report strategies are necessary. Longitudinal comparative work on of adaptation to parenthood for father (and mothers) of at-risk and non-risk infants would be particularly fruitful.

ACKNOWLEDGMENTS

Preparation of this paper and the work on the development of preterm infants were supported by grants from the March of Dimes Birth Defects Foundation, National Institute of Child Health and Human Development HEW PH5 05951 and PHS 5P01

HD05951-12 and National Institute of Child Health and Human Development Training Grant HD 07205-05. Thanks to Karen McGuire and Wilma Hardin for assistance in manuscript preparation.

REFERENCES

Anderson, E. (1984). *The fathers role in the development of preterm infants.* Unpublished honors thesis, University of Illinois.

Andrew, G. (1968). Determinants of Negro family decisions in management of retardation. *Journal of Marriage and the Family, 30,* 612–617.

Arbuckle, M. B. (1983). *The effects of educational intervention on fathers' relationships with their infants.* Unpublished doctoral dissertation, University of North Carolina at Greensboro.

Bloom-Feshbach, J. (1979). *The beginnings of fatherhood.* Unpublished doctoral dissertation, Yale University.

Bronfenbrenner, U. (1979). *The ecology of human development.* Cambridge: Harvard University Press.

Bronfenbrenner, U., & Crouter, A. C. (1982). Work and family through time and space. In S. B. Kamerman & C. D. Hayes (Eds.), *Families that work: Children in a changing world* (pp. 39–83). Washington, DC: National Academy Press.

Brooks, V., & Hochberg, J. (1960). A psychological study of "cuteness." *Perceptual and Motor Skills, 11,* 205.

Brown, J. V., & Bakeman, R. (1980). Relationships of human mothers with their infants during the first year of life: Effects of prematurity. In R. W. Bell & W. P. Smotherman (Eds.), *Maternal influences and early behavior.* Holliswood, NY: Spectrum.

Canning, C. D., & Pueschel, S. M. (1978). An overview of developmental expectations. In S. M. Pueschel (Ed.), *Down Syndrome children: Growing and learning.* New York: Andrews & McMeel.

Caputo, D. V., & Mandell, W. (1970). Consequences of low birth weight. *Developmental Psychology, 3,* 363–383.

Carver, N., & Carver, J. (1972). *The family of the retarded child.* Syracuse: NY: Syracuse University Press.

Cochran, M. M., & Brassard, J. A. (1979). Child development and personal social networks. *Child Development, 50,* 601–616.

Cowan, P., & Cowan, C. (1984, August). *The process of family formation.* Paper presented at the Meeting of the American Psychological Association, Toronto.

Crinic, K. A., Greenberg, M. T., Ragozin, A. S., Robinson, N. M., & Basham, R. B. (1983). Effects of stress and social support on mothers and premature and full-term infants. *Child Development, 54,* 209–217.

Crockenberg, S. B. (1981). Infant irritability, mother responsiveness, and social support influences on the security of infant-mother attachment. *Child Development, 52,* 857–865.

Cummings, S. T. (1976). The impact of the child's deficiency on the father: A study of fathers of mentally retarded and of chronically ill children. *American Journal of Orthopsychiatry, 46,* 246–255.

Egeland. B., & Brunnquell, D. (1979). An at-risk approach to the study of child abuse: Some preliminary findings. *Journal of the American Academy of Psychiatry, 18,* 219–235.

Elder, G. H., & Rockwell, R. (1979). The life course of human development: An ecological perspective. *International Journal of Behavioral Development, 2,* 1–21.

Entwisle, D., & Doering, S. G. (1981). *The first birth.* Baltimore, MD: Johns Hopkins University Press.

Farber, B. (1959). Effects of a severely mentally retarded child on family integration. *Monographs of the Society for Research in Child Development, 24,* whole number 71.

Farber, B. (1960). Family organization and crisis: Maintenance of integration in families with a severely mentally retarded child. *Monographs of the Society for Research in Child Development, 25,* whole number 75.

Friedrich, W. N. (1979). Predictors of the coping behavior of mothers of handicapped children. *Journal of Consulting and Clinical Psychology, 47,* 1140-1141.

Frodi, A. M., Lamb, M. E., Leavitt, L. A., Donovan, W. L., Neff, C., & Sherry, D. (1978). Fathers' and mothers' responses to the faces and cries of normal and premature infants. *Developmental Psychology, 14,* 490-498.

Goldberg, S. (1979). Premature birth: Consequences for the parent-infant relationship. *American Scientist, 67,* 214-220.

Gottlieb, B. H. (Ed.). (1981). *Social networks and social support.* Beverly Hills: Sage.

Grossman, F. K., Eichler, L. S., & Winickoff, S. A. (1980). *Pregnancy, birth and parenthood.* San Francisco: Jossey-Bass.

Hareven, T. (1977). Family time and historical time. *Daedalus, 106,* 57-70.

Hetherington, E. M., Cox, M., & Cox, R. (1982). Effects of development on parents and children. In M. E. Lamb (Ed.), *Non-traditional families* (pp. 233-288). Hillsdale, NJ: Lawrence Erlbaum Associates.

Holt, K. S. (1957). *The impact of mentally retarded children upon their families.* Unpublished doctoral dissertation, University of Sheffield, England.

Kennedy, J. (1973). The high risk maternal infant acquaintance process. *Nursing Clinics of North America, 8,* 549-556.

Klaus, M. H., & Fanaroff, A. A. (1979). *Care of the high-risk neonate* (2nd ed.). Philadelphia, PA: Saunders.

Klaus, M. H., & Kennell, J. H. (1982). *Parent-infant bonding.* St. Louis, MO: Mosby.

Lamb, M. E. (1979). The effects of social context in dyadic social interaction. In M. E. Lamb, S. Suomi, & G. R. Stephenson (Eds.), *Social Interactional analysis: Methodological issues.* Madison, WI: University of Wisconsin.

Lamb, M. E. (1981). *The role of the father in child development* (2nd ed.). New York: Wiley.

Lamb, M. E. (1984). Fathers of exceptional children. In M. Seligman (Ed.), *A comprehensive guide to understanding and treating the family with a handicapped child.* New York: Grune & Stratton.

Legeay, C., & Keogh, B. (1966). Impact of mental retardation on family life. *American Journal of Nursing, 66,* 1062-1065.

Leiderman, P. H. (1981). Human mother-infant social bonding: Is there a sensitive phase? In K. Immelman, G. W., Barlow, L. Petrinovich, & M. Main (Eds.), *Behavioral development.* New York: Cambridge.

Leiderman, P. H. (1982). Social ecology and childbirth: The newborn nursery as environmental stressor. In N. Garmezy & M. Rutter (Eds.), *Stress, coping, and adaptation* (pp. 133-159). New York: McGraw-Hill.

Leiderman, P. H., & Seashore, M. J. (1975). Mother-infant separation: Some delayed consequences. *Parent-infant interaction.* CIBA Foundation Symposium 33. Amsterdam: Elsevier.

Lewis, M., & Feiring, C. (1981). Direct and indirect interactions in social relationships. In L. Lipsitt (Ed.), *Advances in infancy research* (Vol. 1) Norwood, NJ: Ablex.

Lonsdale, G. (1978). Family life with a handicapped child: The parents speak. *Child: Care, Health, and Development, 4,* 99-120.

MacDonald, K., & Parke, R. D. (1984). Bridging the gap: The relationship between mother and father play and peer competence. *Child Development, 55,* 1265-1277.

Marion, R. L. (1981). *Education, parents, and exceptional children.* Rockville, MD: Aspen Systems Corporations.

Parke, R. D. (1978). Parent-infant interaction: Progress, paradigms, and problems. In G. P. Sackett (Ed.), *Observing behavior: Theory and applications in mental retardation* (pp. 69–95). Baltimore: University Park Press.

Parke, R. D. (1980). *Becoming a Family* (Film). University of Illinois.

Parke, R. D. (1979). Perspectives on father-infant interaction. In J. Osotsky (Ed.), *The handbook of infancy* (pp. 549–590). New York: Wiley.

Parke, R. D. (1981). *Fathers.* Cambridge, MA: Harvard University Press.

Parke, R. D. (1984). The development of at-risk infants. Program report to National Institute of Child Health and Human Development, Washington, DC.

Parke, R. D., Grossman, K., & Tinsley, B. R. (1981). Father-mother-infant interaction in the newborn period: A German-American comparison. In T. M. Field, A. M. Sostek, P. Vietze, & P. H. Leiderman (Eds.), *Culture and early interactions* (pp. 95–113). Hillsdale, NJ: Lawrence Erlbaum Associates.

Parke, R. D., Hymel, S., Power, T. G., & Tinsley, B. R. (1980). Fathers and risk: A hospital-based model of intervention. In D. B. Sawin, R. C. Hawkins, L. O. Walker, & J. H. Penticuff (Eds.), *Psychosocial risks in infant-environment transactions* (pp. 174–189). New York: Bruner/Mazel.

Parke, R. D., & O'Leary, S. E. (1976). Father-mother-infant interaction in the newborn period: Some findings, some observations, and some unresolved issues. In K. Riegel & J. Meacham (Eds.), *The developing individual in a changing world* (Vol. II) *Social and environmental issues* (pp. 653–663). The Hague: Mouton.

Parke, R. D., Power, T. G., & Gottman, J. M. (1979). Conceptualizing and quantifying influence patterns in the family triad. In M. E. Lamb, S. T. Suomi, & G. R. Stephenson (Eds.), *Social interaction analyses: Methodological issues* (pp. 231–253). Madison, WI: The University of Wisconsin Press.

Parke, R. D., & Sawin, D. B. (1976). The father's role in infancy: A reevaluation. *The Family Coordinator, 25,* 365–371.

Parke, R. D., & Sawin, D. B. (1980). The family in early infancy: Social interactional and attitudinal analyses. In F. A. Pedersen (Ed.), *The father-infant relationship* (pp. 44–70). New York: Praeger.

Parke, R. D., & Tinsley, B. R. (1982). The early environment of the at-risk infant: Expanding the social context. In D. Bricker (Ed.), *Intervention with at-risk and handicapped infants: From research to application* (pp. 153–177). Baltimore, MD: University Park Press.

Parke, R. D., & Tinsley, B. R. (1984). Historical and contemporary perspectives on fathering. In K. A. McCluskey & H. W. Reese (Eds.), *Life-span developmental psychology: Historical and generationals* (pp. 203–248). New York: Academic Press.

Pascoe, J. M., Loda, F. A., Jeffries, V., & Earp, J. A. (1981). The association between mothers' social support and provision of stimulation to their children. *Developmental and Behavioral Pediatrics, 2,* 15–19.

Pastor, D. L. (1981). The quality of mother-infant attachment and its relationship to toddlers' initial sociability with peers. *Developmental Psychology, 17,* 326–335.

Pedersen, F. A., Anderson, B. J., & Cain, R. L. (1980). Parent-infant and husband-wife interactions observed at age five months. In F. A. Pedersen (Ed.), *The father-infant relationship: Observational studies in the family setting.* New York, Praeger.

Power, T. G., & Parke, R. D. (1982). Play as a context for early learning: Lab and home analyses. In I. E. Sigel & I. M. Laosa (Eds.) *The family as a learning environment* (pp. 223–241). New York: Plenum.

Sameroff, A. (1982). The environmental context of developmental disabilities. In D. Bricker

(Ed.), *Intervention with at-risk and handicapped infants* (pp. 141–152). Baltimore, MD: University Park Press.

Slade, C. I., Redl, O. J., & Manguten, H. H. (1977). Working with parents of high-risk newborns. *Journal of Obstetric and Gynecologic Nursing, 6,* 21–26.

Smith, C., Leiderman, P. H., Selz, L., MacPherson, L., & Bingham, E. (1981, April). *Maternal expectations and developmental milestones in physically handicapped infants.* Paper presented at the Biennial Meeting of the Society for Research in Child Development, Boston.

Stern, M., & Hildebrandt, K. A. (1984). Prematurity stereotype: Effects of labeling on adults' perceptions of infants. *Developmental Psychology, 20,* 360–362.

Stoneman, Z., Brody, G. H., & Abbott, D. (1983). In-home observations of young Down Syndrome children with their mothers and fathers. *American Journal of Mental Deficiency, 87,* 591–600.

Tew, B. J., Lawrence, K. M., Payne, H., & Rawnsley, K. (1977). Marital stability following the birth of a child with spina bifida. *British Journal of Psychiatry, 131,* 79–82.

Unger, D. G. (1979). *An ecological approach to the family: The role of social networks, social stress and mother-child interaction.* Unpublished masters thesis, Merrill-Palmer Institute.

Vietze, P. M., Abernathy, S. R., Ashe, M. L., & Faulstich, G. (1978). Contingent interaction between mothers and their developmentally delayed infants. In G. P. Sackett (Ed.), *Observing behavior: Theory and applications in mental retardation.* Baltimore, MD: University Park Press.

Vietze, P. M., MacTurk, R. H., McCarthy, M. E., Klein, R. P., & Yarrow, L. J. (1980, April). *Impact of mode of delivery on father- and mother-infant interaction at 6 and 12 months.* Paper presented at the International Conference on Infant Studies, New Haven, CT.

Walker, J. A. (1982). Social interactions of handicapped infants. In D. Bricker (Ed.), *Intervention with at-risk and handicapped infants* (pp. 217–232). Baltimore, MD: University Park Press.

Yogman, M. W. (1982). Development of the father-infant relationship. In H. Fitzgerald, B. Lester, & M. W. Yogman (Eds.), *Theory and research in behavioral pediatrics* (Vol. 1, pp. 221–279). New York: Plenum Press.

Research on Men's Transitions to Parenthood

An Integrative Discussion

Phyllis W. Berman
Frank A. Pedersen
National Institute of Child Health and Human Development

Research on paternal behavior has had a short history compared with research on mothers. However, after modest beginnings, investigations into fathers' interactions with their children have multiplied at an accelerating rate, a trend that has been particularly evident in the last decade. One of the most interesting areas of recent research on fathers is concerned with men's transitions to parenthood, their responses to the many changes taking place in the year or two after the birth of a first child, and their interactions with their babies. The conference that gave rise to this book was planned because it appeared to be an appropriate time to take stock, to survey what had been studied, how the research had been carried out, to ask what is now known, what information is needed, and what the best methods are with which to proceed.

This chapter focuses on questions raised in the Introduction and throughout this book. These include questions about fathers' behavior with babies, their emotional responses to their changed role and status, variables associated with different outcomes for fathers, the influence of their wives and marital situations, and early changes in fathers' experience and behavior. However, when evaluating the data presented here it is important to keep in mind which measures were used by each investigation, the populations sampled, and the research strategies used. Attention to methodology should provide a better basis for answers to research questions, help us to understand the limitations upon our answers, and should suggest new and improved ways to conduct future research.

METHODOLOGICAL ISSUES

Almost all of the authors of the preceding chapters have conducted research that followed fathers' transitions to parenthood over some period of time, and recorded fathers' self-reports or observed their behaviors on two or more occasions. Each of the chapters represents a somewhat different approach from the others, with varied samples, methods, time of observation, and so on. Few have studied the same phenomena in the same way. This situation leads to some frustration when making comparisons but, at the same time, provides a complex and varied picture that is a rich source of new hypotheses. It is very helpful to consider this complexity when future research projects are designed. Tables 10.1 and 10.2 present information in summary fashion about each research project and the methods used. It is important not only to compare the substantive issues studied, but also to evaluate the full range of methods used by the group of researchers as a whole.

Samples

Despite the diversity of approaches taken, most of the chapters in this volume are concerned with the parents' first baby and relatively similar populations have been studied. Although we undoubtedly have benefited from this replication in some ways, it is important to keep in mind that there are limits to which we may generalize from these data. Many forms of families exist. These differ in size, ethnicity, social class, traditionality, and work roles, to name just a few important variables, which have been studied very little, it at all. There are families with many different kinds of parental arrangements, but we do not know much about how these families function or the dimensions and antecedents of father behavior within them. Certainly, there is good reason to believe that differences do exist based on differences in parents' race, ethnicity, social class, education, parental work arrangements, and many other factors (cf. Allen, 1985; Cazenave, 1979; Piotrkowski, 1978; Pleck, 1979; Pleck & Staines, 1983; Presser, 1986; Presser & Cain, 1983; Russell, 1982). However, it can be seen from Table 10.1 that the eight research projects described here have studied very largely white, nonminority, middle- to upper middle-class populations. Most of these relatively well-educated parents had deferred childbearing until they were close to 30 years old. The extent to which we can generalize from the data presented in this book must remain an open question until comparative work is undertaken with a broader range of populations.

Moreover, most of the samples are relatively small. This limitation is somewhat offset by the fact that most of the families have been studied

TABLE 10.1
Description of Research Project Samples

Project:	N (Families)	Race	SES/Education	Birth Order	Mother's Employment[a]	Age in Years at Birth (Father/Mother)
Belsky & Volling	64	White	Mainly Middle to Lower Middle Class	First	33% in Year 1	28/26
Cowan & Cowan	96[b]	15% Minority	Wide Range	First	54% in Year 1 & 2	30/29
Dickie	46	White	Mainly Professional	70% First Born	30% in Year 1	Early 30s
Feldman	30	White	Well Educated	First	32% at 6 Months	31/28
Grossman	58	White	Mainly Middle to Lower Middle Class	53% First Born	Mainly Husband Primary Provider	30/28
Parke & Anderson	44[c]	White	Mainly Middle to Lower Middle Class	First & Later	39% by End Year 1	29/27
Pedersen et al.	25[d]	White	Well Educated	First	44% in Year 1	32/30
Yogman	20[e]	Majority White	Mainly Middle & Upper Middle Class	First & Later	—	30/27

[a]Park & Anderson, Feldman & Pedersen et al.: Mothers employed 20+ hours/week; Dickie: Some mothers employed part time; Cowan & Cowan: 67% working mothers employed ½ time at 6 months, 50% half time at 18 months, remainder full time.
[b]Expectant couples randomly assigned to 1 of 3 conditions: 1) an intervention, 2) assessments without intervention, 3) assessment only after birth. A fourth, non-pregnant control group also was evaluated.
[c]Twenty-four full-term and 20 relatively healthy preterm infants.
[d]Eleven fathers who had experienced blues and 14 with no blues in the first 4 postnatal months.
[e]Ten full-term and 10 preterm infants.

TABLE 10.2
Reported Information about Subjects, Timing and Types of Measures Used by Researchers

| | Time of Measurement | | Subjects | | | Types of Measures | |
Project:	Prenatal	Postnatal	Mother	Father	Infant	Self-Report	Observation
Belsky & Volling	Yes	1, 3, & 9 Months	P	P	N	P[a]	P[b]
Cowan & Cowan	Yes	6, 18, & 42 Months	P	P	N	P	S[c]
Dickie	No	4–8 Months	P	P	P	P	P
Feldman	Yes	6–8 Months	P	P	N	P	S
Grossman	Yes	1, 2, & 5 Years	P	P	N	P	P[d]
Parke & Anderson	No	Birth, 12 Months	P	P	N	P	P
Pedersen et al.	No	3–4 & 12 Months	P	P	S	P	P
Yogman	No	1, 3, 5, 9, & 18 Months	P	P	P	P	P

Note. P = Primary, S = Secondary, N = None
[a]prenatal; [b]postnatal; [c]at 42 months postnatally; [d]at 2 and 5 years postnatally

intensively, with repeated measurements over time and, most often much attention has been devoted not only to the father, but also to the mother and, in some instances, to the baby.

Research Strategies

Several different types of strategies for disentangling the relationships between fathers' behaviors and their antecedents and correlates are represented in this volume. These are described in Table 10.2. The first strategy is to follow fathers' and mothers' self-reports and/or observed behaviors from the prenatal period to one or more periods postnatally. With this method, no comparison groups are studied, but the variables that are measured prenatally, and even at early postnatal points, can be traced to later outcomes and the predictive power of the earlier measures can be assessed. Statistically, these designs attempt to trace relationships with correlational or multiple regression strategies. The chapters by Feldman, and Belsky and Volling illustrate this approach.

Another strategy involves comparison of two or more naturally occurring groups. This approach was used by Pedersen and his colleagues, distinguishing between groups based on the fathers' emotional responses to parenting during the first 3 months of their babies' lives. Pedersen actually compared extreme groups, those who reported experiencing no "blues" and those who reported experiencing brief periods of definite, although subclinical, depression. These two groups of men were then followed and later outcomes were assessed.

Still another strategy involved comparing the responses to parenthood of groups of men who experienced different events. Cowan and Cowan, for example, assigned men and their wives to a treatment (an intervention group) or a control group. Couples who enlisted in the study during pregnancy were assigned to groups on a random basis. Because the couples were assigned randomly, the favorable outcome for the treatment group, compared with the control groups, is assumed to be due to the intervention itself.

Yogman, and Parke and Anderson studied the effects on paternal behavior of a naturally occurring event, preterm delivery. It is not clear to what extent the occurrence of preterm delivery might be considered to be random or, at least, not systematically linked in some way with those father behaviors that are considered to be outcomes of premature delivery. However, groups such as Yogman's and Parke and Anderson's have relatively homogeneous samples and there is little difference in socioeconomic status (SES) and education between families of preterm and full-term babies. The assumption is made that the behavioral differences between fathers of preterm and full-term infants result from the risk status of the babies and not from pre-existing psychological characteristics of the fathers themselves.

It is, of course, difficult to make assumptions about the direction of effects or causality when only one group is studied with correlational techniques. That is, we know that certain antecedent states, events and behaviors, for example, in the prenatal period are associated with later outcomes after the child is born. Grossman, Feldman, and Belsky and Volling have all followed one group of families in this way, paying particular attention to the marriage relationship and how aspects of the wife's behavior and the marriage relationship before and after the child's birth were related to father behavior. An interesting feature of Belsky and Volling's study was the repeated measurement when the infants were 1, 3, and 9 months old; although limitations to the assumptions that can be made about causality remain, cross-lag analyses allowed somewhat stronger inferences about how the marriage relationship affects parenting than were possible with the other studies.

Types of Data

It is important to keep in mind the distinction between self-reports and observational data in this volume. Each type of data supplements the other and tells us something different. For example, Feldman used "strain" as her central outcome measure. Strain was defined by self-report responses to five items: feeling overwhelmed, tense, inadequate, sad for no reason, and discouraged. Mothers and fathers who were high on strain responded that they had mood states such as these relatively often although the general level of disturbance for the group was not extraordinarily high. Strain, as Feldman measured it, is important because it affected the emotional tone of parents' other behaviors. That is, if the only measures were observations of how much parents were doing with the baby, the parents who reported this sort of strain could look very well adapted to parenthood. In fact, mothers and fathers who scored high on strain also scored high on caretaking. But the other correlates of strain included elements of dysphoria, including low self-satisfaction, decline in energy and appearance for the wives, both parents feeling puzzled by the baby, and worried. Feldman's study shows that it is particularly valuable to have both self-report measures and behavioral observations to assess the same realm of parenting.

Dickie's chapter on interrelationships within the mother–father–infant triad is intriguing in that it illustrates considerable methodological as well as conceptual innovation. Conceptually, Dickie tried to disentangle aspects of parenting, aspects of the marriage realtionship and characteristics of the infant. She then asked how the three subsystems connect with one another for both the mother and the father. It is a very complex conceptual model and there are separate measures in all three realms. In almost all of the realms, except, of course, for the infant, there were self-report measures coupled with observers' ratings. One example of the consequences of this strategy is that parenting was assessed by observers' ratings of parent competence (defined by a number of rating scales that were then factor analyzed and yielded a single summary score for parenting competence). Parenting was also assessed by self-report measures. The self-report measures did not address competence itself, but instead parents' decisions about how to distribute childcare between husband and wife and their expectations about what constituted an optimal distribution of child-care responsibilities. Thus, in the parenting realm there were observer ratings of competence and also self-reports of what the parents did and what they thought would be optimal. Similarly, in the marriage relationship there were observer ratings of how supportive parents were with one another. Three different aspects of marital support were also assessed by self-reports: those that addressed emotional support, communication, and marital satisfaction. What emerged was very complex with each source of data yielding a somewhat different picture of reality.

This type of study avoids the interdependencies that restrict interpretation of results when all the data come from one source. For example, if all the data were based on observers' measures, there could be biases, such as halo effects in observers' judgments about how the family functions. Similarly, if all the data were self-reported, relationships that obtain would have been filtered through the eyes of the parents themselves. Having both self-report and independent observations provides us with markers of psychological factors that tap different phenomena. The use of multiple levels of description helps us to understand the constructs that have major limitations when defined at only one level.

SUBSTANTIVE ISSUES

Comparisons Between Mothers and Fathers

From the beginnings of research on fathers, maternal and paternal roles have been compared for both quantity and quality of parent investment. The projects reported here were no exception. Although spouses did not always agree about how much parental responsibility each shouldered, it is clear that fathers less frequently engage in caretaking—feeding, changing diapers, bathing, and so on—than mothers do, even when the situation affords equal opportunity to each. All of the chapters that reported a comparison between mothers' and fathers' caretaking found large significant differences between the sexes (see chapters by Belsky & Volling, Cowan & Cowan, Dickie, Parke & Anderson). Dickie reported that mothers took twice as much responsibility for childcare as fathers. This division of child-care responsibility may well be more traditional than either partner expected it to be (Cowan & Cowan). It can also be the source of considerable marital conflict, and considerable disparity is sometimes found between spouses reports of how much responsibility each takes for childcare (Dickie).

Belsky and Volling noted that the mothers in their sample interacted more with their babies than fathers did, even though the observations were in the early evening and most of the mothers had been at home with the baby all day. These findings replicate many other studies that found generally low father–infant interactions. However, if one compares these findings with mother–father differences in more highly educated, urban, professional level families (cf. Pedersen, Anderson, & Cain, 1980) the latter appear to have a more egalitarian mother–father distribution of care. It certainly seems to be a commonplace observation that mothers interact with infants more often than fathers do, even when both parents have equal opportunity. Nevertheless, education, SES, early experience with offspring, and presence or absence of the mother may modify this generalization appreciably. What is more, many other variables have hardly been researched at all. Among these, ethnicity, culture and ideology, early training and sibship, fathers' previous experience with earlier born children and many other factors await investigation.

Marital Support

An important change in parenting research is increasingly obvious in this book. Unlike most of the past work in which childcare was considered to be the mother's domain, and research concerning the father's role in the family was restricted to evaluating his provision of economic resources, the work represented here focuses on the father's role as a parent and his direct interaction with his children. As this work proceeds, it becomes evident that there is an important set of variables concerned with support for the father in his relationship with the baby, in this case, emotional support. In this volume Belsky and Volling, Feldman, Cowan and Cowan, and Dickie all attended to these variables.

When variables associated with emotional support for mothers and similar support for fathers are compared, it appears as though fathers are in particular need of support in the parenting role and that, under conditions of low support, fathers' parenting competence decreases disproportionately compared with mothers' competence under similar circumstances. This reverses the traditional conceptualization of parenting in which fathers have been seen as a source of support to mothers. In fact, the data show that fathers' parenting is more dependent on spousal support than mothers' parenting is. The idea that fathering is more vulnerable than mothering has been expressed in several chapters. That is, deleterious influences are more apt to interfere with the father–child relationship and fathering behavior than with the mother–child relationship and maternal behavior. Another way of stating this is to say that the mothering system is more buffered or resilient than the fathering system.

In Belsky and Volling's and Dickie's research, the marital relationship appeared to be more closely associated with the father's relationship with the infant than the mothers'. Either both marriage and parenting are correlates of something else, perhaps the ability to invest in relationships with significant persons such as spouse, children, or others, or marriage may in fact be more central to parenting for fathers than it is for mothers. In either case, Belsky and Volling and also Dickie found that marriage and parenting were more closely related to each other for men than for women. Women seemed more able than fathers to maintain greater competence with their infants when things had gone awry with their marriages. Feldman, on the other hand, suggested that for mothers more than for fathers a poor marriage relationship was critically related to a subjective sense of strain as a parent.

This is especially interesting because conventional thinking about fathers has centered on their provision of economic and emotional support for the mother. Although these are undoubtedly important functions, the present findings attest to the fact that the father's role is more sensitive to influence from marital factors than is the mother's role. These empirical findings are somewhat the reverse of conventional wisdom and, one could speculate about why this is so. From an evolutionary perspective it has been suggested that the mother–infant bond may be so intense, so programmed for the survival of the offspring, that there may be some biological basis for this connectedness. Whether or not this is so, little is known about any biological mechanisms that make mothering less vulnerable than fathering behavior in humans. However, females generally have more consistent long-term preparation for the parenting role, so that by the time they arrive at parenting women are often regarded by men as experts. With this status accorded to them, the mother often interprets the child's needs and behaviors and models parenting behaviors for the father.

In this historical period there is also great ambiguity about what is an appropriate paternal role in the family. The traditional emphasis on the father's provider role has been challenged and there are new expectations that fathers will assume direct nurturing roles with the young. However, men are entering this arena with little preparation and experience and with few role models. In Dickie's words, men are coming into 1980's role expectations with 1950's preparation. Because of this, they may depend on marriage relationships and their wives' expectations to define the paternal role.

In addition, there is a transactional character to this process. The wife's support to her husband seems to facilitate his child-care investment, and the effect can feed back to benefit the wife by lightening her load. This is occurring at a time when women are also extending their psychological investments outside of the family by becoming increasingly involved in careers outside of the family. One contribution of the research reported in this volume is that it provides evidence that support systems within the family function to draw the father into a more direct parenting role. It also follows that benefits may accrue to the mother as she supports greater integration of the father into the family unit.

Belsky and Volling found two areas of behavior in which interparent correlations were substantial, replicated over the three times of measurement. They were Respond (to baby) and a variable that implied ignoring the baby, Read/Watch TV. For both measures there were substantial correlations so that when the mother responded more frequently to baby, the father also responded at a relatively frequent rate, and vice versa, and when one parent ignored the baby relatively often the other also tended to ignore the baby. The psychological connection between maternal and paternal behavior rates occurred even though the *absolute* levels of involvement of mothers and fathers still differed from one another. Given the rarity of substantial relationships that are also replicable over several times of measurement, Belsky and Volling's findings are noteworthy.

Considerable learning probably took place with the mother modeling baby-directed behavior for the father, and vice versa. As Belsky and Volling note, there also might be another transactional process taking place. The mothers' stimulation of the baby may generate readiness to respond on the part of the baby and this, in turn, can promote the fathers' interactions with the baby. Furthermore, Belsky and Volling found a relationship between the nature of spousal communication and father involvement with the baby at 3 months. Positive communication about the baby between husband and wife when the infant was 1-month-old promoted later "stimulating, responsive, affectionate" father involvement. It is possible that such communications "prime" or sensitize fathers to experience positive emotions when interacting with an infant.

Strain and "Blues"

The families described in the foregoing chapters were generally well functioning and successful in meeting the challenges of parenthood. Most of them experienced considerable pleasure and delight with their babies. Nonetheless, several of the chapters (Belsky & Volling; Cowan & Cowan; Feldman; Pedersen et al.) speak of the strain also experienced by new parents. None of the projects have investigated families with parents who could be described as "clinically depressed" although there are certainly differences between project samples. Pedersen et al. studied fathers who, not only reported experiencing "blues," but at the same time interacted less with their babies at 3 months than did a "no blues" control group of fathers. In contrast, for both mothers and fathers in Feldman's sample, higher rates of infant caretaking were positively correlated with self-reported feelings of being overwhelmed and strained. Those parents who reported feeling strained were doing much caretaking but were unhappy, worried, puzzled, showed little affect, and were dissatisfied and low in playfulness. Their involvement had none of the zest, spirit, and positive affect that is characteristic of positive adaptation. At the high end of the strain ratings there was, then, an overburdened group of families who met their duties to the baby but certainly did not experience much joy doing so.

When Feldman examined self-reports from the prenatal period, she found very specific predictors of later strain for both sexes. The most important single predictor of lack of strain for men was planfulness of the pregnancy. For men planfulness may be a marker of psychological readiness to move on to a parental role, and to forego being the recipient of his wife's exclusive interest. It could also involve economic concerns, feeling satisfied with career choices that are necessary because of the economic responsibility associated with parenthood. Feldman also included a psychologically similar variable predictive for women. She called this *emotional rehearsal* for parenthood. Preparation such as this directs attention to parenthood rather than just pregnancy. Emotional rehearsal for parenthood may have psychological content that men are less able to articulate or is less clearly formulated by men. Men's experience during the first pregnancy may be such that they are less able to express emotional rehearsal for parenthood, although they are able to express a more concrete notion of planning the pregnancy.

The best predictor of strain for women was the marriage relationship, a factor that seemed to be central for women. With the transition to parenthood, women often redefined their roles to be more completely involved with family activity. They were usually economically more dependent than before on their husbands. Many of the mothers in Feldman's sample gave up jobs, careers, and the accompanying rewards and were therefore very heavily invested in the marriage. The centrality and continuity for men of career commitments may somehow insulate them from defining their sense of well-being to the extent that women do in terms of the adequacy of the marriage relationship.

It is intriguing that mens' reports of the adequacy of their marriage relationship predicted their involvement with the baby but *not* strain of parenthood. It is probable that accepting major responsibility for parenting is experienced as discretionary by men more often than it is by women. A non-supportive marital relationship may lead to a father's disengagement from his baby, but possibly not be a major determinant of parenting strain. That is, fathers may feel little strain in parenting precisely because they are disengaged. In contrast, not many mothers may feel that they have such a choice. Instead, mothers may continue to take responsibility for child care, but feel considerable psychological distress as a concomitant of the more obligatory nature of the maternal role.

Cowan and Cowan have described some of the burdens borne by first-time parents during the early months of their infants lives. Division of child-care responsibility was the major cause of disagreement. Self-report data from the pregnancy period show that there is often great discrepancy between fathers' ideal image of parenthood and their real experience. As our culture has changed, fathers' expectations have also changed. Fathers now expect to participate more than before in child rearing but there has been little increase in the support available to fathers for greater participation in this activity. At a time when men are raising young children they are generally also engaged in the establishment of relatively new careers. Although mothers may have the option of taking maternity leave during their children's early infancy and returning to work later, paternity leaves are rarely available. Parents may also perceive that it is financially desirable for husbands to invest more time and energy in their careers than their wives do. Unfortunately, although fathers anticipate that they will spend more time with their children than their own fathers did, the pressures for men to engage fully in work roles have not abated. This may be due to institutional policies or personal ambitions. Changes may take place as social conditions change, but at this point in history the ideology of parenthood has outstripped the conditions that would make possible fathers' fuller participation in childrearing.

This set of circumstances presents a problem to clinicians engaged in family interventions. Dickie has emphasized that more father participation does not necessarily result in greater family happiness. Those fathers who are most competent with their infants and participate most fully in caregiving may experience less marital satisfaction than others. They may undertake more parental tasks without fully communicating their own needs to their wives. Under some conditions then, the father's relationship with his child may be at a cost to his relationship with his wife. There is a finite amount of time and energy that any one person has to give to relationships. Thus, the marital relationship and parent relationship may compete with each other in some ways for time and energy. Dickie makes the point that one can not always have an extensive and optimal relationship with the child and the spouse without a cost to either.

There may be for each couple an optimal point of balance between child-centered and spouse-centered attention and activities. The point may be different for each family and may, in fact, change over time as new mothers and fathers adjust to their own infants, circumstances and personal preferences. This would be conceptually consistent with Pedersen's finding that men who had described feeling "blue" shortly after the birth of their first baby were at 12 months actively interacting with the baby, and also felt significant improvement in the spousal relationship. These men perceived improvement in the quality of the spousal relationship and in having an appropriate amount of time available with the spouse.

Apparently the additional responsibilities carried by new parents often make inroads in their sense of self-esteem. The Cowans found that for both mothers and fathers self-esteem declined from pregnancy to 6 months postnatally and, again, to 18 months. For both parents, self-esteem and marital satisfaction during pregnancy accounted for about 60% of the variance in later satisfaction with child-care arrangments. Most couples became more traditional following the first birth (Feldman & Aschenbrenner, 1983) and it is noteworthy that being responsible for chores that are typically believed to be the responsibility of the other sex was predictive of strain for both husbands and wives. For example, when the wife seemed to be responsible for things that are typically "male" tasks as Feldman defined them, or when the husband was responsible for much of the household work (which our culture defines as typically in the woman's domain) then both groups showed higher strain scores. It could be that when one parent does work that characteristically is the domain of the other, he or she may simply be overloaded. Another interpretation might be that there is some sense of injustice; the work itself might not be burdensome, but "cross-sex" work might not be perceived as belonging to one's self. In this case, the most important element might be a self-defined sense of injustice, rather than sheer amount of work, a sense that the marital partner is not doing his or her "share."

The Cowans found that, when the baby was 18 months old, paternal involvement satisfaction and, inversely, stress at 18 months had multiple predictors as well as concurrent correlates. Many of these were from the marital realm, such as participation in household tasks, satisfaction with couples' decision making, a global measurement of marital satisfaction and child-centered parenting attitudes. At face value, higher scores on these measures contribute to an image of a highly cohesive and interdependent family unit. This suggests that important patterns of father roles can be distinguished. One pattern is found in relatively cohesive and inter-dependent family units. However, there are families with fathers who are more disengaged from the child-care role. Disengaged fathers are also lower on nonchild-care measures that are broadly related to cohesive interdependent, interconnected family systems. One hypothesis that remains to be tested is that there are other family forms that are also adaptive psychologically for the child's development, including well-functioning family units where parents are more differentiated in their roles.

Changes With Time

Although the studies included in this book have concentrated mostly on the first year or so of the baby's life, it is important to note that phenomena such as strain, stress or anxiety, that appear to be similar (but are measured differently at different times) may in actuality be different depending on the infants' age and, at the same time, the parents' developmental changes with the evolution of the family unit. For example, the Cowans found changes in the composition of measures based on parents' perceptions and self-reports of stress in the 18-month period, compared with earlier periods.

The chapter by Pedersen and his colleagues is consistent with the view that there is no simple trajectory over time that can be predicted early on from parents' prenatal behaviors, feelings, self-reports, or from similar measures soon after birth. Phenomena associated with the negative consequences of the addition of a baby to the family are likely to change. Some adjustments take place within individual parents, within the marriage, and possibly within even a larger community support system. There are also obvious changes in the infant. The baby becomes a different person to be reckoned with in terms of the demands made on the family and in terms of interactional ability. These changes may be particularly important to fathers. Men, for example, may have very different expectations for different stages of parenthood than women do. Women still grow up thinking of themselves as primary caregivers although they may have no idea how much work is involved or what the demands on them well be. Mothers may also expect less from young infants than fathers do, while fathers' engagement in play may be particularly dependent on feedback from the baby.

Other changes may have to do with development of the father's career, and other nonfamily types of behaviors as well as his marital development. There is some indication that this is a very important area of change for the father because we see in several places that the addition of a second child involves less change for the father than the first child. There is less predictability from measures taken during the second pregnancy than the first. For example, Grossman found that the relationships between measures of autonomy, affiliation and other psychological measures in the individual, marital, and parental roles were generally stronger among first-time parents than those with more than one child. This suggests that there may be an interplay among family members that is more tightly interwoven during the initial transition to parenthood. Perhaps there is some special emotional impact in these experiences the first time around. There are few cultural guidelines for negotiating the transitions to parenthood that specify what is appropriate behavior for either parent. Thus, it is likely that behavior early after the birth of a first child is directed largely by the parents' own psychological makeup and the way it interacts with their situation and baby. The parental role with later borns might be more influenced by previous experience and habits. For example, even if later parenting is inadequate and adaptation less than optimal, some habits should be in place. Experienced mothers and fathers with later children may be more able to adjust to the individual temperament of a baby, a talent learned by being parents of a previous child. Because of this there should not be as strong a relationship between their behavior and their own preparental characteristics as is true for first-time parents.

In some respects, experiences following the birth of a second child may change even more radically for fathers than for mothers. At the time of the first birth, the father's relationship with his wife is most often redefined more radically than at later births. When a second-born enters the family, the father may experience a further intensification of responsibility for the older child while the mother devotes herself more exclusively to the needs of the new baby. If there is a major change in role that occurs, the connections with the father's preparental characteristics can be weakened, complicating the picture. Mothers' and fathers' early adaptations to parent-hood are interdependent. That is, one partner's adjustment depends on the other's. This means that prediction from early postnatal measures is attenuated. Often, one parent's behavior in some way generalizes to the other's. Parents may model behavior, instruct and learn from each other. In this case the behavior rates between mother and father tend to be posi-tively correlated with one another (Belsky, this volume). This is a sort of additive family experience so that these families have more redundancy in the way each parent relates to the baby.

However, other processes are sometimes responsible for a kind of com-pensatory pattern found by Pedersen and his colleagues. This pattern was characteristic of the families of fathers who reported early blues. That is, the fathers reported dysphoria following the birth of a first child and had less involvement with their babies than did control group fathers. At the same time, the wives of men with blues were more involved with their babies resulting in a negative association between the baby-related activi-ties of fathers and mothers. How this pattern is established is not known. It is possible that the wives of mildly depressed men interacted more with their babies because of their conviction that the infants' needs would not otherwise be met. In this case, a self-righting effect may operate if, in response to their wives' increased support, fathers increased their nurturant interactions with their babies.

A competing hypothesis is that the fathers' low involvement with their babies was the result, rather than the cause, of the mothers' high involvement.

The mother may have left little room for the father to express what may have been initially a rather tentative involvement. A very sensitive research design would be needed to test these alternative interpretations. Nonetheless, it might be feasible through a careful longitudinal design with frequent and early measures from birth on or perhaps a design with an intervention. Considerably more information is needed about the processes responsible for interdependent parent behaviors before it is possible to accurately predict patterns of consistency and change in parents' involvement with their babies from early infancy on.

Infant Characteristics

The major foci of most of the studies described in this volume are mothers' and fathers' experience and development. Except for the two chapters concerned with premature infants, the role of infant characteristics has been given less attention. Both the Yogman and the Parke and Anderson chapters on fathers of preterm babies express a rather similar conceptual model. That is, when the burden of child care is heightened, the father may be drawn into caregiving more actively. Both studies reason that child care for the premature infant is more demanding than care for the full-term baby, both in the practical aspects of nurturing babies and also the psychological burden that parents experience. Parents' separation from the baby, and the uncertainty about baby's health and the fact that premature status has been implicated as a contribution to long-term developmental problems, all may mobilize the father and enlist his participation in more active caregiving than is the case with full-term babies. The evidence for this hypothesis is, however, at this point minimal. Parke and Anderson's data do not support this hypothesis and Yogman's data show, at best, a trend. In the caregiving realm, Yogman's findings are suggestive, and because very few of the results met adequate statistical criteria, they should be thought of only as trends. However, fathers of premature babies appeared to provide more caregiving than fathers of term babies.

Parke and Anderson's study of full-term and preterm infants followed from birth to age 12 months may be compared with Yogman's. As a group, Parke and Anderson's preterms seem to have been less at risk than those Yogman studied. Methods for evaluating participation in caregiving activities used in the two studies were also quite different. Parke and Anderson observed families of infants at ages 3 weeks, 3 months, 8 months, and 12 months with observations of feeding episodes and unstructured activities. Ten-minute caregiving segments were used and conclusions were extrapolated from these data. There was only one consistent finding, namely that mothers were more active than fathers in all facets of caregiving across all time points for both full-term and preterm infants.

In contrast, Yogman collected self-report data that, in theory, encompassed the father's full experience with the baby. Although Parke and Anderson's procedures may be more objective and less subject to distortion, the base of observation is smaller and perhaps less likely to uncover differences between fathers of premature and full-term babies. Parke's findings are somewhat at variance with Yogman's. Parke found that premature status had nothing to do with paternal caregiving, whereas Yogman's sample of preterms elicited more paternal caregiving than this full-term sample did. There does not appear to be a major difference in the demographic characteristics of the two samples. However, Yogman's preterm infants were described as being at greater risk than Parke and Anderson's. If the difference between the results of the two studies is true and reliable, and not the result of differences in the measures used, then risk status of the premature infant may have had an effect on the father's involvement. Compared with the more robust full-term infant the small, sick premature baby may more actively draw the father into the caregiving role.

J. L. Gaiter (personal communication, June 1, 1984) suggested that one of the unique roles that the father fills when the premature infant is still hospitalized is to serve as a link between the institution and the family. The father seeks and gets information about the baby's condition, care, and prognosis from the experts at the hospital. This may be needed only in the very early stages of the infant's life when this baby is still sick and the prognosis may be in question. This process might be particularly operative with later born prematures when there already are children at home and the mother must devote energy and time caring for them. The father could then be the family member who visits the hospital and seeks information about the premature baby, particularly when it is difficult for the mother to go. In fact, Parke and Anderson distinguished between informal support systems, including family and friends, and formal institutional support systems. Women tended more often to use informal, and men, formal systems. The father's tie with institutions seems strongest early in the baby's life. This is the time when support from formal systems is most necessary for the families of preterm infants. Perhaps men are more comfortable than women dealing with medical institutions, especially the well-educated fathers studied in these projects because they have traditionally occupied work roles associated with institutions such as these.

A major focus of Yogman's chapter is on father–infant play and its relation to the infant's later development. Laboratory interactions between fathers and babies were videotaped and coded in very fine detail to assess features of fathers' play patterns with their term and preterm babies. Fathers of prematures tended to play fewer games and played for shorter durations than did fathers of fullterms. Various measures of fathers' involvement in play with their 5-month-old babies were positively and significantly correlated with the infants' Bayley scores at age 6 months and 18 months. The total number of games, number of arousing games, the duration of the games, and the duration of the arousing games all were positively correlated with the Bayley 9-month, and particularly 18-month scores. That is, fathers who played more often and longer, more arousing games had infants with higher scores. A feature in these results that gives them special credibility is that there were no significant correlations between fathers' play and the infants' Bayley Psychomotor Development Index (PDI), but rather the relations were just with the Mental Development Index (MDI). Other researchers (Yarrow, Rubenstein, & Pedersen, 1975) have also found that the MDI is more strongly associated than the PDI to differences in amount of social stimulation provided by the parent.

It is noteworthy that the findings of significant correlations between father's games at 5 months and infants 18-month Bayley scores are in particular for the arousing games, not the unarousing games. We might speculate that the father adds something very unique to the infant's development by a kind of stimulation in arousing games that is quite different from the less arousing stimulation typical of other environments, particularly the baby's stimulation from the mother. It has been a consistent finding (Parke, 1981) that fathers spend proportionately more of their time with infants in play than mothers do. Belsky and Volling found little early differentiation between maternal and paternal stimulation on the infant, but, by the time the baby was 9 months old, the father emerged more prominently in the role as playmate and stimulator. That is, with the baby's maturation fathers' activity with the baby became increasingly different from mothers' activity. Both Yogman's and Parke and Andersons' chapters discuss fathers' play with infants who were at risk. By the time these children were 9 months old, fathers and infants had become much more reciprocal play partners. It may be that at this age fathers perceived that a new role was possible for them, a role that is distinctly different from the caretaking role that predominated in the first few months.

Another factor contributing to parental role differentiation may be the baby's increasing robustness. The absence of parental role differentiation in the baby's first 3 months could be related to the father's perception that the baby is relatively fragile, and has limited motor response capabilities. As the infant's capacities emerged more clearly the father could engage the baby in a more stimulating manner. Oddly enough, this paternal behavior did not appear to depend on the sex of the child. Past research has suggested that this stimulating behavior of fathers is most evident with male offspring, but it is not certain at what age sex differentiation emerges. In Lamb's (1980) work, the interaction between paternal role differentiation and sex of child did not emerge clearly until around the second year.

Pedersen (1980) speculated that the psychological basis for paternal behaviors that are differentiated by sex of child may depend on the child's age, and that there might be a curvilinear relationship between the child's age and paternal behaviors. Early in life, fathers with very young infants may distinguish between male and female offspring on the basis of stereotypes about babies. About the middle of the first year, this type of differentiation might wane as stereotype-based responsiveness diminishes and the father relates to his infant in terms of its unique characteristics. More clear-cut differences in fathers' behavior to boys and girls might later re-emerge in response to growing behavioral sex differences, but in the middle of the infant's first year there may be a short-lived lack of differentiation between male and female offspring.

Parents' Work Roles

Most chapters in this book have paid little attention to areas of parents' functioning outside the family, yet it is understood that fathers in all studies had continuing ties to the work world that were quite different from the mothers'. This was true particularly when the baby was quite young, that is, at the time that received the most attention in these research projects. The data in Table 10.1 show that when families were studied many of the mothers were either not working at all outside the home or they were working less than full time. Feldman has emphasized the effects of increased dependence on the marriage of mothers who have withdrawn from careers and work satisfactions. This dependence takes place at a time when mother and father must adapt to the demands and satisfactions of new parenthood. It would be helpful to learn what effect the mother's work situation has upon the father's role with his child. This is difficult to ascertain from the data presented here because, although a considerable proportion of the mothers who were studied returned to work, the samples were small and there may be many critical differences among these families depending on such factors as the baby's age at the time of the mother's return to work, whether work was full or part time, and the availability and nature of substitute childcare.

Cowan and Cowan in their chapter have touched on the work aspects of parents' lives. Although they do so only briefly, the chapter clearly shows that mothers are often ambivalent about the father's role with the child and the finding is buttressed by clinical interview data. This is particularly true of those mothers who do not have fully developed career roles that may serve as a source of rewards from outside the family. Although the father's child caretaking may offer respite from the heavy demands of major responsibility for the infant, the husband's efforts may be viewed as an encroachment upon the only domain that mothers feel fully belongs to them. It is important in this regard that men in the Cowans' sample who were most involved in parenting, and felt their identity in the father role to be greatest, had wives who felt less of their total identity to be in the mother role. By inference this may mean that there were other identities in which the wives of these child-oriented men were invested. The husbands, then, might have had more opportunity, and possibly felt more need, to enter into a close relationship with the baby.

A parallel process may occur when the mother is the primary breadwinner and the father, the primary child caretaker (K. Pruett, personal communication, June 1, 1984), although there is not much information on these atypical families. Fathers in these families may be similarly ambivalent about the mothers' role with the child. Thus, it is not likely that this phenomenon is restricted to parents with culturally normative sex-differentiated roles. Rather, after the birth of a child, particularly a first child, there may be a reshuffling of roles and the accompanying psychological investments and rewards that accompany these roles. The mother's and father's orientations to the child that emerge from this process may largely be defined by the particular balance between work- and child-care roles that each marital partner assumes.

Participation in paid work outside the home also affects individuals' characteristic ways of dealing with the world. Grossman, for example, focused on fathers' tendencies to be affiliative and/or autonomous. Affiliation is the tendency to be connected with others, to participate in and enjoy empathic relationships. Autonomy is the tendency to be separate and distinct from others, to feel efficacy in one's self, and enjoy activities that are carried out alone or separately from others. It is obvious that the world of work demands the development of a good deal of autonomy and that it is necessary to develop affiliative tendencies in order to assume the role of a nurturant parent. In the past, these two dimensions have been seen as polar opposites. An individual was thought to be either high on affiliation or autonomy. Grossman has presented data showing that affiliation and autonomy are different spheres of development that can coexist and, in fact, the measures of affiliation and autonomy in her study showed a moderate, but positive correlation with each other.

Grossman also found that both characteristics are important for fathers' adaptation to parenthood. However, she makes the point that it is often a problem for men to be affiliative, a characteristic that is demanded of new parents. Affiliative tendencies are important, not only for fathers' adaptation to parenthood, but also for their relationships with their wives and children. Grossman found that men who were more affiliative during pregnancy were more nurturant and physically stimulating to their children at age 2. Moreover, affiliative and autonomous characteristics (measured before the birth of the child) have long-term implications for men's relationships with their children more than 5 years later. The nature of these effects depends on the sex of the child, a finding that attests to the implications of autonomy and affiliation to sex-role socialization.

Early Development of Nurturance to Children

By the time men and women become parents they have had years of experience that prepare them to assume particular sorts of roles with their children. Little of this experience is formal in nature but it is pervasive in a growing child's experience as the recipient of parental nurturance and in expressed expectations within a particular culture and family. Although most of the investigations reported here have focused on the periods just preceding birth and the year or two following birth, it is important to attend to the earlier experiences and learning opportunities that precede the pregnancy and early parenthood periods. Cowan and Cowan have devoted considerable attention to men's early experiences with their own parents and the effects of these experiences on later involvement with their own children.

There is some data that show important relationships between a father's experience in his own primary family, as he remembers experiencing it, and his attitude to his own parental identity and even his relationship with his infant. The Cowans raise an interesting question: some authors (cf. Radin, 1981; Radin & Sagi, 1982) suggest that there may be a compensatory motivation for fathering. That is, those men who wish that their own fathers had been closer to them when they were children become more heavily invested in fathering. Another hypothesis, although these hypotheses are not exclusive (Soule, Standley, & Copans, 1979), is that the more nurturance a man received from his father, the more he witnessed and was the object of fathering as a child, the more probable it is that he will be a heavily invested and good father. These seem to be two possible mechanisms that can operate independently and also coexist.

It is important to study men's early experience as the recipients of mothering, as well as fathering, and not to make the assumption that the only, or even the primary, factor in an individual's preparation for future parenting comes from the same-sex parent. Transfer across sex should be expected in this early learning and, in fact, this type of transmission of patterns of nurturance should be very effective in an adaptational evolutionary manner as a means of refueling the origins of parenting from generation to generation. There may be two somewhat distinct learning avenues in men's early experience, one involving the experience of nurturance from mothers, and the other, from fathers. The process of learning from the two parents may be somewhat different for men. Learning from fathers may involve considerable modeling, while learning nurturant roles from the mothers may involve more complex differentiations between the self and the role model (cf. Lynn, 1969).

Several types of early experience are probably important to men's future parent roles: These include learning not only patterns of nurturance from parents and caregivers, but also learning about the connection between patterns of nurturance and gender roles. In other words, children learn what it is to be a man who relates to babies and children and what it is to be a woman who relates to babies and children. They learn what is an acceptable and well-reinforced parent role in a particular society, cultural group, family, and situation. A substantial literature has been established showing that children learn cultural and family proscriptions very early that serve as guidelines for responses believed to be appropriate for males and females in particular situations with children (e.g., Berman, in press; Berman & Goodman, 1984; Berman, Smith, & Goodman, 1983; Edwards, 1986; Melson, Fogel, & Toda, 1985; Weeks & Thornburg, 1977; Whiting & Whiting, 1975).

CONCLUSIONS

This chapter began with an acknowledgment that research on fathers has grown past its infancy. It has taken first steps into several areas of specialization. Eight of the chapters in this book represent facets of one of these areas: fathers' transitions to parenthood and into the first months and years of their children's lives. It is instructive to evaluate the progress of the research projects on which this book is based, not only for what can be learned about this specialized field, but also because it may to some extent serve as a barometer for the progress of father research in general. It is time to ask what can be concluded from an examination of the reports of these eight projects about substantive questions concerning men's transitions to parenthood and about methodological issues. Finally, we might ask what can an evaluation of these projects tell us about the state of the field and what recommendations can be made for future research.

At the outset it is important to note that the very fact that eight projects of this quality and magnitude exist reflects major progress in father research within the last decade. Although few of the research projects used exactly the same measures, there are several points of convergence, and some tentative conclusions can be reached.

First, the mothers and fathers studied differ from each other in many respects. When comparisons were made it was found that mothers interacted with their infants more than fathers did and took more responsibility for caregiving. Moreover, mothers and fathers differed in that mothers' competence in the parent role was more resistant to stress than fathers'.

A major theme of several of the chapters was that the transition to parenthood is often very difficult, even for the nonclinic populations studied. This transition is marked by changes in mothers' and fathers' work lives and family relations, and often by overload, conflict, strain, dysphoria, and even, at times, inroads into parents' self-esteem. It is possible to predict parent strain at least moderately well from preparental characteristics, and consideration of characteristics of both marital partners increases the accuracy of prediction of parent strain for either mothers or fathers. However, some of the characteristics that best predict strain differ for mothers and fathers.

Several chapters emphasized the centrality of the marriage relationship and wives' support for men's involvement with their infants. Many processes may be set into motion that tend to "correct" a father's early depressed involvement with his child. Some of these could involve increased spousal support, and possibly the wife's modeling of infant caregiving, increased input from support systems outside the immediate family unit, and perhaps the increased responsiveness of the infant as a result of his or her increased interactions with the mother. It is difficult to isolate the variables that ameliorate paternal withdrawal when it occurs during the child's early months; some improvement in the father's relationship with the baby might be expected simply as a result of the developing baby's increased capacity to give positive feedback, and also the baby's decreased demands for care. Nevertheless, several of the researchers have written of the difficulty some new parents may unexpectedly encounter when attempting to manage "optimal" relationships with each other and the new baby at the same time.

The role of infant characteristics was not a major focus of the studies in this book except for the effects of prematurity. The two projects that studied fathers' interactions with premature infants were not in full agreement and the findings were inconclusive. There is some suggestion that infants who are at greater risk may draw the father into a more active role than do full-term babies or premature infants who are at less risk do. This is a hypothesis of great importance, but still in need of validation.

In addition to shedding light on substantive issues, the research projects also have used methods which typify the considerable advances made in father research the last few years. Research on fathers proceeded rapidly from case histories, clinical studies, and studies of paternal deprivation, to cross-sectional studies of fathers' interactions with their children. The present volume represents a long step forward because it is, with only one exception, composed of reports of longitudinal studies. Although some of the samples were small, many of the investigators observed and/or interviewed mothers and fathers at three or more points in time. What is more, the measures of mother, as well as father characteristics and behavior present a fuller picture of the connections between marriage and parenthood than would otherwise be possible. Converging measures that are composed both of observation and self-reports offer some protection from the types of bias peculiar to the use of each type of measure alone and allow greater insight into the underlying meaning of the father's behavior within his own phenomenological framework.

One problem encountered by most of the researchers is that the lack of experimental control makes it impossible to determine the direction of effects and causality, and caution must therefore be exercised in interpretation. A more serious problem is that these studies are limited, by and large, to very restricted populations. This allowed enough replication that we now have substantial information about transitions to parenthood in populations that are largely white, nonminority, middle-class, traditional nuclear families with parents who are highly educated and have deferred childbearing until the beginning of their third decade of life. However, it is not known whether these data are typical of a broader spectrum of populations or whether they are determined by some set of circumstances characteristic of the restricted populations that have been studied thus far. This is all the more a problem because there is reason to believe that race, ethnicity, socioecononmic class, type of family and traditionality, education, and age of parents, are all variables that can be expected to affect fathers' responses to parenthood and relationships with their children.

In summary, the studies described in this book represent several very important advances for research on fathers. By and large the studies are longitudinal. They view fathers in the context of the larger family unit and in relationship to other family subsystems, such as the mother–child relationship and the spousal relationship. They study what fathers and mothers do, that is, their overt behavior, and the meaning of this behavior to the parents themselves, that is, their ideology, attitudes, and feelings. Although few of the researchers used identical procedures or measures, many of the studies dovetailed in such a way that a coherent picture has emerged of fathers, and to a lesser extent, mothers in the transition to parenthood.

What is now needed is a picture that is somewhat larger, one that will put our current understanding into broader perspective. First, more details are needed about the contribution of the infant to fathers' perceptions and behavior. The foregoing research has made us aware that variables such as infants' age, sex, social competence, and risk status are all important, but we have little clear (and replicated) data on the specifics of the operation of these variables.

We also know that the time from pregnancy through the first year or two after the birth of a first child is one of many changes for fathers, as well as for mothers. However, it is recognized that the father's role is shaped, in part, by contributions from his earlier history, going back to his early childhood. The father's role also has a future life course of change. Changes are fed by the rapid growth of the child, changes in the marriage relationship and in the father's own developmental status, not only as father and husband, but in the work world and in relation to the father's family of origin, peers, and wider community. The birth of a subsequent child affects the father's relationship with his first child and is, of course, a very different sort of transition for the father than is the first birth. Further research on the life course of fatherhood and the many variables that contribute to its development will certainly help us to understand the transitions and short-term changes discussed in this book. Finally, widening the base of popula-tions to be studied will give us still another perspective and will provide comparisons and contrasts to what has been discovered in the studies described in this book, deepening our understanding of the causal relation-ships that determine father's roles.

ACKNOWLEDGMENT

The authors are grateful to Dr. Earl Huyck for his helpful editorial suggestions.

REFERENCES

Allen, W. R. (1985). Race, income and family dynamics: A study of adolescent male socializa-tion processes and outcomes. In M. B. Spencer, G. K. Brookins, & W. R. Allen (Eds.), *Beginnings: Social and affective development of black children* (pp. 273–291). Hillsdale, NJ: Lawrence Erlbaum Associates.

Berman, P. W. (in press). Children caring for babies: Age and sex differences in response to infant signals and to the social context. In N. Eisenberg (Ed.), *Contemporary issues in developmental psychology*. New York: Wiley.

Berman, P. W., & Goodman, V. (1984). Age and sex differences in children's responses to babies: Effects of adults' caretaking requests and instructions. *Child Development, 55,* 1071–1077.

Berman, P. W., Smith, V. L., & Goodman, V. (1983). Development of sex differences in response to an infant and to the caretaker role. *Journal of Genetic Psychology, 143,* 283–284.

Cazenave, N. A. (1979). Middle-income black fathers: An analyses of the provider role. *Family Coordination, 28,* 583–593.

Edwards, C. P. (1968). Another style of competence: The caregiving child. In A. Fogel & G. F. Melson (Eds.), *Origins of nurturance* (pp. 95–121). Hillsdale, NJ: Lawrence Erlbaum Associates.

Feldman, S. S., & Aschenbrenner, B. (1983). Impact of parenthood on various aspects of masculinity and feminity: A short-term longitudinal study. *Developmental Psychology, 19,* 278–289.

Lamb, M. E. (1980). The development of parent-infant attachments in the first two years of life. In F. A. Pedersen (Ed.), *The father-infant relationship: Observational studies in the family setting* (pp. 21–43). New York: Praeger.

Lynn, D. B. (1969). *Parental and sex-role identification: A theoretical formulation.* Berkely: McCutcheon.

Melson, G. F., Fogel, A., & Toda, S. (1985). *Children's ideas about infants and their care.* W. Lafayette, IN: Department of Family Studies, Purdue University.

Parke, R. D. (1981). *Fathers.* Cambridge, MA: Harvard University Press.

Pedersen, F. A. (1980). Overview: Answers and reformulated questions. In F. A. Pedersen (Ed.), *The father-infant relationship: Observational studies in the family setting* (pp. 147–163). New York: Praeger.

Pedersen, F. A., Anderson, B. J., & Cain, R. L. (1980). Parent-infant and husband-wife interactions observed at age five months. In F. A. Pedersen (Ed.), *The father-infant relationship: observational studies in the family setting* (pp. 71–86). New York: Praeger.

Piotrkowski, C. S. (1978). *Work and the family system.* New York: Free Press.

Pleck, J. H. (1979). Men's family work: Three perspectives and some new data. *Family Coordinator, 28,* 481–488.

Pleck, J. H., & Staines, G. L. (1983). *The impact of work schedules on the family.* Ann Arbor, MI: Survey Research Center, Institute for Social Research, The University of Michigan.

Presser, H. (1986). Shift work among American women and child care. *Journal of Marriage and the Family, 48,* 551–563.

Presser, H. B., & Cain, V. A. (1983). Shift work among dual-earner couples with children. *Science, 219,* 876–879.

Radin, N. (1981). Childrearing fathers in intact families: I. Some antecedents and consequences. *Merrill-Palmer Quarterly, 27,* 489–514.

Radin, N., & Sagi, A. (1982). Childrearing fathers in intact families: II. Israel and the USA. *Merrill-Palmer Quarterly, 28,* 111–136.

Russell, G. (1982). Highly participant Australian fathers: Some preliminary findings. *Merrill-Palmer Quarterly, 28,* 137–156.

Soule, B., Standley, K., & Copans, S. A. (1979). Father identity. *Psychiatry, 42,* 255–263.

Weeks, M. O., & Thornburg, K. R. (1977). Marriage role expectations of five-year old children and their parents. *Sex Roles, 3,* 189–191.

Whiting, B. B., & Whiting, J. W. (1975). *Children in six cultures.* Cambridge, MA: Harvard University Press.

Yarrow, L. J., Rubenstein, J. L., & Pedersen, F. A. (1975). *Infant and environment: Early cognitive and motivational development.* Washington, DC: Hemisphere, Halsted-Wiley.

Author Index

Complete references are listed at the end of each chapter.

A

Abbott, D., 200, 205
Abernathy, S. R., 200
Abidin, R., 155
Abrahams, B., 13
Adamson, L., 7, 180
Ainsworth, M. D. S., 6
Albrecht, S., 118
Aldous, J., 10
Allen, V. L., 149
Allen, W. R., 218
Almgren, P., 15, 30
Als, H., 7, 179, 180
Anderson, B., 41, 120, 165, 205, 224,
Anderson, C., 118
Anderson, E., 197–212, 221, 223, 232, 233, 234
Andrew, G., 202
Anzalone, M. K., 89, 93, 95, 97, 99, 107
Araji, S. K., 145
Arbuckle, M. B., 209
Aschenbrenner, B., 17, 23, 32, 42, 92, 107,
    120, 121, 136, 146, 148, 229
Ashe, M. L., 200
Atkinson, A. K., 32

B

Backman, E., 145

Bailyn, L., 108
Bakan, D., 91
Bakeman, R., 178, 200
Bales, R. F., 13
Ball, F. L. J., 117, 118, 169
Bandura, A., 149
Barber, L., 116
Barnett, C., 122
Barnett., R. C., 146, 148, 149
Barry, W. A., 119
Baruch, G. K., 146, 148, 149
Basham, R. B., 208
Baumrind, D., 123
Beck, A. T., 66, 67
Beckwith, L., 178, 179, 190
Bell, R. Q., 5
Belsky, J., 10, 14, 29, 37–61, 68, 73, 83, 120,
    121, 124, 136, 139, 146, 148, 153, 205,
    221, 222, 223, 224, 225, 226, 231, 234
Bem, S. L., 16, 17, 20, 97
Benedek, T., 14, 93
Benson, L., 91
Berman, P. W., 217–241
Bernard, J., 107, 113, 153
Bibring, G. L., 14
Bierman, J. J., 178
Biller, H. B., 3, 91, 113
Bingham, E., 200
Biringen, Z., 13
Block, J., 3, 121

Block, J. H., 3
Bloom-Feshbach, J., 113, 211
Boles, A. J., 117, 118, 146, 147, 152, 153, 154
Bornstein, M. H., 69
Boukydis, C., 190
Bowlby, J., 6, 9
Bradley, R., 189
Brassard, J. A., 198
Braverman, J., 68
Brazelton, T. B., 7, 115, 179, 180
Bringle, R. G., 3, 4
Brody, G. H., 200, 205
Broman, S. H., 3
Bronfenbrenner, U., 114, 119, 198, 207
Brooks, V., 199
Brown, J. V., 178, 200
Brunnquell, D., 200
Burton, R., 6

C

Cain, R. L., 41, 65–86, 120, 165, 205, 224, 226,
    227, 230, 231
Cain, V. A., 218
Cairns, R. B., 6
Caldwell, B., 189
Campbell, A., 13
Campbell, D., 9, 51
Campbell, J. D., 6,
Campbell, S. B., 65, 66
Canning, C. D., 199
Caputo, D. V., 178, 199
Carmichael, L., 145
Carter, C., 190
Carver, J., 206
Carver, N., 206
Catalyst, 167
Cazenave, N. A., 218
Celhoffer, L., 190
Chadwick, B., 118
Chandler, M. J., 2, 5, 69, 179
Chiriboga, D., 13, 14
Chodorow, N., 107, 108
Clarke-Stewart, K. A., 7, 40, 41, 145, 120, 177
Cleaves, W. T., 41
Cochran, M. M., 198
Cohen, S. E., 178, 179, 190
Cohn, J., 190
Coie, J. D., 91, 124, 151
Coie, L., 91, 124, 151

Cole, S., 113
Coleman, R. P., 95, 97
Colman, A. D., 14
Cook, N. I., 122
Cook, T. D., 9, 51
Copans, S. A., 237
Cowan, C. P., 15, 30, 31, 41, 42, 84, 91, 92,
    114, 115, 117, 118, 124, 145–171, 199,
    221, 223, 224, 226, 228, 229, 230, 235,
    237
Cowan, P. A., 15, 30, 31, 41, 42, 84, 91, 92,
    114, 115, 117, 118, 124, 145–171, 199,
    221, 223, 224, 226, 228, 229, 230, 235,
    237
Cox, M., 207
Cox, R., 97, 207
Coysh, W. S., 117, 118, 146, 147, 152, 153, 154,
    155, 165, 167, 168
Crawley, S., 40, 183
Crinic, K. A., 208
Criticos, A., 183
Crockenberg, S. B., 114, 139, 208
Crouter, A. C., 148, 207
Cummings, S. T., 202
Curtis, J. A., 14
Curtis-Boles, H., 117, 118, 146, 147, 152, 153,
    154

D

Darwin, C., 6
David, J., 116
Detre, T., 66
Deutscher, M., 14
Dibona, P., 145
Dickersheid, J., 38
Dickie, J., 113–140, 205, 222, 223, 224, 225,
    228
Dieterman, B., 118, 121
Dixon, S., 7, 40
Doering, S. G., 117, 118, 121, 122, 199
Donovan, W. L., 199
Drillien, C. M., 178
Duvall, E. M., 13,
Dwyer, T. F., 14

E

Earp, J. A., 208

Easterbrooks, M., 42
Edwards, C. P., 238
Egeland, B., 200
Eichler, L. S., 15, 30, 89, 93, 95, 97, 99, 107,
    114, 119, 121, 122, 146, 148, 167, 202
Elder, G. H., 198
Emerson, P. E., 6
Emms, E. M., 68
Entwisle, D. R., 117, 118, 121, 122, 199
Erbaugh, J., 66
Erikson, E., 13, 30
Erikson, E. H., 91
Eron, L. D., 4

F

Fanaroff, A. A., 198, 199
Farber, B., 206
Fasteau, M. F., 91, 93, 108
Faulstich, G., 200
Fedele, N. M., 91
Fein, R. A., 15
Feiring, C., 198, 204
Feldman, H., 15
Feldman, S. S., 13–33, 42, 65, 68, 84, 92, 93,
    107, 113, 118, 120, 121, 136, 139, 146,
    148, 149, 221, 222, 224, 225, 226, 227,
    229, 235
Field, T. M., 66, 178, 179, 189
Fisher, H. E., 84
Fisher, L., 146
Fletcher, J., 68
Fogel, A., 238
Foy, J. L., 92
Frank, E., 118
Frankel, J., 40
French, F. E., 178
Freud, S., 91, 104
Friedman, S., 183
Friedrich, W. N., 205
Frodi, A., 39, 47, 178, 199
Frodi, M., 39, 47, 178,
Furstenberg, F. F., 10

G

Gaiter, J. L., 179, 233
Galligan, R., 31
Gamble, W., 14

Garcia, R., 66
Garland, T. N., 93
Garrett, E., 117, 118, 146, 147, 152, 153, 154
Gay, L., 66
George, L., 13,
Gerber, S. C., 116, 120, 121, 124
Gilligan, C., 30, 90, 91, 94, 118, 136
Gilstrap, B., 39, 42, 43, 47, 48, 54, 68, 73
Gjerde, P. F., 3
Gofseyeff, M., 89, 93, 95, 97, 99, 107
Goldberg, S., 179, 199
Goldberg, W., 42
Goldsmith, R., 149
Goldstein, K. M., 178
Goldstein, S., 66
Goode, M., 124
Goodman, V., 238
Gordon, K., 14
Gordon, M., 178
Gordon, R. E., 14,
Gorsuch, R. L., 97
Gottlieb, B. H., 208
Gottman, J. M., 169, 198, 204
Greenbaum, C. W., 39, 47
Greenberg, M. T., 208
Greenberg, N. H., 14
Grimm, E. R., 15
Grossman, F. K., 15, 30, 42, 89–110, 114, 119,
    121, 122, 136, 146, 148, 167, 202
Grossman, K., 204
Gutmann, D., 91, 94, 113

H

Haber, A., 178, 179
Hamburg, D. A., 66
Hareven, T., 198
Hartford, C., 14
Hartman, A., 14
Heinicke, C. M., 146
Heming, G., 117, 118, 146, 147, 152, 153, 154
Hertzog, C., 43
Herzog, E., 3
Herzog, A., 66
Herzog, J., 149
Hess, R. D., 2
Hetherington, E. M., 207
Hildebrandt, K. A., 199
Hobbs, D., 113, 120
Hochberg, J., 199

Hoffman, L. W., 93, 113, 122
Hoffman, M. L., 5, 113, 122
Hollingshead, A. B., 2
Holmes, T. H., 13
Holt, K. S., 198, 202, 206
Hoogerwerf, K., 118, 121
Hopkins, J., 65, 66
Humphrey, M. E., 176
Huntington, D., 14
Huston, T. L., 148
Hwang, C., 39, 47, 178
Hymel, S., 116, 209

I

Iacobbo, M., 183

J

Jeffcoate, J. A., 176
Jeffries, V., 208
Jessner, L., 92
Johnson, A. A. S., 107

K

Kaij, L., 29
Kaplan, S., 90, 94
Kegan, R., 91
Kennedy, J., 198
Kennedy, W. A., 3
Kennell, J., 178, 198
Keogh, B., 198
Keylor, R. G., 99
Kimmel, D., 97
Klaus, M. H., 178, 198, 199
Klein, R. P., 114, 202
Kohn, M. L., 2
Kohut, H., 90, 94
Kokes, R., 146
Kopp, C. B., 179
Kotelchuck, M., 39, 40, 116, 177
Kramer, E. L., 65, 67, 68, 70, 72, 82, 83, 120
Kunz, P., 118

L

Lacoursiere, R. B., 66
Lafiosca, T., 155
Lamb, M. E., 7, 39, 40, 41, 42, 47, 94, 113, 114, 122, 145, 149, 177, 178, 199, 200, 202, 205, 234
Lancaster, J. B., 84
Landau, R., 39, 47
Lang, M., 41
Lawrence, K. M., 206
Leavitt, L. A., 199
Lefkowitz, M. M., 4
Legeay, C., 198
Leiderman, P. H., 122, 198, 199, 200, 206
Leifer, M., 15
Lemasters, E., 14
Lester, B., 7
Lester, B. M., 179
Levenson, R. W., 169
Levin, H., 6
Levine, J. A., 113, 114
Levinson, D., 91, 92
Lewis, M., 33, 113, 119, 122, 198, 204
Lewis, R., 113
Lidz, T., 13
Liebenberg, B., 93
Lloyd, J. K., 176
Locke, H., 97, 152
Loda, F. A., 208
Loesch, J. G., 14
Lonsdale, G., 206
Lowenthal, M. F., 13, 14
Lunde, D. T., 66
Lushene, R. E., 97
Lynn, D. B., 237
Lytton, H., 41, 123

M

Maccoby, E. E., 5, 6
MacDonald, K., 204
MacPherson, L., 200
MacTurk, R. H., 114, 202
Magnus, E. M., 14
Mahler, M. S., 90
Mandell, W., 199
Manguten, H. H., 198
Manis, J. D., 93
Marcus, M., 65, 66

Marion, R. L., 198
Martin, J. A., 5
Martinez, I., 118, 121
Marton, P., 176, 189, 190
McCarthy, M. E., 114, 202
McLaughlin, J. E., 3, 4
McQuiston, S., 114
Melson, G. F., 238
Mendelson, M., 66
Miller, B., 41
Miller, W. B., 31
Minde, K., 176, 189, 190
Minuchin, P., 10
Mock, J. E., 66
Moos, B. S., 157
Moos, R. H., 66, 157
Morrison, A., 121
Most, R., 124
Myerowitz, J. H., 15
Myers, B. J., 115

N

Nash, J., 145
Nash, S. C., 13, 17, 20, 23, 29, 30, 32, 42,
    92, 93, 113, 118, 120, 121, 136, 146,
    148, 149
Neff, C., 199
Neugarten, B. L., 13, 95, 97
Nichols, P. L., 3
Nicolay, R., 14
Nilsson, A., 15, 29, 30
Niswander, K. R., 178

O

O'Leary, S. E., 15, 38, 40, 204
Olson, J. P., 122
Osofsky, J. D., 6
Overton, W. F., 68

P

Palkovitz, R., 8, 146, 148, 149
Paloma, M. M., 93
Parke, R. D., 7, 15, 31, 38, 40, 116, 119, 122,
    145, 146, 149, 165, 176, 177, 178, 179,
    189, 197-212, 221, 223, 232, 233, 234

Parmelee, A. H., 178, 179
Parsons, T., 13
Pascoe, J. M., 208
Pastor, D. L., 208
Paykel, E. S., 68
Payne, H., 206
Pedersen, F. A., 1-10, 38, 39, 41, 65-86,
    113, 119, 120, 124, 134, 165, 177,
    217-241, 205, 221, 224, 226, 227, 229,
    230, 231, 234
Pedhazur, E. J., 158
Perrotta, M., 176, 189
Phillips, D., 38
Phillips, S. L., 146
Piotrkowski, C. S., 218
Pitt, B., 29, 67
Pleck, J. H., 113, 114, 145, 149, 218
Pollack, W. S., 90, 99
Power, T. G., 40, 116, 177, 178, 198, 204,
    209
Presser, H., 218
Pressman, R. A., 93
Pruett, K., 92, 145, 236
Pueschel, S. M., 199

R

Rabinovich, B., 65-86, 226, 227, 230, 231
Radin, N., 5, 15, 31, 99, 113, 145, 149, 166,
    237
Radloff, L., 153
Ragozin, A. S., 208
Rahe, R. H., 13
Ransom, D. C., 146
Rapoport, R., 91, 92, 107, 108
Rapoport, R. D., 91, 92, 107, 108
Rassaby, E. S., 68
Rawnsley, K., 206
Redl, O. J., 198
Redlich, F. C., 2
Reese, H. W., 68
Rendina, I., 38
Retterstol, N., 14
Richardson, L., 183
Richardson, M. S., 113
Rickels, A. V., 32
Rigler, D., 69
Robin, A. A., 14
Robins, E., 14
Robinson, J., 94, 145

Robinson, N. M., 208
Robson, K. S., 38, 39, 177
Rockwell, R., 198
Rogers, P., 183
Rogosa, D., 51
Rollins, B., 31
Rosenblatt, P. C., 41
Rosenblum, L. A., 113, 122
Roux, J. F., 68
Rovine, M., 39, 41, 42, 43, 47, 48, 54, 68, 73
Rudd, P., 146
Rubenstein, D., 118
Rubenstein, J., 124, 234
Russell, C., 30, 113, 120
Russell, G., 8, 15, 31, 145, 148, 149, 218
Rustad, M., 145
Ryder, R. G., 15

Spock, B., 1
Staines, G. L., 218
Standley, K., 237
Stafford, R., 145
Stechler, G., 90, 94
Steinberg, J., 178
Stern, D., 177, 178
Stern, M., 199
Stevens, J. P., 72
Stoneman, Z., 200, 205
Strassberg, S., 149
Strelitz, Z., 91, 92, 107, 108
Sudia, C. E., 3
Suwalsky, J. T. D., 65–86, 226, 227, 230, 231
Svanum, S., 3, 4
Szinovacz, M. E., 145

S

Sagi, A., 113, 237
Sameroff, A. J., 2, 5, 69, 179, 198
Sandberg, D., 66
Sarbin, T. R., 149
Sargent, S. P., 89, 93, 95, 97, 99, 107
Sawin, D. B., 7, 38, 145, 200–201, 209
Schaffer, H. R., 6
Schang, B., 121, 122
Schooler, C., 2
Schuurmans, S. M., 121, 122
Sears, P. S., 3
Sears, R. R., 6
Seashore, M. J., 206
Selz, L., 200
Senn, M., 14
Sharon, N., 113
Shea, E., 190
Shereshefsky, P. M., 15, 67, 114, 119
Sherry, D., 199
Sherwood, K., 40
Shinn, M., 3
Sigman, M., 69, 179
Slade, C. I., 198
Smith, C., 200
Smith, V. L., 238
Sollie, D., 41
Soule, B., 237
Spanier, G. B., 41, 43, 99, 113
Speilberger, C. D., 97
Spinetta, J. J., 69

T

Taub, H. B., 178
Tasch, R. J., 15
Tew, B. J., 206
Thoman, E. B., 122
Thompson, M., 183
Thornburg, K. R., 238
Thurnher, M., 14
Tinsley, B. R., 31, 116, 146, 176, 189, 197, 198, 200, 204, 209, 210
Tod, E. D. M., 68
Toda, S., 238
Trebub, S., 190
Tronick, E., 7, 40, 180, 190

U

Unger, D. G., 208

V

Vaillant, C., 91
Vaillant, G., 91, 96
Valentine, A. F., 14
Vanderveen, F., 97
Van Gent, E., 118, 121
Vega-Lahr, N., 66
Venet, W. R., 15
Vietze, P. M., 114, 200, 202

Volling, B., 37–61, 83, 205, 221, 222, 223, 224, 225, 226, 234
Vondra, J., 42

W

Wainwright, W. H., 14, 66
Walder, L. O., 4
Walker, J. A., 200, 204
Wallace, K., 97, 152
Walters, R. H., 149
Wandersman, L. P., 114, 120
Ward, C. H., 66
Watson, J., 6
Weeks, M. O., 238
Weigert, E., 92
Weinberg, S. L., 113
Weingarten, K., 93
Weinraub, M., 40, 119
Wente, A., 114, 139
Werner, E. E., 178
West, S., 38
White, R., 190

Whiting, B. B., 238
Whiting, J. W., 238
Winickoff, S., 15, 30, 89, 93, 95, 97, 99, 107, 114, 119, 121, 122 146, 148, 167, 202
Wise, S., 180

Y

Yalom, J. D., 66
Yarrow, L., 4, 15, 41, 67, 114, 119, 124, 202, 234
Yarrow, M. R., 6
Yogman, M. W., 7, 40, 145, 148, 175–193, 201, 202, 203, 221, 232, 233, 234

Z

Zaslow, M. J., 65–86, 120, 226, 227, 230, 231
Zelazo, P. R., 116
Zilboorg, G., 176
Zimmerman, J. L., 155

Subject Index

A

Affiliation and autonomy, 89–110, 230,
    236–237
Age, 102, 104, 105
    see also Strain
Autonomy and affiliation, 89–110, 230,
    236–237

B

Baumrind's observation schedule, 123
Bayley tests, 179, 180, 186, 187, 188, 189, 190,
    192, 234
Beck depression index, 66
Bem satisfaction scale, 16, 17, 20, 23
Bem sex role inventory, 16, 17, 23
Boston university pregnancy and parenthood
    project, 89, 92, 95
Brazelton's neonatal behavioral assessment
    scale, 115

C

Caldwell HOME scale, 189, 207
Career (work), 33, 91, 149, 152-153, 158, 164,
    167-168, 227, 228, 235-237
    balance of, with family, 92, 93

Caregiving
    actual vs. ideal, 118–119, 125–130
    balance with career, 92, 93
    competence of parents, 38, 48, 127-135,
        139, 167, 228, 238
    father involvement in, correlates of,
        158-161, 162-163
    interrelation of maternal/paternal
        behavior, 48-53, 60, 61, 188-189,
        226
    intervention, 156, 209-210, 221
    mother/father comparison, 38-39, 40,
        47-48, 59, 114, 125, 145, 155, 202,
        223-234, 238
    paternal, lack of correlation to play, 186
    postpartum blues relation to, 67, 72-79,
        85
    satisfaction, paternal, 161, 162, 163
    self-esteem and, 148, 161, 162, 163, 167
    sex-role identification and paternal,
        8-9
    traditional family vs. nontraditional, 39,
        47-48, 178
    see also Parenting
    see also Preterm infants
Center for the epidemiological study of
    depression scale, 153
Child care
    see Caregiving
Cox adaptation scale, 97

Cross-lag panel analyses, 48, 51, 52, 53, 57, 58, 59, 222

D

Dyadic adjustment scale, 99

F

Family environment scale, 157
Family system (family triad), 15, 37–61, 93, 109, 110, 113–143, 165–170, 197, 204–206
   see also Handicapped infants
   see also Preterm infants
Father-absence studies, 3–4
Father behavior rating scale, 99
Femininity, 95, 102, 104, 105, 107
First borns
   fathers of 93–94, 95, 101, 104, 107, 108–109, 230–231

G

Gender
   child's, relation to parenting, 7, 48, 109, 116, 122, 136–138, 140, 149, 209, 234–235
Gesell test, 179

H

Handicapped infants, 197–211
   caregiving by father, 202–3
   family system, 204–6
   marital relationship and, 205–6
   mother/child relationship and, 198–200
   support system, 206–211
HOME scale, *see* Caldwell HOME scale

I

Identity and intimacy, 91
Infant characteristics, 122
   irritability, 113, 204, 208
   social competence, 122, 137–138, 140
   see also Gender

   see also Handicapped infants
   see also Preterm infants
Intimacy and identity, 91

L

Lamaze, 114
Later borns
   fathers of, 93–94, 95, 104, 107
   parenting of, 231
Locke-Wallace marital adjustment inventory, 97

M

Marital
   conflict, 115, 118, 152, 170, 224
   relationship, 114–115, 128–129, 131–136, 146, 147, 164, 168–170
   relationship and parenting, 41–42, 53–59, 60, 119–121, 128–129, 131–136, 139–140, 148–149, 225, 227–228, 239
   satisfaction, 15, 94, 107, 113, 114–115, 118, 119–120, 122, 132, 134, 148, 152, 153, 154, 156, 161, 163–164, 169, 205, 228, 229
   stress, 113, 170
   support, 130, 224–226, 131–135, 205
      cognitive, 121, 131–135, 137, 139
      emotional, 9–10, 119, 121, 131–135, 137, 139, 224–225
      physical, 121, 131–133, 137
   see also Postpartum blues
   see also Preterm infants
   see also Strain
Masculinity, 93, 95, 102, 104, 105, 107, 110
Motherese, 38

O

Object relations, 90, 94
Obstetrical risk index, 201

P

Parenting
  actual vs. ideal, 119, 130
  change, 152-153
  competence (skill), 115-117, 119, 120, 121,
      127-135, 205, 224-225
  consistency, 153
  earlier experiences (family of origin) and,
      149, 158, 160, 161, 162, 163, 165-166,
      237-238
  gender differences, 153-154
  identity, 118, 125, 127, 130, 131, 137, 139,
      236-237
  intervention, 114-117, 138-140, 152,
      155-156
  parental agreement, importance of, 121
  role expectations, 119
  satisfaction, 115-116, 118, 167
  stress, 115, 156, 157, 162, 163, 167, 225
  transition to, 13-15, 114, 239
  see also Caregiving
  see also Gender
  see also Later borns
  see also Marital
  see also Strain
Parenting stress index, 155, 156
Pennsylvania infant and family development
      project, 43
Play
  actual vs. ideal, 126
  effect of, on development, 186-188
  fathers and, 118, 125
  intervention, 116
  mother/father comparison 7, 40, 177-178,
      234
  mothers and, 127
  see also Preterm infants
Postpartum blues
  follow-up observations, 65-86
  marital relationship and, 68, 83-84, 85, 229
  maternal, 65-66, 67-8
  paternal, 65-86, 120
  relation to spouse's behavior, 67, 76-77,
      78-79, 82-83, 231
  sense of competence and paternal, 84
  see also Caregiving
  see also Marital
Preterm infants, 188-189, 197-211
  caregiving, mother/father comparison, 176,
      203-204, 232

caregiving of, by father, 176, 183-184,
      188-189, 201, 232, 233
case studies, 190-193
family system and, 204-206
marital relationship and, 205-206
mother/child relationship and, 198-200
mothers interaction with, vs. mothers inter-
      action with full-term infants, 179, 203
parents of, vs. parents of full-term infants,
      176, 183-184, 201, 203, 232, 233, 239
perceptions of, vs. perceptions of full-term
      infants, 199
play comparisons of preterm infant
      fathers/full-term infant fathers, 184-6,
      189, 203-4, 233-4
play, mother/father comparison, 189
social variables and play impact on
      development of, 178-179, 186-188,
      190-192, 233-234
stress and, 175-176, 183, 192, 198-199, 206
support systems, 206-211, 233
see also Handicapped infants

R

Research methods,
  autonomy and affiliation, 95-100
  family systems, 43-45, 123-124, 150-151
  overview, 217-241
  past approaches, 1-9
  paternal caregiving satisfaction and stress,
      154-155, 157-158
  postpartum blues and parenting, 70-72
  predicting strain, 16-28
  preterm infants, caregiving and play of,
      179-183
Roles
  disruptions, 113
  division, 113, 115, 125, 139, 152
  expectations, 113, 114, 117-119, 124-131,
      138-139, 225
  parenting and spousal, 42, 114
  satisfaction, 118
  transition, 13-14

S

Second-order effects, 33, 40-41, 119, 177, 188,
      205

Social class (SES), 2, 39, 98, 102, 104, 105, 107, 108, 224
Stanford-Binet test, 5
State anxiety scale, 97
Strain, 156, 163, 222, 227
  age and, 25, 26, 27, 28
  cross-sex household tasks performance and, 25, 32, 229
  expectancy experience impact on, at parenthood, 25, 26–28, 29, 30–31
  maternal behavior relation to paternal, 30
  marital relationship and, 25, 26, 27, 28, 30–31, 154, 225, 227–228
  stress and, 26, 27, 28, 31
  unplanned pregnancy impact on, at parenthood, 28, 31–32

  see also Stress
Stress, 222
  see also Parenting
  see also Preterm infants
  see also Strain

T

Teenage parents, 42

W

Work
  see Career